Muddy Tracks

Muddy Tracks

Exploring an Unsuspected Reality

Frank DeMarco

HAMPTON ROADS PUBLISHING COMPANY, INC.

Cover design by Marjoram Productions
Cover photo by Frank DeMarco

For information write:
Hampton Roads Publishing Company, Inc.
1125 Stoney Ridge Road
Charlottesville, VA 22902

Or call: 804-296-2772
Fax: 804-296-5096
e-mail: hrpc@hrpub.com
Web site: www.hrpub.com

If you are unable to order this book from your local
bookseller, you may order directly from the publisher.
Call 1-800-766-8009, toll-free.
Library of Congress Catalog Card Number: 00-109657
ISBN 1-57174-257-3
10 9 8 7 6 5 4 3 2 1
Printed on acid-free paper in the United States

I should not talk so much about myself if there were anybody else whom I knew as well. Unfortunately, I am confined to this theme by the narrowness of my experience. Moreover, I on my side, require of every writer, first or last, a simple and sincere account of his own life, and not merely what he has heard of other men's lives; some such account as he would send to his kindred from a distant land; for if he has lived sincerely, it must have been in a distant land to me.

—Thoreau
Walden

For my friends who have gone on ahead:

Dave Schlachter (1947–1970)
Suni Dunbar (1924–1996)
Ed Carter (1915–1996)
Joyce Johnson-Jones (1946–1997)
Dave Wallis (1938–1998)

Especially for Bob Monroe (1915–1995)
who made so much possible
for so many

Contents

Foreword
Colin Wilson ix

Introduction
"I of my own knowledge" xix

One
Upstairs, Downstairs 1

Two
Of God and Shirley MacLaine 32

Three
Past Lives, Present Life 44

Four
Guidance 59

Five
A Matter of Focus 100

Six
Gateway Voyage 128

Seven
An Altered Reality 174

Eight
Inner Connection 217

Nine
(Non) Ordinary Life 236

Ten
Connection Between Lives 252

Eleven
Connection Between Individuals 298

Twelve
Connection Across Time 320

Thirteen
Interim Report 340

Afterword
Pointing at the Moon 351

Appendix I
Monroe's Toolbox 357

Appendix II
Mapmakers 361

Appendix III
Author's Note 364

Foreword

by Colin Wilson

When Frank DeMarco told me he intended to write a book about his experiences of The Monroe Institute, I immediately offered to write this introduction, for I needed no convincing that Robert Monroe is one of the most important figures in modern paranormal research. What I had not expected was that the book I had so casually offered to introduce, sight unseen, would be itself as remarkable as any of Monroe's books.

I met Frank on March 17, 1995, in the New York apartment of the distinguished paranormal researcher Alexander Imich. As it happens, it was the day Robert Monroe died. I remember the date because my taxi had gotten stuck in the Saint Patrick's Day parade, and I was two hours late for the party. Fortunately, it was still going strong. But the only one of the guests I mentioned later in my diary was Frank DeMarco. And that was partly because he had sent me a novel he had written called *Messenger*, a sequel to James Hilton's *Lost Horizon*, and that, unlike most sequels, it was totally absorbing. It was the story of a young American pilot whose spy plane crashes in Tibet in 1962, and who is taken to the monastery of Shangri-La. It was obvious that DeMarco had written it partly because he felt that James Hilton had missed some important opportunities. His young pilot attempts to escape but is caught, then decides to make the best of it and begins to practice mental and spiritual disciplines. The book made it clear that DeMarco knew a great deal about such disciplines, and had practiced them himself. And I sensed this as I talked to him—mainly about Monroe—at the party.

Back in England, I reread Monroe's book *Journeys Out of the Body*, which I had first read twenty years earlier. The book had deeply impressed me, and I wrote about it in *Mysteries* (1978), a sequel to *The Occult*. Monroe was a Virginia businessman who, in the late 1950s, began to have spontaneous out-of-the-body experiences—probably because, as a broadcasting executive, he had been experimenting with sleep-learning using two earphones. What was so interesting about Monroe was that, unlike many classic "astral travelers"—for example, Sylvan Muldoon and Oliver Fox—Monroe set out to discover how to teach others to leave their bodies, through the process he called "Hemi-Sync," or hemisphere synchronization, the use of patterns of sound to synchronize the left and right halves of the brain, and to induce a deep calm that is conducive to "altered states" and out-of-the-body experiences.

Monroe was able to "project" himself to other locations—like a neighbor's house—but soon found journeys in "this world" oddly boring. But he quickly discovered a region where he felt more at home, a timeless realm he calls "Locale II," and which seems to be the place we go to after death. In Locale II there are apparently many thoroughly bewildered people who do not know they are dead. Monroe began to help such people—although he occasionally needed help himself, as he came to realize that Locale II was also peopled by some very strange and occasionally terrifying entities.

Monroe will remind many readers of Emanuel Swedenborg, whose books contain descriptions of a realm beyond death that bears a remarkable resemblance to Monroe's Locale II. But readers of *Heaven and Hell or The True Christian*

Religion will occasionally experience doubts about Swedenborg, whose Christian standpoint makes us wonder whether he was a religious crank. What is so impressive about Monroe is that his work carries a ring of total honesty, a man who is trying to tell precisely and exactly what he has experienced, insofar as it can be conveyed in ordinary language.

In 1986 I had bought Monroe's second book, *Far Journeys*, but had found it disappointing compared to his first, and never finished it. It was full of weird neologisms like "I plied," "he flickered," "I smoothed." But when Frank DeMarco directed me to a strange and fascinating chapter called "Hearsay Evidence," which offers a symbolic—and uncomfortable—history of why humans were created, I was so impressed that I went back to the beginning and read the whole book. After that I went on to read Monroe's third and most mind-boggling book, *Ultimate Journey*, in which he tries to take us just about as far as words can go. It is certainly one of the oddest and most fascinating books I have ever encountered, and I deliberately read it slowly because I was enjoying it so much.

At about this point, Frank sent me an account he had written of his stay at The Monroe Institute in 1992. This I also read straight through, totally gripped, because what he had to say was so amazing. In his younger days, Frank had practiced amateur hypnosis (as described in this book), and become convinced that it was possible to access past lives. He had been to visit Emerson's house in Concord, and had an impression that he had once visited Emerson there. Now, at The Monroe Institute, he began using Monroe's techniques to mentally project himself to Emerson's house.

He says that it was like watching a movie, with realistic playback. He saw himself—as a Dr. Atwood—arrive at the back door and be introduced to Mrs. Emerson, who seemed vaguely familiar. After that he talked to Emerson, until their conversation was interrupted by Thoreau, who at the time lived in the

Emerson household, and who seemed to regard Atwood with mild suspicion as a possible rival.

I shall not describe all this further, because it is in this book. But when I came to write a book about the enigma of "alien abduction," and felt the need to write a chapter on "remote viewing," I asked Frank's permission to quote his story, and did so in Chapter 9 of *Alien Dawn*.

When Frank began to send me chapters of his new book, I felt exactly as I had felt on reading Monroe: that as weird and strange as all this sounded, it made an impression of complete truth and authenticity.

That was in the autumn of 1997. But after that, I gathered the book was not going so well. Although it seemed to me that all he had to do was keep on telling his story and the book would write itself, he apparently found that this was not so, and was getting himself into that tangle that happens to writers when they have too much to say.

Then, suddenly, it began to flow fast, and he began to e-mail it to me at the rate of more than three chapters a week. This, it soon became clear, was due to the help and support of what he called "The Gentlemen Upstairs" (TGU).

This in itself strikes me as one of the most interesting and important things about this book. Who are "The Gentlemen Upstairs?" Angels? Spirits? His own "superconscious mind"? I suspect that he himself is not quite sure.

If I had read this book in the late 1970s, I would have come down on the side of the "superconscious" hypothesis, for I was at that time fascinated by the phenomenon of multiple personality, and had come to the conclusion that every one of us possesses many levels of personality, and that our evolution as individuals means climbing what I called "the ladder of selves." But then I came upon the work of Max Freedom Long, particularly that astonishing book with the atrocious title *The Secret Science Behind Miracles*. Investigating the religion of the Hunas of

Hawaii—which had been suppressed by the Christian Church—
he learned that the kahuna (Huna priesthood) believed that man
has three souls: lower, middle, and high. The middle self is what
we call "I," the everyday personality; the lower self is what Freud
called the "unconscious"; but there is also a "high self," which is
as far above the everyday self as the unconscious is below it. This
high self can even foresee the future, which must mean that, in
a sense, it is outside our time realm.

Long came to feel that the kahuna system explains multiple personality far better than our Western psychology. He cites
a case recorded by Dr. James Leapsley of a girl whose original
personality alternated with another personality every four years.
Experts hypnotized her in an attempt to solve the problem in
the standard way, by getting the two personalities to blend, or
to persuade one of them to go away. Then an unfamiliar but
authoritative voice spoke through the girl's mouth, identifying
itself as the guardian of the two girls. It told the experts that if
they did not stop interfering, it would simply withdraw the two
girls and leave them with a corpse. The experts recognized that
it could do exactly as it said, and gave up.

The case convinced me that many multiple personalities
are, in fact, possessed by "spirits." I agree that sounds like a
hopeless backward step into the dark ages of superstition; but
since that time, many similar case studies have convinced me
that it is true.

So I would be inclined to feel that Frank DeMarco's
"Gentlemen Upstairs" could be either Frank's own "Higher Self"
or another person entirely. But even this may be a simplifica-
tion. In 1907 an architect named Frederick Bligh Bond was
commissioned by the Church of England to try to locate the
remains of the ancient chapel at Glastonbury Abbey. He used a
medium who specialized in automatic writing, and was soon
getting messages from dead monks that enabled him to locate
the ruins precisely. And one of these monks remarked, "Why

cling I to that which is not? It is I, and it is not I, butt parte of
me which dwelleth in the past and is bound to that which my
carnal soul loved and called 'home' these many years. Yet I,
Johannes, amm of many partes, and ye better parte doeth other
things. . . ."

Are we all "of many partes?" Certainly, Frank's strange
story of Katrina suggests as much. If Katrina was one of Frank's
past lives, then how could his present self locate Katrina in
"Focus 27" of that parallel world called Locale II? I asked Frank,
and he admitted he was by no means sure.

It can be seen why I became so excited about this book, and
in spite of a fairly heavy work schedule, printed up every e-mail
attachment as soon as it came and read it straight through.

I was particularly impressed by his section describing the
effect of taking mescaline as a student. To begin with, the drug
produced the same effect described by Aldous Huxley in *The
Doors of Perception*: a deepened sense of reality. Frank writes,
"If I were looking at a candle, say, I would really look at it, really see it, for the first time in my life." Looking at a painting of a
boat, it was as if the front half of the boat was sticking out into
the room.

"The walls, I realized, were alive! Literally. What I had been
taking for dead matter was something much more exciting; it
was somehow alive in a way I couldn't fathom, but couldn't
doubt."

I was reminded of a passage in a book called *The States of
Human Consciousness* by C. Daly King, a student of Gurdjieff,
who describes how, standing on a New Jersey station one morning, he experienced a more intense form of consciousness, in
which the dun-colored bricks of the station "appeared to be
tremendously alive; without manifesting any exterior motion
they seemed to be seething almost joyously inside and gave the
distinct impression that in their own degree they were living
and actually liking it."

Even more important, I think, is the comment DeMarco makes about coincidence—that he had always taken it for granted that life was just a collision of forces on the material plane. Under mescaline he suddenly became aware that there is no such thing as coincidence. "Several times in the course of that long Saturday afternoon I watched the interaction of five people come to perfectly orchestrated peaks and lulls. I refer not to anything externally dramatic, but to the temporary clarity of vision that showed me (beyond later doubting) that more went on between individuals than their ordinary consciousness realized. Thinking about the orchestration I saw then, I for a while referred to God The Great Playwright."

What this passage brought to mind was an interview I had had with the remarkable Australian mystic Barbara Tucker, wife of the painter Albert Tucker, one of whose experiences happened at a party:

"All the people round me were laughing and chatting and doing all the things people do at parties—and then, again, I suddenly saw all the connections between these people—how they all interconnected, how all this show that was going on was not, in fact, idle chatter. It was all interconnecting into their relationships with one another in the most extraordinary way."

Obviously, Daly King, Barbara Tucker, and Frank DeMarco had all had that same sense that our world is not as chaotic as it looks, but is imbued with an underlying meaning.

This book is not, in the ordinary sense, an autobiography, which seems to me in a way a pity, for Frank's experience has been in many ways remarkable, and he has a natural gift for making it come alive. This is autobiography only insofar as it is relevant to his interest in The Monroe Institute and Monroe's own ideas and experiences. When I asked him to let me have a few biographical details for this introduction, he sent me an e-mail ironically entitled "My Fascinating Life." But it provides the necessary background to this book.

He was born in 1946 in New Jersey, the son of a farmer, and brought up a Catholic. He graduated from George Washington University in 1969, and wrote his thesis on Thoreau. He married in that same year and had a son and daughter. After trying journalism and librarianship, he decided to follow the lead of his hero Kennedy, and ran for Congress at twenty-seven, coming fourth of six in the Democratic primary. For two years he worked for the man who was elected, then became a computer programmer, and finally became the co-founder of the Hampton Roads Publishing Company in Virginia. This was in 1989, and in the following year he made his first trip to The Monroe Institute, and got to know its founder—which is virtually the starting point of this book.

My own work had played a part in his development (as described in the first chapter), which is how I come to be writing this introduction. It helped to crystallize his own feeling that there is something oddly wrong with "this life," and that there has to be some alternative, some other way. I had experienced the same odd sense of suffocation during my own teens (in the 1940s), and for me it had crystallized in T.S. Eliot's phrase, "Where is the life we have lost in living?" I began to collect material about what I called "Outsiders," misfits who had experienced this same sense of not really belonging to our down-to-earth reality. The romantics of the nineteenth century felt the same, and often committed suicide, or died of a kind of self-induced despair at the thought that there is no alternative.

What fascinated me so much were these glimpses of overwhelming delight and affirmation, the kind of thing that led Van Gogh to paint "Starry Night" and made Nijinsky write in his diary: "I am God, I am God." Were they sheer illusion—as Van Gogh believed when he committed suicide? In states of depression and fatigue, it was easy to believe this. But then there were those other moments, states of immense happiness and confidence, in which it was obvious that human beings are far stronger than they realize.

It was this question—what Thomas Carlyle called "Everlasting No versus Everlasting Yes"—that led me to write my first book, *The Outsider,* in 1955, whose publication in 1956 led to the vertiginous and not wholly pleasant experience of overnight success—the question that I later dramatized in the science fiction novel *The Mind Parasites* in the mid-sixties, and that Frank stumbled on a few years later.

Although I became deeply interested in "the occult" in 1969, when asked to write a book about it, and so discovered the work of Robert Monroe, I have never attempted to follow Frank into the exploration of these curious powers of the mind. In fact, although writing *The Occult* and *Mysteries* left me in no doubt whatever of the reality of out-of-the-body experience, I remained oddly skeptical about the whole notion of life after death, feeling that perhaps human beings ought to devote their attention to finding out why we are alive and what we are supposed to do now that we are here. Writing a book on the poltergeist in the early 1980s convinced me beyond all doubt that poltergeists are spirits, and not some manifestation of the unconscious minds of disturbed teenagers. And finally, researching a book called *Afterlife* convinced me that human beings somehow survive their death.

Yet what continues to obsess me is the notion that human beings are on the verge of a new step in their evolution, and that it is in the process of occurring at this moment. It seems clear to me that for well over three thousand years, human consciousness has been trapped by survival needs in a narrow "left brain" vision, and that it is now virtually in a cul-de-sac. Research into a book on the so-called alien abduction phenomena has convinced me that something very strange is happening, and that we are on the verge of some great change. It seems to me that there is much evidence that the "aliens"—or some of them—are attempting to "midwife" the human race to a new stage of consciousness.

Why do I feel that Monroe's insights are so important to the present time? I can illustrate the answer by pointing to a recent book called *The Threat* by my fellow researcher David Jacobs, who is convinced that the human race is about to be taken over by the aliens, who will overrun us as the Nazis once hoped to overrun the world. His book left me feeling worried, for thirty years of research have certainly taught him more about UFOs than I shall ever know. Then I thought about Frank DeMarco and his book, and suddenly became aware that Jacobs—with whom I had some interesting conversations at a conference two years ago—is leaving out of account what Monroe knew and what DeMarco knows: that in this strange "multiverse" there are powerful forces for good as well as evil, and that if we remain trapped "downstairs," in a kind of worm's-eye view of reality, we shall inevitably take a pessimistic view of the future. What is so important, and so refreshing, about this book is that it provides a remarkable bird's-eye view of the universe that instantly induces a sense of what G. K. Chesterton once called "absurd good news."

Introduction

"I of my own knowledge"

It was the third of a series of five questions that I had been instructed to ask the universe. *"Who am I?"*

I was at The Monroe Institute, in central Virginia, participating in a residential program called the Gateway Voyage. Given the amazing things that had already happened to me there that week, I asked the question fully expecting an answer.

Who was I? The answer came: "Muddy footprints in the grass." Being in an expanded state of consciousness, I understood the image. It meant that I am here to encourage others to do some exploring. I am here to show you that others have passed through what may appear to be a trackless wilderness.

Muddy footprints. Not muddy as in muddled; muddy as in wet and indistinct. Wet, as one's footprints are wet after being immersed in water. Indistinct, little more than traces. Enough to let you know that you are not the first to tread this ground, but not enough to tell you much about the person who made them.

When you see muddy footprints in the grass, you may not know anything about who made the tracks, or which way the person was headed, or where they came from or where they're going. You may not know if the person who made them knew where he or she was going. What you *do* know is that someone, at some time, for some reason, went that way.

This image came to me in December 1992. The course of that week turned my life, beginning an opening-up to many longed-for abilities and perceptions. Within the next five years I took other courses there, and in August 1997 I received a message telling me to write a book about what I had seen, felt, and experienced, as a way to encourage others. I was even given the title: "Muddy Footprints in the Grass." So shortly thereafter I took off six months from work and set out to write what had happened to me between 1987 and 1997, as a way of demonstrating some of the possibilities open to us all.

I tried to write this book the normal way for five months before I gave up and allowed it to happen. For five months I tried outlines, tables of contents, note cards, endless revisions. Got more and more enmeshed in the apparatus of scholarship. More and more enmeshed in prior versions.

Finally I had to concede I couldn't do it. Not *that* way, anyway. I took all my files off the computer (though I carefully saved them on floppies; what might be called controlled desperation, or perhaps performing *with* a net) and left a blank legal pad on my desk.

I'd tried doing it the right way. I'd tried giving up.

Now I'd have to try living what I was preaching. Or to put it more precisely, to *write* in the way I had learned to *live*. The inner guides I call The Gentlemen Upstairs had been gently mocking me for my fear of trusting the process. You don't need notes to *talk*, they said rightly. Why think you need notes to write?

The process worked; at least it sort of worked. As I began writing this, I had no evidence at all that it could be done. The legal pad was as blank as the unrolling present that we call the future. But the book got reorganized, rewritten, and ready (I thought) for publication in less than a month.

There followed a series of rejections from various publishing houses. Confused, because I knew that at least some of it was good, I consulted various friends whose judgment I valued. Eventually I realized that I was receiving (if not always hearing) a consistent criticism: the book was too much about the journey of brain-wave researcher and out-of-body pioneer Bob Monroe and too little about mine. The book had a split focus, continually alternating between my personal experience and my analysis of Monroe's. At length I resolved to rewrite it with one single focus: what had happened to me, with all this implied about who we are and what our possibilities are.

So now, dear reader, it is up to you to continue. You came to this book for a reason, and you yourself probably don't yet know why. You will learn why, if you persevere. This is not a formal thesis, or a summary of the books of Bob Monroe and others, but mostly a firsthand narrative of what I've learned and how I use it. From work at The Monroe Institute and elsewhere, I learned how to obtain firsthand knowledge of life beyond what our society considers normal. I learned how to extend my abilities in ways that our society considers to be impossible. Most important, my experience sheds new light on the reality underlying this world that has been described (and then repeatedly misunderstood) in scripture the world over.

From my own experience, I have become convinced that we are immortal spirits temporarily inhabiting bodies. This life is not our only life. And although we see ourselves as "individuals" separate from each other, in fact—and not at all metaphorically—we are all connected one to another, by way of our intimate connection with a larger being that cares about us and can be trusted, but that sees things differently. This larger being is a source of foresight and wisdom made available to us both at times of its own choosing and upon our request. Nonetheless, we may often lose communication with it by failing to remember that we are more than we appear to be.

Interestingly enough, this sketch of the way I now see the world encompasses Bob Monroe's description of earthbound individuals as part of a larger being that exists primarily in a region beyond what he calls the Time-Space Illusion. This larger being sends out probes to experience earth life; the probes live as if they were separate beings, and at physical death they reunite not only with the part of the larger being that stayed outside what I call 3D Theater, but also with the others who were in the physical. But Monroe's description also passes for a good description of God as he is understood in the Christian, Jewish, and Moslem traditions. In fact, it corresponds with descriptions handed down by mystics and other wanderers in realms beyond 3D Theater. And that ought to open up many a line of fruitful inquiry, retrieving various babies from the bushes where they landed with the bathwater.

The implications of these few statements are immense, literally changing everything from birth to death and beyond. If you once see us as all connected through a larger being, many otherwise puzzling reports become matters of common sense. They become, in fact, only what is to be expected. Communication with the dead? Telepathy? Distant healing? Ghosts? Our society has *opinions* on all of them; all over the landscape. Knowledge? Not to be found. And this goes double for the ultimate questions. Is there an afterlife? Does God exist? Do spirits exist? If so, in both cases, do they concern themselves with human lives? Of these things our society *teaches* nothing because it *knows* nothing. Indeed, silently, by implication, it teaches that we *can* know nothing. Our society not only lacks a common body of accepted *knowledge*, it lacks a commonly accepted *method* of acquiring knowledge on these subjects. Instead, various elements in society dismiss the questions with contempt, or maintain a benevolent neutrality, or invite us (silently) to form opinions based on the opinions of others, or on blind faith.

But when we find ourselves habitually putting aside entire classes of phenomena that nonetheless continue to be reported over the years—over centuries—we ought to take that as a sign that we need to find or construct a better picture of the world we live in. Only an inadequate worldview forces us continually to ignore inconvenient data or put it into separate boxes that don't communicate with the rest of our mental world or with each other.

Among those inconvenient reports: ghosts; out-of-body experiences. Possession and witchcraft. Telepathy. UFOs. Afterlife experiences including heaven and hell. The power of prayer. The ability to heal by touch, and at a distance. Plenty more.

To my mind, any way of seeing the world that has been believed over time by large numbers of people was not constructed out of whole cloth. It had at least a bit of reality. The trick is to keep the bit of reality and leave the logical structure that was constructed atop it. And the way to distinguish the two is to see which part can be reconciled with other parts. Truth, ultimately, is one. It's a good sign that you're on the right trail when many seemingly separate or even contradictory bits converge.

We now have a way of seeing things that makes sense, and that offers a continuing path for us to explore and refine. It makes our world whole without chopping out large bits that we can't find room for, and does so without requiring watertight mental compartments. That is, it stops us from having to believe mutually incompatible things and think in mutually incompatible ways. What is better, it reconciles and affirms the beliefs of many seemingly incompatible belief systems. Many of the differences in beliefs over which people have killed each other (or in our day, slandered each other) now seem to be little more than difference in nuance. Each saw a different aspect and took it for the whole picture, and each then built a dogmatic structure around it. As a friend of mine whimsically says, how do you describe a blind man to an elephant?

I hope it is obvious that I know better than to think that I—unlike all those others—have caught The Ultimate Truth. I haven't. We can't; not while we are still in the body, at least, and probably not afterward either. But it is quite worthwhile to have found a larger truth, a way of seeing that catches as much reality as possible. To my mind, the most valid system is one that reconciles the greatest number of seemingly incompatible beliefs by showing that each was a partial view of something now seen whole. Or at least *more* whole than before. Given our limitations, that's the best we can do.

My life's experience tells me that we can obtain firsthand knowledge of these things, and that firsthand knowledge is the only kind there is. In ancient Egypt (so says Joan Grant in *Winged Pharaoh*) the priests in the temples taught the people using this formula: "I of my own knowledge tell you that this is the truth." Their formula was not, "This is what I have been taught," but, "I *of my own knowledge* tell you that this is the truth." Where would we find equivalent knowledge today? Where would we find an equivalent institution? Our universities and churches have no training program to produce such teachers. They teach what *is said to be* true, or *might be* true, or *ought to be* true, or what we *wish* were true. But knowledge cannot be transmitted by those who do not know.

Without firsthand knowledge, no one can transmit the true nature of physical-matter reality, or of the worlds beyond physical life, or of what we as individuals and as groups can achieve. No one can teach the meaning of life, as it emerges from a greater understanding of the inner and outer world we live in. In this, both religion and science have failed us. Religion fails us when its priests attempt to teach from faith rather than from personal knowledge, for as a natural result they then demand faith and obedience as substitutes for study and knowledge. Science fails us when it refuses to investigate certain categories of experience or thought (such as what people call the supernatural, whether labeled as religion or parapsychology) because it *believes*, before investigation, that these categories of experience are nonsense. In both cases this failure is not necessarily the result of hierarchies scheming to obtain and retain power. Just as often it is the result of people not realizing that firsthand knowledge is there to be obtained.

It is as well, perhaps, to say explicitly what ought to be obvious: that I am not denying that religion and science have worth, or that they are partly based on truth, or that at best they are based on a desire to find truth rather than belief. Still, it remains true that both become more valuable to humanity when they ground their view of the underlying nature of the universe less on inherited beliefs, no matter how widespread, and more on firsthand experience, firsthand knowledge.

We are starving for that knowledge. In fact, we could kill ourselves—certainly we often kill others—in trying to compensate for lack of knowledge by taking refuge in arbitrary certainty. Those who teach firmly held beliefs, grounded mainly in the strength of the need to have something to believe, produce things like Hitler's beliefs about the master race. It is from uncertainty—and the fear that uncertainty brings—that individuals and societies do desperate things. If you don't *know*, you cannot teach, except by faith. And faith implies doubt. Doubt and the resulting repression of doubt breed fanaticism and intolerance. Worse, they breed ignorance pretending to infallibility, which breeds charlatans and blind followers.

I am not an Egyptian priest, and I cannot transfer my firsthand knowledge. But I *can* tell how you may obtain *your* own firsthand knowledge, and I can offer my own preliminary report of my own findings. This book is a report, in descending order of certainty, of:

• What I have experienced, as best I can reconstruct it.
• What I think that experience means.
• What others have reported having experienced.
• What they thought that experience meant.

• What light I think my own experience sheds on such reports, and vice versa.

Among other things, I share with you some true stories that give a sense of what firsthand experience makes possible, hoping to describe my journey of self-discovery (self-creation?) in such a way as to encourage you, the reader, on your own journey. In this I would be doing for you what Bob Monroe and his institute did for me. It is my hope that my own muddy footprints will help at least a few people to spend less time feeling lost, so that they can spend more time joyfully exploring.

For instance, here's a small example of how I now live. One weekend I was in New York City, and met my agent—an old friend—for breakfast at a little place she knew. As we sat down, she said she didn't know if she could eat anything. Her throat had swelled up overnight and she felt terrible. Now, as it happened, she had just done me two big favors, which added gratitude to affection, which I knew would make the job easier. So (a little self-consciously) I asked if she would mind if I tried to fix it. She said she didn't mind, so I closed my eyes and visualized her throat opening and her returning to normal health. When I opened my eyes, I didn't need to ask. Her eyes wide, she said, "That's amazing!" Then we proceeded to have breakfast. It was no big dramatic deal, you see, just life the way we can learn to live it, helping each other. That was in 1995. Today I am even more offhand about it all.

The psychic abilities I long half believed in and wanted are, if not all within reach, at least a lot closer than they used to be. And my experience convinces me that they are within reach of any who want them. It's only candid to add that the major reason I finally decided to write this book is that I realized that only by doing so could I move to another level of being. And this is what seems to have happened.

I of my own knowledge tell you what follows.

ONE

Upstairs, Downstairs

Do you want psychic abilities? In this book is all you need to learn to experience such abilities on a daily basis, rather than having to rely on second- or third-hand reports. You won't get there without work, but if you choose to pay the price, you *will* get there. The resources, helpers, and abilities that all humans have can transform your life. It's just a matter of your realizing what is there and how it may be used. And if our society as a whole could learn even what I have learned so far, it would have a vastly expanded idea of what we are.

That you may absorb what I know emotionally, rather than merely intellectually, I will tell you stories from my life. These are true stories, whether or not you at first dare believe them. My life now seems magical to me. It didn't always seem that way.

What I was before I slowly learned to change is relevant to what I learned to be, for it is unnecessary to live isolated, as I lived then. I started as a solitary, lonely individual, struggling along, afraid of others, afraid to open my heart, afraid to trust myself. I lived (as I would now say) only Downstairs, without day-to-day connection with my Higher Self or with other levels of being. I did try to believe in God. Many times I believed quite strongly, and learned that I could safely rely on invisible support. At my best, I said, "Dear God, show me the way," and trusted. At my best, I loved. But it was all so intermittent! So hit-or-miss!

I was a member of the last generation to grow up in what I call the medieval Catholic Church. By nature, I was a mystic. The Latin Mass, the sense of the all-pervading infinite world behind this one, the firm belief in an unchanging order of things, including a black-and-white code of behavior, appealed to me at my deepest levels. When, as a teenager, I found myself unable to remain a believing Catholic, I didn't realize that Catholicism was only one specific religion expressing humanity's supernatural connections. I thought it was all or nothing, and I had seen—I thought—that it was nothing.

Atheism didn't suit me. I couldn't see worshiping The Big Nothing, and couldn't see how anyone could say absolutely that There Is No God. I could imagine saying either, "I have experienced God" or, "I haven't experienced God." But how could anyone say, "I have experienced No-God"? It didn't make sense. Atheism seemed a bigger act of faith than believing.

So what was left? I had an affinity for Buddhism, but it isn't my path; at least, not this time. For a while, George Bernard Shaw's brand of spiritual evolution appealed to me, but gradually I came to see it as the expedient of a religious man who was looking for an intellectually respectable way out of the contemporary belief only in material reality. Carl Jung's *Modern Man in Search of a Soul* came to me as a godsend, if that's not too bad a play on words. Here was a mind-scientist who could investigate deeper realities—even those involving church doctrine—without giving up his right to inquire and make independent judgments.

In Henry Thoreau I found a friend, a wise man. Colin Wilson's works bred in me a sense of untapped human potential. Those of Laurens van der Post reinforced my belief in the underlying spiritual, rather than physical, nature of life. So did those of Yeats, and Ouspensky, and Gurdjieff, and Schumacher. So too, Richard Bach.

All of this, though, was only reading, and reading is a most solitary enterprise. I have done way too much reading in this lifetime. It tended to take me ever farther away from the world I was supposed to be living in. Not that a life of much reading is not as worthwhile as any other. But too much reading may lead you to think you *understand* what in fact you merely *recognize*. Without active life as a corrective, you misinterpret what you have read. This is the value of a teacher.

I well remember a day in my early twenties, standing on a city street reading that "when the student is ready, the teacher will appear." I wanted desperately to believe it, and didn't know whether in fact I could. He showed up, in person, within months. Although he made his living by teaching art in the public schools, he did not appear with a sign around his neck saying "Teacher!" He was not a perfect being without problems and neuroses. Nor, over the years, has it been a case of him always teaching and I always learning. More often, he and I have been able to help each other; sometimes at the same time, sometimes alternately. Indeed, the saying about students and teachers hadn't prepared me for relationships in which the roles could unpredictably reverse from moment to moment. But that is the characteristic of assistance between and among equals. Evidently my life is a no-guru zone.

As well as human teachers, I was blessed with other sources of inspiration and assistance. The divinatory arts, for instance: the I Ching, astrology, tarot. Various forms of inner guidance. In time came dreams and dream analysis, very powerful tools indeed. All very powerful. All as readily available to you as to me. And attempts at self-discipline were always available: prayer, fasting, and meditation.

I sought "psychic powers," if only as a proof that there is much more to life than the material world reported by the senses. I sought them, and obtained them, and found that they are not things divorced from ordinary life, but things that *one* culture has refused to admit into its own arbitrarily limited view of ordinary life. To regard them either with New Agers' awe or with religious fundamentalists' fear leads equally to superstition. In fact (reckless generalization number one): if any single thing discredits accounts of extraordinary experience—metaphysical, religious, or spiritual—it is this tendency to treat such experience as somehow disconnected from ordinary life. It isn't. Life is filled with all sorts of things, regardless how hard we try to make it consistent, logical, or "safe."

– 2 –

For more than forty years I endured the long, hard, solitary road. Yet I had gotten a startling glimpse of the existence of a better way of living one night late in February 1970, when I was a few months from turning twenty-four. I was in a drugstore checkout line when a strong impulse led me to pick up a paperback book off the rack. Oddly, for some reason the thought came to me that I might steal it. I still don't know why *that* thought came across, unless merely to underline for me the importance of that book, a science-fiction novel called *The Mind Parasites*, by an author I'd never heard of named Colin Wilson. I bought it, and that moment turned my life.

The plot was simple enough. Two scientists at the end of the twentieth century (then more than thirty years in the future) discover that we are all the unsuspecting hosts to—well, to mind parasites, creatures that sap our vitality and our sense of purpose. After sundry adventures, the scientists learn to defeat the parasites, and for the first time begin to take possession of humanity's unsuspected abilities, including a host of powers then usually called occult.

When I read that book, I was seized with the conviction that the author was telling the truth. We *do* have such powers, and they *are* inexplicably beyond our grasp. What is more, it was clear to me that the author believed it too. The strength of his conviction ran like a strong current beneath the surface of the story, and was spelled out clearly in his preface.

His preface mentioned that he had begun his career (at just about my age then) with *The Outsider,* an international best-seller. I went looking in the local public library for any other of his books, the beginning of a lifelong habit. I soon found that, whatever form he uses—and he has written novels, volumes of criticism, biography, history, essays, plays—the same underlying message comes through. It came through to me that night, and filled me with excitement. Something within me went *click!* and said, "This is how it is."

For a while I pressed this book on all my friends, and was disappointed and puzzled that it didn't turn their lives as it had mine. But it had turned mine because it was the right book for the right person.

Chance? Coincidence? I would have thought so then. I don't now. Today I know that the words "chance" and "coincidence" are shorthand terms covering mental laziness or, perhaps, fear of a world that is seamlessly purposeful. Neither was it predestination, karma, destiny, or fate; at least, not as commonly understood. Today I would call it guidance, but what I mean by that and what I *don't* mean and why I think the way I do now probably will take the rest of the book to explain.

Before I picked up *The Mind Parasites,* I had it in mind to become a writer and politician. I still had within me the dream I'd had since I was thirteen or fourteen of structuring my life like Winston Churchill's and John F. Kennedy's, combining writing and statesmanship. This was ridiculously unrealistic for several reasons, the very least of which was that they had been born into riches and powerful connections while I was a farmer's son. But at the time I had no idea of how life really is; had no idea what hidden springs move society; had no idea what motivates people, what deters them. I had had a quiet, sheltered boyhood, almost a cloistered life, surrounding myself with books instead of people. I look back now, all these years later, and I smile at the vast number of things that everybody else knew and I didn't know. I knew lots that the people around me didn't know, but that didn't mean that what I knew was useful. (Much of it wasn't even true.) But it took time for me to discover that.

My ambition to lead a life imitating two others from different social strata and different times met a snag before I had even graduated high school. In the spring of 1964 I took a bus from my hometown in southern New Jersey to nearby Philadelphia, and took the physical and other tests to enter the armed service. I was thinking to go to Vietnam and emerge a military hero—à la Churchill and Kennedy, of course—as a beginning to my illustrious political career. I didn't realize that this war was going to be unprecedentedly different, and I certainly didn't suspect what life in the armed forces might have done to me. I didn't get a chance to find out.

After going through the entire battery of physical and mental tests, I was at the very last desk. The man there looked up from my form, asked if I had asthma as I had indicated, and said, "Of course, you realize that this washes you out." I was given a 1-Y deferment. No military career for me. This was in early 1964, months before the Gulf of Tonkin incident and the beginning of America's large-scale military involvement in that quagmire. The armed forces were a lot choosier than they would be a few months hence. In attempting to enlist those few months earlier than my eighteenth birthday I was lucky, perhaps. But it didn't seem so to me at the time.

I rode the bus home in a state of shock. Never to wear a military uniform? Never to go to war and come back a hero? What happened to that instinctive certainty I had about my career? This on top of the murder of John F. Kennedy a few months previously. Asthma had hospitalized me in my boyhood, and it still gave me bad nights, sometimes several nights and days at a time. I wasn't a perfect picture of health. But I wanted to be in the army! Back home, I quietly asked an army recruiter if I should lie about having asthma and join anyway. He turned decisive thumbs down. "You'd be a menace to yourself and your buddies," he said, and I took that as the last word. What in the world was I going to do with my life?

What I did was work in factories for a year, then go to George Washington University, so that I could be in Washington, D.C. There I worked for my congressman, first as a volunteer in my freshman year, then as an intern that summer, hoping to find my way into politics. But the congressman was defeated in the 1966 elections. Another plan gone west. (It has been pointed out to me that the congressman's defeat was perhaps a bigger piece of good fortune for me than the fact that my lungs kept me out of Vietnam.)

I emerged from college in 1969 with a B.A. in history and still no idea what to do. I took for granted that I would run for Congress in 1974, at age twenty-eight, basically since Kennedy had first run for Congress at age twenty-nine. (Our two lives had no other parallels, but I didn't notice.) But I laid no groundwork, and wouldn't have known how to go about doing so.

That was entirely typical. I was *very* unworldly. All the time I was in college, I never gave a thought to how I would make a living afterward. Particularly shortsighted it was, in that I had had to work my way *through* college. It wasn't as if I didn't know the value of money, or how hard it could be to earn. But my ideas were as limited as my experience. I seriously thought that I might have to go back to work in the factories after I graduated college. I couldn't imagine a path.

But things happened, as they do. In the Washington, D.C., race riots of April 1968, I took a walk past police lines into the riot zone, wrote up my impressions, and sent them to the editor of my hometown newspaper. The following year, I began working for that paper as news reporter, beginning the Monday after my last exams, a week before the graduation ceremony, which I didn't bother to attend. A couple of months later I was married, and in February of 1970 there I was, buying this book by a man named Colin Wilson.

– 3 –

Wilson's entire body of work revolves around the same premise that is central to the story line in *The Mind Parasites*, a premise that could be summarized as follows: *"There is something wrong with life.* The unsatisfactory way we live isn't the way it should be or has to be. We possess vast unsuspected powers and abilities of which we are slowly becoming half-aware. It is our task to exert the intelligently directed will to learn to develop and use these powers."

That message filled me with excitement partly because it was pretty much without precedent. I had read Jess Stearn's *Edgar Cayce—the Sleeping Prophet*, and Ruth Montgomery's *A Gift of Prophecy,* but to the best of my recall now, all these years later, not that much else that could be called parapsychology or occult (or now, New Age). There must have been some, but my science fiction stage had not yet been replaced by fondness for what I call weird stuff. My mental world was filled with history, biography, politics, current affairs. After all, I was going to be a statesman!

The only thing in my life touching on the paranormal was the fact that in college I had hypnotized a couple of my fraternity brothers, eliciting stories that purported to be past lives of theirs. (More about this later.) As to drugs, George Washington University was a very conservative school, slow to catch up with the times, and I was a very conservative person—and a timid one—who had his future political career to consider. I graduated without having tried any drug stronger than alcohol and tobacco. So much for what I would now call a Downstairs view of things. Upstairs saw it differently, as it usually does.

I suppose I will have to explain how and why I use the terms Upstairs and Downstairs, though many will find them self-evident. Others use Inner and Outer. Either way, it's a spatial analogy describing a noncorporeal yet intimate relationship. In the 1970s I had no idea that I *had* an Upstairs. I lived in, and operated from, the kitchen, so to speak, and thought that was all there was.

As a naturally pious, naturally mystical Catholic in the time before Vatican II—that is, in the 1950s—I participated thoroughly in that mental and spiritual world. The Latin Mass and all it symbolized—the entire theology—was as real to me as secular, technological America. And that was the gift of the situation. I lived with one foot set firmly in twentieth century postwar America and the other set equally firmly in a medieval worldview whose assumptions about reality were radically different. My freedom from both came from the fact that I had embraced both without feeling tension between them. Looking back, I realize that most of my contemporaries and probably most of the clergy lived by constructing separate mental compartments and making sure the contents of one stayed separate from the contents of the other. But I—for reasons I never troubled to examine, because I never realized the situation—did not. To me, there was no split between being a good medieval Catholic and a good twentieth century technological American. For one thing, I was very metaphysically oriented by nature. (I didn't discover how much so, and why, until I was forty-seven.) Also, I was either intellectually lazy about reconciling different compartments of my mental world, or was particularly shielded. Or both.

I left Catholicism intellectually with a violent lurch in my teens, though it took much longer to leave it emotionally. My reasons (my Downstairs reasons, I should say) don't do much credit to my emotional maturity or even common sense. Certainly they show that eleven years of Catholic school had left my theological understanding essentially untouched. I didn't want to believe in a God who could let Kennedy be killed.

(That's how closely I identified with JFK!) I didn't any longer believe that the Church's rules were ordained by God. And I couldn't believe that God would condemn people to hell when I knew *I* wouldn't. I had many reasons. In fact, as I see it now, Downstairs I was disappointed in God and creation. Upstairs, though, had its own agenda, which involved being sure that I would be free to go where I needed to go.

This seeming digression about Catholicism is mostly to assure you that my Upstairs/Downstairs concept is not a disguised remnant of theology. This will become obvious after a while, but it seems as well to spell out the fact now. And there is another, seemingly contradictory, reason. What I had been taught in the medieval Catholic Church was not merely fairy tales made up to enhance an institution's control of its members. I from personal experience learned that what I had been taught was someone's best shot at describing what I now see and experience in a radically different framework.

About Downstairs. I came to learn that I as an individual am much more than I used to think I was. A man was born in 1946 and eventually died. (In 2023, as I have been told? We'll see.) He formed around an ego that centered, by design, in one particular time and space. That self, what Carl Jung used to call self number one, is the self I usually think of as me. It isn't as simple as that, but for a shorthand description, it will do. This intellectual and emotional and physical unity, I call Downstairs. (Some today might think this a description of the functioning of the left brain, but that is so vast an oversimplification as to amount to falsehood.)

This unit operates on sensory data, and logic, and emotion. It plans and executes. It functions, and unconnected millions are aware of nothing more than this level of functioning. Certainly, for much of my life, despite substantial clues to the contrary, I stumbled along thinking that this unit was all there was to me. This Downstairs consciousness thinks it is alone, and struggles through its life, alone, as best it can. It may form close emotional bonds with family or friends; may fall in love; may identify with the idealized existence of others (as I did with Churchill, for instance, and JFK). Nonetheless, it feels alone. It may believe in God, or the Higher Good, or All That Is, or it may believe in Marxism or history or evolution, and identify with any of those, or even with nothingness. Regardless, it lives and dies feeling alone.

Or rather, it does unless at some point it experiences connection, in which case it discovers Upstairs. Unless and until that connection is experienced, one lives life alone, regardless of *belief,* for I am speaking here not of a theological concept but of an experienced reality. Many a bishop lives only Downstairs, I suspect, and many atheists would be horrified (or possibly amused) to realize that they themselves live more firmly connected Upstairs than do many believers.

So what is Upstairs? For now, let us say that we Downstairs individuals are to Upstairs as individual computer terminals are to computers that are networked together. Upstairs has access to vastly more data and wisdom, and remembered purpose. It has the wider view of our lives, our personalities, and our meaning. Upstairs is where unsuspected "coincidences" nudge our lives to keep certain possibilities continually available to us. Available, not inevitable, for it is up to us to choose. That is what we are here for, Downstairs: to choose. And, as I see it now, nudging is exactly what was going on when I picked up Colin Wilson's book that night, shortly before Dave Schlachter's father called to tell me that Dave was dying.

— 4 —

Dave had been one of my closest friends in college; in some ways the closest. There were things we could share with each other that couldn't be shared with anyone else. For instance, in the autumn of 1968, when the guys in our fraternity house came back to school, it was Dave and I who stayed up into the early hours one night, talking about how we had reacted to the news that Bobby Kennedy had been killed, and how we had spent the rest of that long summer. In that regard and in others, Dave and I were instinctively on the same wavelength, even though he was a well-motivated, scholastically successful, solidly middle-class Jewish Midwesterner, and I was none of these.

(That we were on the same wavelength we took for granted; only in 1987, in the course of a past-life regression by an amateur hypnotist, did I startle myself by seeing me as having in another lifetime been Dave's star pupil. I told myself then that *that* explained why he and I were so close in certain ways. Not that I was fully convinced, and not that I see things quite that way now, particularly the question of reincarnation. But that's getting far ahead of the story.)

In our senior year, only a few weeks before he was to graduate, Dave suddenly began seeing double. He was hospitalized, and within hours became paralyzed. The doctors said this was the result of the sudden growth of a brain tumor that must have been lying in wait since he was perhaps two years old. An operation removed the paralysis by removing the pressure of accumulated fluids, but it also revealed that the tumor was in an inoperable place. A few weeks later Dave walked out of the hospital and was able to return home, but the doctors made it quite clear that there was no long-term hope. He might live a year, two years, even twenty—who could know?—but ultimately it would kill him.

My reaction was fierce: Fight this thing! Something told me that Will would have more to do with Dave's survival than anyone was admitting. And I wanted desperately to help. Had the feeling that I *could* help, if I only knew *how*. But no one could tell me how. Our mutual friends were defeated by it. I read in their eyes that they thought I was merely refusing to accept reality. We were in our early twenties, what did we know? The doctors knew. The adults knew. Dave had been given a death sentence.

The worst of it was that I could see that Dave thought so too. I told him to fight it, the last time I saw him, the last time we had a few quiet moments together while he was in GWU hospital that summer. But he was too weak, too discouraged, and there was nothing around him to give him any realistic reason to think he could successfully fight fate. In those days, even more than today, the surrounding culture called despair realism. The terms "alternative medicine" and "distant healing" hadn't even been coined then, so far as I know. In any case, they weren't current with anybody *I* knew.

In 1970 the consensus was that his only hopes were medical intervention or spontaneous remission (whatever *that* was supposed to mean) or a miracle. Medical intervention had failed, spontaneous remission wasn't happening, and I don't think anybody in Dave's hospital room believed in miracles. I did, I suppose, but I sure didn't know how to summon one.

He would have many more options today. Nearly thirty years later another friend of mine, Dave Wallis, was hospitalized at the University of Virginia Hospital in Charlottesville after an accident. What a difference! During the two days he was in a coma, his friends, instead of having to sit in a waiting room holding up the walls, spent time around his bed, sending healing energy. We each did what we knew to do, doing a lot of energy work. Not only did the UVA hospital personnel not object, they were supportive. They had seen therapeutic touch and other therapies work before. In fact, an orderly told me that one of the doctors on staff wouldn't operate without the assistance of prayers from the patient's loved ones. Charlottesville in 1998 was a far cry from Washington in 1970. We as a society have come a certain distance along the road.

Indeed, one time in 1998, when three of us were around Dave's bed, sending him healing energy, I looked around and got choked up as it hit me how beautiful it was. I thought, "This is how it's *supposed* to be. This is how it *will* be." The doctors will use their skill and others will send love and support and will use what they know, and the whole process of recovery from illness and accident will be so much more human. Also, we'll be able to *do* so much more.

How I wish I could have given Dave Schlachter anything of what I know now. If that was his time and pattern to go, all right, but in different circumstances, it might have had a different result. Circular logic, of course.

Dave died in his hometown on March 2, 1970. Several of us had come out to Iowa to be with him. In those last moments, one of our friends held his mother, another held his girlfriend, and I put cooling cloths on Dave's head and stroked his forehead, and maybe talked to him, though I don't remember. Then it was over and we walked out of his hospital room feeling terrible. The following week we were in northern New Jersey, where his father had family, and on a bitter Friday we buried him, as the rabbi and his father said the ancient words that probably none of his friends believed in.

My friend Dennis, who was Dave's closest friend, was there, having obtained compassionate leave from the army. (He had been drafted soon after graduation.) While we were standing as pallbearers, he leaned over to me and quietly quoted Kahlil Gibran: "Pain is the breaking of the shell that encloses the understanding." I had plenty of pain, but not much understanding. I couldn't even understand why I had pain. Intellectually, I knew Dave was better off dead than trapped in a malfunctioning body. Intellectually, I believed he was now free. Intellectually, I believed in reincarnation, so intellectually I couldn't see death as a tragedy, right? (This from the same brain that was still lacerated from the murders of JFK and RFK, two famous men it hadn't even met!)

Intellectually was one thing. Emotionally was another. Emotionally, I was a wreck. I said I *shouldn't* feel, and thought that ended it. Many years later, I treated myself to a spell of

Jungian analysis, and there I finally learned that feelings can be ignored, but not dictated, and that we ignore them at the price of deadness.

– 5 –

So what does this have to do with Colin Wilson? At this point, I have no idea. I thought I knew, when he first came up, but I see now I am blank about it. Let's have a word from Upstairs. Gentlemen, can you assist me here?

Of course. And welcome to you, reader. What Frank calls The Gentlemen Upstairs, at your service. Perhaps he will not mind if we cast some of this in the third person. It will be easier for him to hear, and easier therefore to slip it through his mental filtration.

Frank was functioning exclusively Downstairs, as he calls it, all the years from the time he was shut down at about age seven until he gradually learned to consciously reopen the tap as a middle-aged man. The point of these early sections is to remind him—and you—of what it is like to live continuously Downstairs, without conscious access to other levels of your being. It isn't "wrong" to do so, in any moral sense. It isn't even "incorrect" to do so, for all paths are good, and all lead to growth one way or another. But while it isn't wrong, and isn't incorrect, it certainly is doing things the hard way. People do things the hard way sometimes because they are stubborn, and sometimes because they feel they have no choice. But usually they stop doing it the hard way when they learn that there is an easier way.

One purpose of this book is to convince you to try the easier way.

When Frank's friend died, and in a way even more so when his earlier "friends"—his heroes—were killed, he had to deal with it exclusively from his Downstairs resources, and not even all of those. Because he thought he *shouldn't* fear death, or mourn it, he convinced himself that it *shouldn't* hurt, and that therefore it *didn't*.

Unable to acknowledge his feelings, he was of course unable to process them, and they remained violently alive within him. (So it seems to you in bodies, anyway.) Repressing awareness of feelings takes enormous amounts of energy, even when much of the emotion becomes locked into the physical structure. The violent unacknowledged feelings sloshing around inside made him prone to violent, unpredictable, uncontrolled mood swings, as those who were around him then could well testify. And the situation divorced him increasingly from the world around him, as he tried to cope with the world—with others—strictly from unacknowledged, therefore unknown, feelings. People were already a puzzle to him; they became even more so. He had no *feel* for who they were, or why they were as they were. He couldn't understand the simplest things about what motivated them. And he had no idea how he appeared to others. Some were attracted to him, some were contemptuous, some puzzled. In no case did he have any idea why.

What all this has to do with Colin Wilson jumps the gun a bit, chronologically. Frank's helplessness in the face of his friend's death appalled him—though he scarcely realized it. And his dissatisfaction with his own life was so acute, his belief in the reality of any realistic path so nonexistent, that he was feeling trapped. He *thought* in terms of writing books, making lots of money, and living an independent existence not requiring him to go to work five days a week, but to his puzzlement he made little attempt to do the writing that would lead to the goal. He *thought* in terms of running for Congress in 1974, but made no attempt to lay any groundwork for the plan. He was stranded. At a deeper level, he was purposeless. (We speak here strictly of the Downstairs level that he experienced.)

Colin Wilson's books gave him an opening he could believe in: the development of mental powers! The achievement of supernatural abilities, paranormal skills! He didn't know whether he could believe in them or not, but here was a writer who was investigating reports of such things, and doing so from a point of view quite similar to his own: open and inquiring, yet skeptical and wanting to make sense of it all, rather than merely accepting someone's word for it.

Wilson's book came into Frank's life—something he is about to learn as we bring him to write this—at just the time needed to provide him a bridge across despair. The Catholic Church had failed him, or so he would have put it, in that its rules and its perceived completeness and rigidity left no room for things he somehow *knew* were not as they had been described. (He called that knowing intuition then, not yet thinking in terms of layers of being.) The materialist worldview had no appeal; he similarly *knew* that was even less true than what he took the Catholic Church's position to be. He was looking for a way out of his logical prison that said, "There is no God; or anyway, not as I have been taught; yet we are more than the accidental collection of chemicals."

Wilson was there, to lead him to many others. *The Mind Parasites* inflamed him with the nonrational certainty that mental powers were there waiting to be developed. *The Outsider* and the succeeding books in Wilson's Outsider cycle were crammed with references to others who seemed to see the world, if not just as Frank saw it, at least closer than anyone he knew in the flesh.

– 6 –

Well, there you have a sample of The Gentlemen Upstairs (TGU) as I experience them. They and I function as close friends, joking with each other, but serious at the same time; trusting in each other's good intent and basic ability. I gently make fun of them sometimes, and they return the compliment. There's a lot of play in our relationship, in both senses of the phrase. I'm a little surprised they didn't sign off by saying something like, "We now return you to our regular programming." They're well capable of it.

For a long time I wondered if "they" were "real"—meaning were they truly independent intelligences offering assistance, or were they part of my own subconscious or semiconscious mind, helping me to fool myself. Particularly when I would ask them a question about the future and get either a wrong answer or a refusal to answer, I would strongly suspect that it was all an internal mind game. I persevered for good reason: They are good company, and they are wonderful at analyzing situations. In fact, my business partner and I got into the habit of consulting TGU when we were facing decisions, or whenever we happened to want counsel. They wouldn't necessarily tell us what to do (not that we would have listened in any case) but they *would* extensively analyze the background, the context, and the ramifications of what we were asking about.

As in the sample above, they often tell me things I don't know about my own background or motivations. It is quite an interesting sensation to write the words "something he's about to learn as we bring him to write this" and have no idea what will follow—and then to reread what follows, and learn something.

And perhaps this is as good a place as any to describe the process of connecting Upstairs, so that you may decide if you want to try it for yourself. It isn't difficult.

Consider how you write ordinarily. Writing to a friend, say. You sit with pen in hand, or hands poised over typewriter or computer or word processor, and—what happens? Do you first think out your sentences and paragraphs and then write them? I doubt it. If you function as I do, you sit down to write, and you write. You have an idea of what you are going to say, and you begin to say it, and each thing suggests another. (Another way to view it: writing one thing allows the next connection to well up within you.)

This is precisely how you learn to talk to your friends Upstairs.

Usually I ask a question, writing or typing it to focus my mind on it. Then I let Upstairs respond. By now the response, the alternation, is essentially instantaneous. But in the beginning, when I was becoming accustomed to it, here's what I did.

I wrote the question and sat with pen in hand waiting for a word or phrase to surface. At first only a disconnected word or phrase would come, and I would write it down *as if* I knew the rest of the sentence. (I suppose I might as easily phrase it, "in faith that the rest of the sentence would come".) Word by word the sentence would come. Sometimes I would get a great bit, other times only a word at a time. My attitude was the important thing: I sat with my mind quiet, open and expectant, not trying to force something to happen, but not second-guessing what came, either. I thought, "If what comes is nonsense, so be it, but let's see what comes." And if I were to lay down one rule for all this, it would be, "Don't criticize too soon!" Criticism, even doubt, inhibits the process. If you're going to try something, really try it! Expect it to succeed. And give it more tries than one. What doesn't work one day may work another day. Keep trying. Then comes the next step, which is harder and requires more practice. You need to learn to tell the difference between good information and contamination from your own anxiety-ridden, or egotistic, or off-the-beam thoughts.

It ought to be unnecessary to point out that in such matters you are not required to check your common sense at the door. (Note, I said it *ought* to be unnecessary.) If when you try automatic writing you get a message telling you to kill yourself or others, or to put everything you own on Baby Shoes in the seventh at Hialeah—are you going to listen? If you get messages saying you are God (more than the rest of us, I mean) or that you are a slave of Satan and must now follow orders—are you going to believe it?

Not if you are in your right mind.

If you're in your right mind, stay there. Don't throw common sense out the window. Contacting Upstairs is a resource that can enhance life Downstairs; it's not a substitute for *living* here. That means using your best judgment and making your own choices, neither becoming a robot for beings on the non-physical side of life nor succumbing to psychic inflation, letting your ego swell because you have come into contact with something so exciting, profound, and beyond everyday life.

Let me add a few words more, since not everyone *is* in his or her right mind. What occultists call the astral plane, and what Monroe-speak calls Focus levels 22 and 23, contain many kinds of souls, among them the delirious, the perplexed, the malicious, and the obsessed. You really don't want to be contacting them unknowingly. Upstairs has its low-rent and high-crime districts just as we do here, and an unprepared soul can be more helpless there than in the equivalent areas on this plane. For one thing, in visiting other planes, you are, at least in the beginning, functioning basically blind. For another, unless you use your judgment, your very (necessary) attitude of openness may leave you vulnerable to being conned. It is because these dangers do exist that some belief systems—notably fundamentalist religions—warn against contact with the other realms.

But if dangers exist, so do rewards. The dangers can be dealt with easily enough; it's a matter of being prepared. And on that note, let's hear another word from our sponsors, who have given me no reason to fear them, and many reasons to value them. I think they will have their own ideas on the subject.

– 7 –

In certain directions, we should say, Frank is quite exceptionally fearless. He jokes (meaning it, however) that his personal motto is "where angels fear to tread." Certainly there is nothing wrong with that, assuming one *knows* (as he does, not questioning *how* he knows) that it is safe to do so. But what is safe for one is hazardous for another. He senses this—hence his call to us, for truly he has no idea how one would protect oneself. This is because *what he is* is his protection, and he knows not how to transfer that immunity.

We cannot give you ground rules and rituals, lest they immediately become superstitions, which in our definition is something done in the hope that it will lead to results if done right; yet done without understanding of *why* it is done. By this rather flexible definition, you might note, even multiplication by the times table may sometimes be superstitious, and we suggest that often it is.

Rather than a rite, then, we will give you the underlying dynamic. You may trust yourselves to devise your own rites—your own habits, we should say—based on your understanding of what is to be accomplished and how. The fact that you will remember that the rite was constructed by yourself for specific purposes will to some degree (depending on your level of being, and your acculturation) protect you from the superstition of worshiping as an idol a psychological protection ritual.

The situation is this. You are a spirit encased in a body. That body is *shielding*. You wish, for specific purposes of growth and exploration, to step beyond the shielding. Well and good—only, bring a portable form of shielding with you.

Frank (though he doesn't know it yet, or didn't till we gave him this!) will explain Monroe's concept of focus levels and vibratory levels. We, though, have the somewhat trickier task of trying to explain to you how to obtain equivalent protections and results without employing the terminology and technology—and mental technology, we could call it—that Frank found so good a set of training wheels. It is true that he proceeded independently before becoming acquainted with Monroe's work, but Frank is not a typical person, and we aim this more for the bold but uninstructed who *may not* have particular protection.

We digress for a moment to point out that on what Frank calls the Upstairs level, all of you are protected; all of you have the knowledge, and the ability. You might do it as safely and surely as he has done it. Sleepwalking, he calls it—walking securely in the dark, knowing and not knowing how he knows, but trusting. If you are in touch with your own Upstairs, you can do it too—for the same intelligence that put you here will guide you. One day all will be able to live like that. But if you were on speaking terms with Upstairs, you wouldn't have to be learning how to get into touch, would you? Hence the need for precautions. To proceed:

1. You are a spirit. Your body protects you (insulates you) from the vibrations of discarnate spirits except in unusual situations, which we will not discuss here.
2. To venture safely beyond the protecting body, you need to provide yourself with an insulating chamber in which to travel. Hear us clearly: This is neither a physical container nor a metaphor, but a change in vibration or rather a setting of vibration. You are to set your vibrations so "high" (vibration, after all, being only an analogy) that "lower" vibrations cannot enter to displace or molest you. The verbs are chosen carefully.
3. You, Downstairs, do not know how to do this. Your Upstairs knows full well. Setting your firm intent *prior to* opening yourself to other realities opens the channel to allow your Higher Self to protect you. We are sorry if this sounds circular to you—we are attempting to give you an understanding that will serve you, rather than a cookbook-approach ritual that would equally well serve, but would allow you to proceed without understanding what was happening.
4. Construct some visualization that will serve to symbolize protection from external entities. You might visualize a sphere of white light with yourself in the center. Many do this. Or you might see yourself pumping energy from yourself into the surrounding area (so that lesser energy cannot get to you, you see). Or you might visualize the protecting hands of God, or Christ, or Saint Christopher, or your Aunt Nelly. We say this not to ridicule but to emphasize that the *visualization* is *subjective*; the *protection* flows in from your Higher Self—your Upstairs; call it what you will—and is *objective*. No matter how you see it, once you generate it, by asking for it and visualizing it, it is there.
5. With your protective image in place, *then* open up to what your friends have to say. You may in fact add to your visualization a comforting and focusing statement of intent such as Monroe uses.

This is the essence of the process of going Upstairs, or talking to your Higher Self. It is called automatic writing; it is called many things. Our last *caveat* to you is that you remain conscious even while remaining receptive. A tranced communication is not what is desired here; but rather, an opening or widening of the accepted channels of communication between your Downstairs and Upstairs selves.

And now—if only to satisfy Frank's humor—we return you to our regularly scheduled broadcast.

– 8 –

Rereading that section was very interesting to me; I learned something. I of course was aware that I pay little attention to protection rituals, but I never much thought about it. Their explanation rings true. I feel protected. I have nothing to fear. Yet it is also true, I was uneasy at the thought of sending others out without protection. Something told me it wasn't safe. Now I see why. I am safe because of something that comes from well within me. Anyone else coming from that same place is equally safe, but it is not reasonable to expect others to know whether or not they are coming from safety when I myself never knew. It is for those who do not know that my friends provided their explanation and suggested procedure. And I think their helpful nature comes through. I have often noticed that they are even longer-winded than I am, though not prolix. Whenever I ask them a question, I can be sure to get a summary of the situation as well, unless it is so simple that they tell me, in essence, "You know what to do, why are you dithering about it?" But usually they don't do that. They're more likely to say, "We can only advise. *You* must act." They say that's what we're here for: to act. To choose, and choose, and choose again, and thus shape what we become.

– 9 –

We've come a long way from what we were discussing, which is that in 1970 I was living my life exclusively Downstairs.

I found it hard enough. Yet I could find no way—no intellectually respectable way—out of the trap I was in. I believed in
material life; I believed in supernatural powers, or wanted to.
But I had no access, and no way of gaining access. Besides—
though I didn't realize it then—my idea of supernatural powers
was closer to Superman comics than to the real thing. I had no
guide, no idea where to go or what to do. At least, I didn't
Downstairs. Upstairs had it figured out in advance, or impro-
vised brilliantly as we went along, using whatever became available. As it very efficiently used my one experience of mescaline
to teach me several interrelated lessons.

My first and only experience with mescaline came within a
few weeks of Dave Schlachter's death. I had come down to D.C.
mostly to see Dennis, who had gotten a weekend leave. It was
the first time I had seen him since Dave's funeral, and we both
knew that he was going to Vietnam soon. There was a very real
possibility that I'd never see him again. We met at the apartment of one of our younger fraternity brothers who was still in
school, along with another senior I knew slightly, and my ex-
roommate Bill. One thing led to another; we were offered a
chance to try the psychotropic drug mescaline, and we took it.

Dennis and I had gotten through college without trying
drugs; our younger contemporaries were somewhat patronizing
about our lack of experience. But now Dennis was going to do it
and I wanted to stay with him, even though I was somewhat
scared of the idea. So we paid our money (all of two dollars in
1970) and swallowed the capsules along with a little orange juice,
and waited for something to happen, which soon enough it did.

It woke me up in a big way! Mescaline (or whatever it was
we took: we were *told* it was mescaline) instantly and entirely (if
temporarily) altered the way I experienced the world. It had the
effect of magnifying my perception of things while at the same
time reducing my field of focus. If I looked at a candle, I really
looked at it; really *saw* it, for the first time in my life. Until then

I had gone through life looking at things, experiencing things, rather lazily. My attention was more on abstractions and ideas and thoughts and memories than on what was right there in front of me.

Mescaline grabbed me and said, "*Look!* Notice! Pay attention to the outside world!" And so, for nearly the first time in my life, I did. And I was astounded at how much was going on that I was missing. It was like the time I picked up the prints from my first roll of color film, and walked down an autumn street really *seeing* the turning leaves, drunk from sudden awareness of so much color in the world.

Now I looked at a print of a painting of a boat on the seashore, beached head-on—and suddenly experienced the front half of the boat sticking straight out into the room ahead of the plane of the painting. Every time I noticed the painting (for I kept forgetting about it and noticing it anew), this happened. I realized that the artist not only was able to paint it that way, out of his skill; he was able to *see* it that way.

A friend put on some classical music; a flute trilled, and I heard it as a bird singing in a garden, and *knew* (on no other evidence) that this was what the composer was describing in a language normally all but closed to me. I liked classical music, but this was a revelation. Close to tears, I said to my friend, "It's so beautiful!" He knew that I had appreciated the music before, but he could see the sudden difference in comprehension. "That's what I've been trying to tell you," he said.

The walls, I realized, were alive! Literally. What I had been taking for dead matter was somehow alive in a way I couldn't fathom, but couldn't doubt. Reality wasn't what I had thought it was. My Downstairs view of reality took a couple of serious hits.

For one thing, I had always taken for granted the idea of coincidence. A child of my times, I viewed life (never much thinking about it) as a collision of forces, unpredictable and only somewhat manageable. Only the superstitious considered every little incident to be an omen, or an integral part of the grand scheme of things. One of mescaline's many effects on me was to shatter my belief in coincidence.

Several times in the course of that long Saturday afternoon I watched the interaction of five people come to perfectly orchestrated peaks and lulls. I refer not to anything externally dramatic, but to the temporary clarity of vision that showed me (beyond later doubting) that more went on between individuals than their ordinary consciousness realized. Thinking about the orchestration I saw then, I for a while referred to God The Great Playwright. I didn't anymore know if I believed in God or not, but it was suddenly very clear that *something* was ordering the patterns I saw around me.

I awoke in a different way that afternoon. At one point I looked over at Dennis and started to say something about Dave, and he said thickly, "Don't!" He explained, "It'll tear us up, and I don't want to do that." For that moment I saw the depth of his feelings; for that moment, his inner self was real to me. But I soon went back to slumbering.

At one climactic point, as I realized how far above my usual mental routines I had been lifted by the energy set free by the drug, I said, "I'm not going back to that prison!" And I meant it. But one of my younger friends, who was angry at me for many reasons, said contemptuously that I had no choice. And of course I didn't. The drug wore off, and in a few hours I was back in ordinary consciousness.

But everything was different. I had had a glimpse of what lay beyond. I didn't know how to get back there, but I *knew*, now, that my intuitions on reading *The Mind Parasites* had been correct it, though my understanding had been inadequate. There *was* more available. Only—how to find it?

Drugs were a dead-end path for several reasons. They were illegal, number one; I didn't want to go down that road if I could help it, regardless what I might do once. Also, because they were illegal, they were unregulated, hence unpredictable; regardless what you were promised, there was no telling what you were going to get. And worst of all, they wore off. Although they could show you the promised land from across the river, they couldn't bring you over to live there.

In fact, as I realized later, by their very nature they were a dead-end path even for exploration. For one thing, the drug-weirdness distorted what you were being shown. They produced effect at the expense of function. One couldn't, by definition, function normally under drugs, *because* that functioning was drug-dependent. Mescaline tremendously stimulated perception, but it equally strongly suppressed continuity of awareness. At any given moment, I could see deeper into the nature of whatever had my attention than I ever had, but at the price of forgetting the very existence of whatever had occupied my attention previously. Only later was I able to piece together a more or less continuous picture of what had happened. At the time, I was riding the edge of Now, and hanging on for dear life.

The mescaline trip was a great one-time wake-up call, but it could not be a way of life. It was a shortcut, a glimpse, not a permanent gain.

– 10 –

Many years later a psychic would tell me that she saw me as a shaman of a tribe, at an undetermined time, in the desert somewhere in the southwestern United States or northern Mexico, "always going off by yourself on vision quests." At the time this didn't make much impact, because how was I to know whether what another person saw was accurate? But a few weeks later, in researching this book, I got a shock when I reread my notes from a Monroe Institute program I took in 1995 and saw that I had recorded a vision of myself as a shaman in just that place.

I won't swear that either her vision or mine is accurate, but it would explain something that pleased and puzzled me during that mescaline trip. Despite having no intellectual preparation Downstairs, and no experience, and no conscious connection Upstairs—not knowing Upstairs even existed!—nonetheless *I always knew what I was doing!* One reason my friend got so angry with me that day was that I continually "stumbled" into knowings. He had read about occult things since before high school, but he didn't have the same ease with it that I did. I was right at home, even while being amazed at myself.

Auras, for instance. I don't think I'd even heard of them, though this may be memory playing me false. But as soon as I realized that we live in the middle of an energy sheath, I knew several things without knowing how I knew them:

- I knew that the energy field would be there to be sensed later, when I was no longer influenced by the drug. In other words, it really existed, it wasn't an illusion. And indeed, from that day I have always been able to sense the field, and to teach others how to sense it.
- As I moved my hands across the aura of another person, I could feel a gentle friction, and I knew from somewhere that this was what Friedrich Mesmer was doing with his "mesmerizing" passes over people's bodies in the 1700s. He was aligning the energy somehow. (Mesmerism was the eighteenth- and nineteenth-century precursor to hypnotism.)
- I brought my hands near the temples of a friend who had not taken the drug, and knew that somehow this would enable or assist telepathic communication between us. (And this was before *Star Trek* movies. I didn't get the idea from Spock.)

Jumping to conclusions, all this. Yet they were accurate conclusions! How?

It soon became apparent that the things I have sketched above were the least of what might be found—if I only knew how to do the finding! If I knew, Downstairs!

For instance . . . At one point in the long afternoon of that drug experience, all the conversation in the room died down at the same time; not a sudden hush, but a culmination, for no apparent reason. I had just time to notice the sense of anticipation—clearly, we were all waiting for something, though we didn't know what—when there came a quiet knock on the door.

A knock. But the mental pause, the hush, had come first, although I don't think there had been an audible clue from outside. I think that if we had heard it, in our heightened state of awareness we would have known that we had heard it. Easy enough for me to understand today: it was Upstairs, giving us a peek at the next page of the script. In other words, I suspect that each of us was cooperating Upstairs, which is what orchestrated the play, even though the respective Downstairs editions hadn't a clue as to what was going on. Twenty-seven years later, at a Monroe program, I would experience exactly the same sense of anticipation in the middle of an event, and I would realize suddenly that in this context too, the scenario was being scripted elsewhere. At the time, I saw the orchestration clearly, but I wasn't thinking in terms of us having an Upstairs and Downstairs version. Jumping to conclusions, I came up with the idea of God The Great Playwright. (I jump to conclusions at a moment's notice. My redeeming grace is that I am equally willing to jump away from the original conclusion, given new evidence.)

But this wasn't the only conclusion I was jumping to. My first thought was, "Oh my God, it's the police. I'll be arrested. Now I'll never be able to run for Congress."

It's funny now. It wasn't funny then.

Fortunately, it wasn't the police, it was my old friend/adversary whom I will call "Ben Speaker," bringing us his sunny, cheerful presence as he came to see what was going on.

As usual, he looked wide-eyed, mischievous, and innocent. As usual, there was no telling what he was really up to. Or so I thought at first. But when I focused on him, I realized that he wasn't a mystery at all. Suddenly I understood him. I said "Ben! You don't *need* drugs, do you?" He shook his head, smiling. "I'm always like this." And that explained some things.

Ben's ordinary consciousness was artistic, quirky, sensitive, irritable. His motivations and reactions often baffled his fraternity brothers. Speaker was Speaker, we had decided; a law unto himself. He was, in fact, naturally high, more truly an individual than anyone else in the fraternity. More individual even than I was, and I in my own way was weird enough. With drug-powered insight, I could see that Ben literally lived in a different world. That glow in his eyes reflected great depths; it was the glow of someone who was truly conscious. As I had *not* been truly conscious.

No wonder Ben stole so many people's girlfriends! (He had stolen mine in the course of a casual conversation at a party, after I had made a point of introducing them.) He did it without effort, almost without intent, merely by the fascination of what he was. He was alive! He was conscious! He had no shortage of faults, and who could describe them better than those who knew him best then? But he was a fascinating personality, precisely because he was alive to the moment, rather than entranced.

All this I saw instantly. And when I went on to demonstrate to him the aura I'd just discovered—putting my palms near his, and then putting my palms near his temples to see if it would aid mental contact between us—Ben was right there with me. He didn't retreat into caution or attempt to be the authority. He knew who he was and he was willing to play. It was a revelation. Today I would say that Ben naturally lived with one foot in normal everyday consciousness and one in another layer of consciousness, as we'll discuss later. At the time, I had no framework. The best I could do then was to say that his nerve endings had no protective skin covering, so to speak. He was alive to the world more directly than I was. This was hopeful in a way, for it showed that some, at least, could get there without drugs. But he had been born that way and I hadn't. What was I to do, once the drug wore off?

For most of the rest of this book, we will look at what I did, and what I discovered in the doing. I have hung this narrative on my own life because, as Thoreau put it, I am confined by the narrowness of my own experience. But that doesn't mean my experiences are only my own business. They shed light on who and what we are.

The world changes when you look at it through what Bob Monroe used to call a Different Overview. I think you will find that things that had been inexplicable become understandable, even commonplace. Reports and ideas that had seemed fanciful become seen as a straightforward attempt to speak plainly about extraordinary experience. Our everyday reality reveals itself as simultaneously utterly mundane and utterly strange and wonderful. And we ourselves? We become creatures of wonder to ourselves, as we realize again how much more we are than we commonly think.

TWO

Of God and Shirley MacLaine

My mescaline trip took place in 1970. I didn't have another meaningful experience of a connection with something beyond my conscious self until Shirley MacLaine's Higher Self Seminar in January 1987. Because I attended, I did contact what might be called my Higher Self. And because I honestly and openly reported what had happened to me there, I set out upon the path that has brought me to a vastly expanded universe. Even the story of how I came to attend is itself instructive.

I was living in Virginia by then, age forty, in my first year as associate editor for the Norfolk *Virginian-Pilot,* happily writing editorials, columns, and book reviews, finally making my living by writing after years of doing things that did not use the one talent I valued above all others. The professional part of my life seemingly was under control. Yet whenever I sat down to work on the novel whose first draft I had written eight years before, or on my study of "Thoreau and Mr. Emerson," begun even earlier, I dried up. Why? And I had other problems, including my marriage and, notably, my health.

My prime comfort—I know this will sound odd—was that I felt I had developed a pretty good working relationship with God. I belonged to no church, being unable to get within a church the spiritual nourishment I needed. But I had learned to live in faith, which I then interpreted in pretty traditional terms. I lived, or tried to live, listening to God, doing God's will, leaving it up to God. My prayer was, "Dear God, show me the way." There are many worse ways to live. Indeed, at my best I live that way now, though I define things differently. That's one of the things that this book is about, new ways of seeing things, for the problem is, religious *experience* unites; religious *opinions* divide.

Anyway, early in 1987 I was experiencing chronic intense back pain. My chiropractor sent me to get X-rays, and one Tuesday she showed me the X-ray films. They showed arthritis, with additional features including insufficient curve in the neck and pelvis and thinning of pads in the hips. The thinning was pretty serious, and the white on the X-rays showed abundant calcium deposited on the bones. It looked like frosting. And nothing could be done to remove it. It looked like I was beginning to become an old man, and I was only forty. Pretty depressing.

I went through the rest of that week in repeated periods of great pain. Any little thing, like building a cold frame for some lettuce seedlings, reduced me to near immobility. I couldn't sit, stand, or lie down comfortably. And along with the pain came depression, I not realizing that this was the low point.

My wife suggested that I might want to watch *Out on a Limb,* the upcoming two-part TV special about actress Shirley MacLaine's spiritual searchings. I dislike television, and I didn't have any particular interest in Shirley MacLaine. But I was in pain, without anything better to do. Why not watch a little TV? So I watched the first night's program (three hours' worth) with intense interest—and the damnedest thing happened. When I got up to go to bed, I suddenly realized that for the first time in days, my back didn't hurt! What's more—to jump the gun on the story—the arthritis of the spine disappeared, and never troubled me again. I had years of back pain yet ahead, but never again from arthritis.

It would be years before I learned the "how" of what had happened, but even at the time I took it as a wake-up call.

Thinking I was leading a God-centered life, I had still let externals distract me. No wonder I felt like I was dying! I decided to go to the first of the Higher Self Seminars, which (in honor of Edgar Cayce) was going to be held in nearby Virginia Beach. It would cost three hundred dollars, no small amount for us then, and I wondered if I was going to be taken for a ride, but decided to make the effort. And so I was one of the six hundred-plus people in the good-natured crowd that filed into the Cavalier Hotel in Virginia Beach.

The newspaper ad had said that the seminar would offer "group meditations, techniques in visualization, chakra-raising sessions, questions and answers relating to past-life recognition, how we create our own reality, and the final connection with the Higher Self." I saw, clearly enough, the expert manipulation that had been used in the wording of the ad, but reading it again all these years later, I judge that what she offered is what she delivered. And she delivered it, as a seasoned showbiz professional, by knowing not only how to employ sound-effect techniques but how to mobilize and use group energy. In the very first visualization exercise, her voice led us to visualize crossing a river to where the Higher Self would be waiting. To my astonishment, there indeed was an image, one I never would have consciously chosen.

My Higher Self appeared as a unicorn! A unicorn, a magical, mythological beast. For the first time, I realized why my father—who could be symbolized as a loyal, dependable workhorse—had always been so dismissive of my beliefs. He thought I was "really" a horse too—and what was he to make of a horse who thought he was a unicorn? My unworldliness had worried him. By telling me (against my active resistance) "the way things are," he had tried to protect me. The gift of the situation, besides all the practical things he did teach me, was that living with him provided me with protection against (that is, understanding of) skeptics and cynics.

On the other hand, I realized that weekend, I'm *not* a horse. I am what I am! I *am* different, and that difference is to be prized. This visualization, more than any single event in my life, removed my shame and doubt about who and what I was. (Also, I got a vision of myself as translator. Somebody to comprehend the time and the energy and the pattern, and help everyone deal with them. Somebody who is empowered from within, one in touch with all levels. Oddly, by the time I got confirmation of this at The Monroe Institute five and a half years later, I had long forgotten it.)

I had asked myself in my journal, that morning, what I wanted from the seminar, and after some false starts had decided that "what I'd chiefly want is to be spiritually, physically, mentally whole. I'm so tired of being a fragment, and a crippled fragment at that." That weekend of healing brought me partway toward wholeness: health. I got something of what I wanted.

I knew I could trust the Higher Self, and knew I could trust God. But each of these labels came with its own emotional nuances, and they didn't fit all that well together. It's too easy for the idea of God to become confused by every bit of half-baked theology that has ever come our way. And although I knew I had connected to *something* at the seminar, I got no sense of a separate individual or group of individuals like The Gentlemen Upstairs as I later experienced them. The Higher Self was a vague concept to me, little more than a smarter aspect of my personal self. It showed me that the long, hard, solitary road wasn't the only road there is, but it didn't give me much more to work with.

When I got home from that weekend, I wrote up a two-thousand-word piece for my newspaper's "Commentary" section, which appeared the following Sunday. I didn't try to describe meeting my "higher self," because for a general audience a thirdhand description would be worse than none at all. (Thirdhand, in that they would have had to interpret my interpretation of my experience.) It is one thing to describe a thing to someone who may use that description as a guide or as a trail marker. It is quite another, futile, thing to describe it to those who will then judge its validity offhand, without having had the experience and without making any attempt to *have* the experience. Yet I didn't hide behind the journalist's facade of pretended impartiality. I was more willing to be called a fool than I was to pretend that nothing had happened to me.

I admit that I had qualms when, on the Friday before publication, I saw the article in page proofs, with my suggested headline made into a subhead and "In the spirit" used as the head. "Oh God," I thought, "what have I done?" Nothing in the piece was phony, shallow, or wrong, though it might have been more carefully hedged. But it was so open and unprotected! I suddenly wasn't so sure I wanted it so widely distributed.

On the Monday following, I went to work braced for a wave of criticism or ridicule. Instead, I got lots of reinforcement. Reporters and editors talked to me (carefully!) in the hallways, showing intense but strictly private interest, even fascination. I might have known. The previous Thursday I had gone up to the newspaper's library, and one of the women there had said, "Look, it's Frank DeMarco!" Great entrance, but not one I was used to. (The newsroom budget for Sunday had mentioned that I would have a piece on the Shirley MacLaine seminar.) It was my first experience of how much underground interest there is in the subject.

This turned out to be my introduction to the local New Age community, because in their experience, a newspaper article giving "inside" (and favorable) coverage of a metaphysical event was unprecedented. The article drew some favorable phone calls, and a local radio host asked me to appear on his show to talk about the seminar. A fellow journalist at another bureau said she was interested in her inner self, and asked if I could suggest a starting place or a book. Another, an older man, called to say that he and his wife had "a certain amount of experience" in the field themselves, had liked the article, and admired my courage in letting it be published. Again, an experience of people's trepidation. It wasn't long before I found out why. The criticism followed in a second wave.

What I found particularly interesting was the fact that, although my article criticized materialism rather than fundamentalism, nearly all the adverse letters came from fundamentalists rather than from materialists. Maybe science worshipers considered the subject beneath their notice. Fundamentalists did, at least, concede that we were dealing with real forces. But they were certain that these forces were of the devil.

My reaction was bemusement. So far as I could see, my piece hadn't attacked their religious beliefs even implicitly. Contacting your Higher Self *needn't* be done within a Christian framework, yet certainly *may be*, and *has been* for nearly two thousand years. As I explicitly said. Like Monroe (and three years before I read his books), instinctively I had written in a very low-key, matter-of-fact manner, sensing that dramatization is falsification, and that descriptions of metaphysical pursuits are very prone to just this error. What could be more matter-of-fact than the reporter's six questions of who, what, when, where, how, and why? I did try my best to get through to as many people as possible. Yet here were people saying that getting in touch with our Higher Selves was the work of the devil.

One man wrote that as "a person's spirit becomes open, the susceptibility to demonic influences increases. I know this to be true because at one time I touched on the occult and received a very bad experience." He suggested that searchers "do it under God's guidance by way of a qualified person such as a pastor or priest in an established church." In other words, like the medieval Catholic Church, he thought one should talk to spirit only through a licensed intermediary of an "established church," as if people like me would have been still searching if we had found what we needed there.

Another said Shirley MacLaine "offers more abstraction and vagueness to a large group of desperate souls in search of a quick fix in their spiritual lives." He said she "came to town to peddle an ancient, rehashed version of sorcery and nether-world indulgence." He added that she had been his favorite actress, but was "now someone who must be avoided at all costs. The Holy Spirit demands it." This name-calling was justified, presumably, because he *knew* what the Holy Spirit demands.

A third writer said Ms. MacLaine had "taken the same detour that disillusioned so many in the 1960s. Eastern religions, despite their seemingly profound inner revelations, can lead to a dead end. Ask the Beatles." (I never did figure this one out.)

A fourth, to cite one last example, said she was "shocked and appalled at the publicity your newspaper gave the seminar," which she termed a "rip-off," and said she was "most anxious to learn the name of her new temple and what false idol will be worshiped there." Ms. MacLaine, she said, had used "various brainwashing techniques such as 'visualization,'" and was "playing with fire. That fire has a name: a destructive cult."

What I found disturbing in this last letter was its misunderstanding of, fear of, and therefore rejection of techniques such as visualization. I was to learn in years to come that many fundamentalist Churches fear—perhaps more than any other single thing—individual attempts to commune with spirit in the absence of whatever version of the Bible that Church happens to believe in. Some teach that meditation is dangerous as "Satan can insert thoughts into open minds." God, apparently, can't.

– 2 –

Now, look how hard it is for fundamentalists, the mainline religious, and what are called New Agers to live together. Although the three groups all believe in the reality of spirit, in a very real sense they live in radically different worlds, because they perceive different realities. But those three at least believe that we are a blend of body, mind, and spirit. Materialists eliminate spirit as "unscientific," whatever that means. Behaviorist psychologists, if I understand their arguments, eliminate even mind, regarding thought and all internal human existence (presumably including their own) as an accidental by-product of chemical processes of the brain.

How can people holding such different viewpoints live comfortably together? We cannot do so very comfortably—strained tolerance is about as well as the various sides usually do. Each sees its own values under assault; each feels that its values are not respected by others or by society as a whole; each (to cite yet a third case of the same thing seen differently) sees others living in a fantasyland and forcing others to live there as well.

This is where wars between cultures begin, and that's precisely what is going on today throughout the world. For each of the participants, the stakes seem infinitely high, because of two connected assumptions. The first is: "It's us against them, and only one can win, and the result will determine human life for the indefinite future." The second, acknowledged or not, is: "We're on our own." And disagreement over high stakes breeds fanaticism.

To resolve this culture war without anyone losing, we'd have to find at least a common starting place, which surely can only be agreement on the facts underlying human existence. If we could agree on the facts, we could fight about interpretations and values later. But where is agreement on the facts to come from? Divine revelation? Scientific theory? Abstract reasoning? Intuitive knowing?

I would argue that it comes a little from each, and mostly from personal experience. What I know because I've been there (even though "what I know" may be wrong) is in a different category from what I only believe. It is in believing that we are tempted to kill one another; for what we are unconsciously unsure of, we defend with redoubled vehemence.

The scriptures say Jesus came that we may have "life more abundantly"—which I understand to mean life deeper, wider, and richer than commonly experienced. Let me say explicitly that I believe that life more abundantly is certainly possible, and that for a certain type of mind and personality, religion is the best, perhaps the only, avenue to that greater life. I am an enemy neither of religion, nor of spirituality, nor of expansion of consciousness, nor of any other way of achieving growth toward becoming what we are meant to be. Nor do I see any necessary contradiction among them.

It is clear to me that, just as humanity comes in different races and nationalities, so it comes in different psychological types, and members of each of these types can fulfill themselves only in a certain way. It's no good expecting fundamentalist Christians to find their spiritual growth in shamanic practices, or to expect Episcopalians and atheists to find their own growth in the same way. A path exists for each, and what is a path for one is trackless wilderness for another. It becomes a matter of personal experience.

But although there are many paths, perhaps it is not too much to say that we all have similar needs and similar intuitive certainties—certain things that seem to all of us self-evident. After all, at a level far beyond our conscious reasoning, we come out of the same world and are part of the same world, within the sensory realm and beyond it. As our experiences are not necessarily mutually contradictory, neither are the explanations—unless one says, "This interpretation is the only valid interpretation."

Which is what usually happens, of course.

— 3 —

The fact is, we have a hard time on earth—in physical matter—because this is not our home. Our bodies are of the earth, our animating spirit is not. And the closer you get into touch Upstairs, the clearer this is. This makes living in physical matter easier, and harder. It is also your guarantee that you do possess "psychic" abilities. No spirit incarnating could exist without them. One might as well suppose that people could live without breath, or heartbeat.

One reason this book has been so difficult to write (and rewrite, and rewrite!) is that everything is connected, which can make it hard to find a natural starting place. So, as in life, let's start where we find ourselves. In my case, both because I became an editor for a New Age publishing house, and because I was conducting my own investigations at The Monroe Institute and with others, I soon numbered among my friends writers and psychics and psychic writers. Various experiences with psychics taught me quickly that a person's psychic abilities, whether natural or developed, do not necessarily reflect a comparable level of maturity or wisdom or even goodwill. The gift does not imply moral or intellectual superiority; it's just a gift. Psychics, like anyone else, can be charitable or patient or wise, or all of these things, or they may be malicious or petulant or foolish—or all of these things.

Psychic's Disease, I call it: the certainty that whatever one feels strongly is true. The unwillingness to question one's own motives. The sometimes hysterical denunciation of anyone perceived to be in opposition. The assumption that anything and everything one wants is obviously for The Higher Good. The identification with God or with the Forces of Light or whatever, not as a matter-of-fact choosing of sides ("I stand with good against evil") but in an inflated manner that often seems merely overcompensation for an inferiority complex.

Now, you ask, seeing that description of common human frailty, how is that different from any other collection of fallible humans? The answer is, only in that genuine psychics have a specific talent that tempts them to regard themselves as set apart from other people, subject to different rules. Indeed, to a degree they *are* subject to different rules, because they experience their lives differently, and live in a manner that, in our tone-deaf time, is outside the accepted way of doing things. By contrast, in an American Indian tribe, for instance, the shaman is recognized as the bearer of a specific gift; his specific social role comes complete with expectations and allowances, somewhat as in our society our expectations and allowances for artists, say, are different from those we have for businessmen.

But in our secular society, psychics have to operate as if they lived in the same world the rest of us live in. Living by listening to the inner voice, experiencing the world in a radically different manner from those who experience it primarily through the senses, they cope as best they can, but in these circumstances it is easy for them to go off the beam, unnoticed by themselves, because they have so little external support to balance them. Someone living closely responsive to the inner voice doesn't easily listen even to constructive criticism by those who live only by external rules. The psychic knows that to live by external rules is death to the spirit. The psychic is correspondingly likely to forget that while in the body one cannot live *exclusively* in the spirit. Cannot. *Should* not. That's not what we're here for.

It can be impossible to get this across to them.

In a society that made an accepted place for these people, those gifts would be more easily available *and* reality checks would be easier for them to come by. They could more easily rely on reality checks not merely from each other, but from the culture at large, as in Joan Grant's vision of ancient Egypt. There is no inherent reason for psychics to have to function on the fringe of society, except that society has made clear to them that they are fakers or freaks, to be tolerated so long as they behave themselves; to be put in mental institutions or prisons if they step too far or express themselves incautiously.

Freaks? My point in this book is that we are *all* psychic. We can't help being psychic; it is inherent in being human. Only our view of what it means to be psychic distorts our awareness of how it fits in with the rest of the life that we take for granted. Thus we misidentify the abilities we use every day, and doubt or deny those that must be developed or that come by unlooked-for circumstances or by fortunate birth.

In this, we are plagued by the consequences of wrong definitions. Adjust the definitions, and much of what "makes no sense" makes perfect sense—without making nonsense of what we thought we knew before. In other words, bring the world into better focus, and many things make sense that previously made no sense at all, and so were largely disregarded.

THREE
Past Lives, Present Life

An example of something that our culture has disregarded because it seemed not to make sense is the concept of past lives, or (given that time is not what we think) other lives.

Why should it matter to us if we were somebody else before? What difference does it make? For a long time, I didn't know *why*, I only knew that it mattered a lot to me, and had from the first time I even *heard of* reincarnation, which was in a book lent by a neighbor when I was fourteen. (And suspiciously enough, his loaning me that book was the only significant interaction he and I ever had. He was two or three years older than I, and we hadn't much in common beyond riding the same school bus. Our lives intersected for just that transaction and then diverged, mission accomplished, apparently.)

The book, *Danger Is My Business*, by John D. Craig, described (very entertainingly) the adventurous life Craig led in the 1920s and '30s as a very young man. Part of that adventure happened in India, when Craig met a sadhu, a holy man, who began to talk to him.

"'You have come a long way,' [the sadhu] said, 'but you have a longer way to go. In your last incarnation you were cooped up in a London countinghouse, as a clerk. In this life you will do all the things of which you dreamed then. Before that you had many lives, but this one is more important. That is, it can be. You have a long way yet to go before you reach The Silence.'"

The sadhu talked to him for several hours, explaining the theory of reincarnation and its ramifications.

"'Thus,' the sadhu pointed out, 'in this interpretation of life all philosophies are included and explained: pantheism, which makes all nature God; monotheism, which calls for a single personal God; evolution, which teaches that man arose from lesser beings; Christianity, which prescribes a superhuman, or God-man; and all the other isms and schisms which snatch at a fragment of truth and build a structure of unreason about it.'"

The sadhu told Craig that he remembered his own lives, and could read Craig's from the Akashic Record.

"'You have many lives to live yet. Some lives later, you will return here to India. You may achieve The Silence then. But that will be a long time from now.' . . .

"On the way back to the mission I walked in a confused world that was not always under my feet. . . .

"I was afraid of the sadhu's philosophy for two reasons: it explained everything, and it solved the problem which had been annoying me. My religious training, such as it had been, and my Scottish Presbyterian blood, revolted against that. The world and the universe should be a mystery, and my personal problems should continue to bother me. But should they?

"That night I sat on my bed looking with glazed eyes at the floor. . . ."

When I read this little passage, I instantly *knew* (whether my knowing was right or not) that this is how things work. That's the only mention of reincarnation in the entire book—scarcely a shot across the bow, so to speak—yet it helped determine my life, for it helped determine what I believe, and hence what would be important to me, and hence what I would act on. Eventually.

It seems clear to me that Upstairs used *Danger Is My Business* to bring to my conscious mind an idea that would become increasingly important to my path. From time to time, as years passed, I would get glimpses of what seemed to be past lives. I have since learned that receiving such glimpses is normal and frequent, but is usually dismissed as "only imagination." But it was a long time before I found any effective way to do any exploration.

At least, it seemed a long time to a very young man. Actually, counting, I see that the summer of 1968 was only eight years later. This was the summer before my senior year at George Washington University. I was taking summer courses and working nearly full-time at a nearby grocery store, when I suddenly got the idea that I ought to be able to hypnotize people. My roommate Bill was willing, so we tried it. He lay down on the bed, and I sat in a chair nearby, hitting a letter opener against the chair to make a monotonous but not unpleasant clanging sound while I told him how he was getting sleepy, etc. Ridiculous procedure, of course, that couldn't possibly work, given that I didn't know what I was doing.

Well, apparently, Upstairs *did* know what it was doing, and did it very effectively, and lo and behold, there was my very intelligent but skeptical roommate talking in the voice of a British slum kid named Jamie MacAllister, who was killed in an air raid in 1942 or 1943.

Did the British suffer air raids as late as 1943? The story didn't sound right. Nonetheless we persevered. By the end of the summer we had recorded a whole series of past lives Bill reported. And not only was I talking to people whom we took to be Bill's past lives, I wound up talking to what seemed to be the spirit that was Bill when he was between lives. This spirit I called the *mismo,* that being a Spanish word meaning more or less "I myself." It seemed to be beyond Bill's everyday self.

Yes, the words Higher Self come to me now. They didn't then.

Nor did we get stories only from Bill. I was able to hypnotize and tape several tales of "past lives" from Dennis, another close friend and fraternity brother. However, to my intense disappointment, no one was able to hypnotize me. I had a feeling that Dave Schlachter might have been able to, had he been there. But he was a thousand miles away.

Not that we believed everything we heard, or even that we *always* believed *any* of it. Of course we had doubt. The stories weren't fraudulent, but were they self-delusion? We never knew how to verify them, and so left the subject in the "interesting-but-unproved" category. And at least once Bill caught his "imaginer" in the act: It had lifted a long drama from a novel he later remembered he'd once read. Bill tended to think this proved it was all made up. Something in me said otherwise, regardless of the evidence. Somehow I *knew,* or felt I knew.

To cut short a long story—and an interesting one, if there were space here for it—the summer came to an end, my senior year came and went, and my friends and I went our separate ways, David to an early grave. I didn't follow up on our summer's experiments. Didn't know how to. And so matters stood for nearly twenty years, until my article about Shirley MacLaine's Higher Self Seminar led me to a local man named Ted who said he could hypnotize me to help me recover past lives. I decided to give it a try.

– 2 –

I had thought that hypnotism always implied unconsciousness. But I never lost consciousness. I had thought I would see pictures, hear voices. Instead, there I was, seemingly free-associating. Ted would ask questions and I would respond, sometimes with emotion, but I never lost consciousness of my present-day self. At the end of the session I figured I had merely demonstrated how the human subconscious strings together input into coherent stories. Waste of time, waste of money.

Or—was it? Something within held on to the stories that had come out. And five years later a newly met psychic would bring forth one of the same stories.

That session brought forth four lives, or anyway four stories. And although I came to these stories looking for verifiable facts, what I got instead was explanations of aspects of my internal makeup. At the time, I took this to be a sign that perhaps I was making it all up. Later, when I had learned a bit more about the process, I found it reassuring. When we go dredging for other lives—past lives, if you will—we find those lives that are the most important to us here and now, which implies that these are the ones closest to us in vibration. (I know that "vibration" is a vague-sounding word, but it will have to do. Words like "gravity" and "electricity" are pretty vague too, when you really look at them, but they get the concept across.) What means the most to us comes first.

First came a "Roman or Italian or something" boy named Clio. I even spelled it out. In response to questioning, I got impressions of his family, but nothing of any evidential value. He had me describe a meal, the house, et cetera. My answers were neither detailed nor convincing. What good is "unleavened bread, some kind of vegetables, wine" as a description of a meal? What good is this as a description of a house: "Impression of stone, one-story or mostly one-story. Sturdy woods. More open than you'd think."

Yet when describing relationships and other matters with emotional resonance, I felt on firmer ground. (And wondered if it was because I could say anything that came to mind, without worrying about whether it checked with the historical record.) I confidently described Clio as the youngest in the family, "sort of overlooked" and "impatient to grow up." I had one clear sense of him lying down looking at clouds, "connected to earth and sky. Irresponsible time." This had resonance from my own boyhood—and therefore gave me cause to suspect it.

I had a clear sense that he was receiving schooling to become a seer. "Kind of religious, but not Christian. Too early for that."

Ted asked how I felt about the training, and I said I felt good. "It takes something and gives me the ability to use it. It's developing something that's only a seed. A seed."

I envisioned myself looking into the fire in a lamp, gazing into the liquid part. "It isn't an exercise anymore, it's the first time for real," I said. And I got that he felt responsibility, rather than pride. "It's—on the one hand it's graduation, a new step, but it's also a sense of beginning—now it's real."

When Ted said, "Go on to the next significant moment," my answer came with great emotion.

"It blots out everything! Just blots out the sun!" I had a clear sense that I was seeing Vesuvius erupt. (But I thought that at the MacLaine seminar, a psychic had said that I had been in that area then. Wasn't I now just making up a story to fit the suggestion?) Ted asked if I had tried to warn anyone. I gave an unhappy laugh. "Yeah, it's my function. The warning was that you're going to die and can't run away fast enough: Accept it. That's not how it was received; people panicked."

"Did you do your best?"

"I'm not sure it was good enough." I had a clear sense of responsibility, of guilt. And in fact in this lifetime, particularly as a boy, I struggled against an exaggerated sense of responsibility for everything, near or far, under my control or not. The emotional resonance to Clio as I was describing him was clear.

Clio's final day I described as the day Vesuvius blew up. He waited for the black gas from the volcano to reach him, not caring to survive and remember. His last feeling was one of responsibility. He could have done better.

Ted asked what lessons were to be learned from that lifetime. "The integrity was there. Carelessness. Rash. Too confident." I said, "It isn't exactly a character flaw, it's part of the character." I ticked off a series of things that resonated in this lifetime, not only the exaggerated sense of responsibility for others, but "some of the things that just come to me, I learned there—how to see things."

Interestingly, when he asked about my training, I thought of Dave Schlachter, and somehow knew that I had been his prize pupil, and that we had been not that different in age. He asked if there was more from that lifetime, and I said, "I am a little too cautious this time. Then too rash, this time too cautious. Too afraid to say what I saw. Trust. Just trust. Trust God, trust the world. Trust the feelings I always had that appearances seemed to contradict. Trust things I can't prove to others but that are plenty apparent to me. More than trusting; have to tell, like in the article, [the writing of which was] a stepping stone."

– 3 –

The second life came because I had asked Ted to help me find the cause of my present development as a writer. This story proved vastly important to me, not least because another psychic would home in on it more than five years later, though with interesting and significant contradictions to the story received in 1987.

As soon as Ted asked, I said, "I'm getting a map of England. Bristol. But not pictures, but a map." A name? "Owen or Evan. Or Ian. Maybe Owen." Owen's home life? I got an impression of sheep and some kind of farmhouse. Perched on mountain. I mentioned that I had a "tendency to drift toward country life-times," and said this was in Wales somewhere, "barren but nice barren. Space and stuff." I said he liked the space, but went to town to learn things.

Owen's father I described as "sort of small, very British— Irish-looking. Sort of happy. Smokes a pipe or something. Cheerful. Takes things as they come, I think. Never in a lot of conflict." I said we got along okay, but "he doesn't understand some things about me. He's happy there and I can't be: 'You've got all this, what else do you need?' I'm not sure he says it in words."

I described Owen's mother as "quick-witted, pert, not old before her time. She is also happy there, but she understands about going away. She's not from there."

I kept getting Chester, or Bath, and didn't know what if anything the towns meant to him. I described Owen as looking "British. Reddish cheeks. Not short like father—middle. Maybe slender build. Good physical condition, taken for granted." What did Owen want to do with his life? "Something other than herd sheep. Although that's all right too—but it's not enough."

At first the story was that he was going to London in 1838 or so to get a job. "He wound up writing for newspaper or something but I don't think that's what it started to be. Just a hope. The big city. Which is where the action is." I got a sense that because he had come from an area of few people, he found it interesting to watch them. I saw him as some kind of reporter: "not just sent around but writes what he wants. Like Charles Dickens, Owen goes around and absorbs stuff like a sponge. But I don't know what he does with it. I'm trying to make it out to be a book but it isn't. I think he's going to wind up on water somehow, on the ocean."

Did he get married? "No, that would wind up being rooted somehow. Owen liked to drift around." Then I said, "China! Why China? And Canton maybe? Talking about the '40s. I know, the Opium War! No, that's forcing it. '47? '48? '48 I think. Trading somehow? Again still looking at all those people. [This seems to me an example of my way of obtaining nonsensory information. I "feel around" for it, feeling for what sounds right and often correcting myself as I find myself trying to force information to meet preconceived logical patterns.] Carried on a ship for some reason but not a sailor and not a merchant. Some kind of observer. Almost like tourist, but not a tourist, just got there. Just went. Hard to sort it all out."

Then came an impression of "maybe New Zealand and Wellington and that, and living there and dying there, spending the rest of his life there. South Island. [Laugh.] Sheep. Sixty-three maybe."

Did he like to travel, then?

"Just like breathing. Saw South Africa some. Went inland some. Saw something. My father [that is, Owen's father] was right too—but it's good to travel."

Then began a wild-goose chase, still unresolved this many years later: "He wrote a book in New Zealand. *Memories*— something like that. His name was Cornish or something like that. Cornwall, Cornwell? Cornpone, for all I know. [The humor was my way of reminding Ted that he was speaking to *me*, not to David.] Cornell. Owen David Cornell?

"*Water Memories. Water-born Memories, Water-born* _____ something. Like pictures or something. The book is only a—can't write what's most interesting. Owen just liked looking at stuff and seeing the world."

His final judgment on that life? "It was an interesting life—he didn't just stay home and count sheep." He died at "sixty-something, maybe— Maybe there ten years. Body just old. Ready to go. Very tranquil life—all that movement but no tension. Contentment that he didn't hurt anything. Life a grace note after all that trauma. [Note that the only trauma described on this day was the lifetime that had ended with the eruption of Vesuvius.] No real connection with people—preferred." I added, "I think he had a beard by the time he died." When and where did he die? "1873. September nineteenth, seventeenth maybe. New Zealand. Maybe even Nelson. Sheep. Like Wales." The moral of the story: "There wasn't anything to be worried about. A lot of trust and it worked out fine."

And what was its bearing on writing?

"It had a bearing on my present interest in New Zealand. And China. Maybe stayed a while. Fascinated. Time and number of people. Cities were crowded. Time—old civilization. Quite different from South Africa, which was all new. Still interested in South Africa and China and New Zealand. And England. Always England. Went to England with reporter's attitude. Just a natural observer. Went there for something. And wound up on the ocean. I know what it might be."

I paused. "Something—somehow he got the opportunity to go away and he took it. That time he was in London. I got that overlay about being a reporter because he wrote about it later. Described standing on the street—bridge—something. Made some kind of comparison between London and Shanghai? Canton? Not Hong Kong. He wasn't reporting at the time, only at end of his life. And he was a talker. He knew more than he could ever say, because no time. Better at looking than at analyzing, but analyzing didn't get in the way of looking.

"If I could remember what went on, I think the texture would help. Like South Africa. I think he spent some time in South Africa. Maybe four to five years. He had ability to work with animals. Could have been—sort of like cattle, but not exactly cattle. Not sheep but he understands them like sheep. Deals with them on foot. Not like cowboy. One thing that made an impression on him."

A significant moment in South Africa?

"He was still a youngish man, standing at the harbor, saying to himself, 'Time to go.' Not 'go *to*,' but moving on."

I added, "I think he was named David Owen and they *called* him Owen."

This life story surfaced again in 1992, as we will see, and repeatedly after that. I have come to believe that David Owen is alive within me, and has had more of an impact on my life than any other "past life" I have yet met. I could almost list the times he took my life in hand and pointed me in a new direction, or rather pointed me toward a new aspect of the one constant direction. And although it is jumping the gun a bit, I should say that I eventually learned that David Owen's life had more significance to me than his writing. Not least, his interest in what might be called psychic matters. But I would be a while learning about that. Until the summer of 1993, I thought of him only as the Welsh writer who had gone traveling.

– 4 –

I had asked Ted to ask what we could find bearing on my interest in spiritual or metaphysical aspects of life. When he had asked the proper questions, I said, "Well, I get the impression of Japan. And at a time I don't know, in a monastery of some kind, forties, fifties. Trying, striving, working. Can't remember when *wasn't* there. Feel unsatisfied, still working. Too heavy, too earthbound. Giving up the hope of doing that. Not giving up like leaving monastery but giving up hope that will get—be— what wanted. Get up, pray, eat, do the same things: work, pray, eat, pray and go to bed and do same thing next day."

I came up with a name that sounded something like "Sanji-san," or "Senji-san." He asked if Senji-san had achieved a certain attainment. "Only theoretically." Did he enjoy the effort? "Sometimes you get inner silence and outer silence and it's nice but not often."

I said that he "never had reflective ability to figure it out. The monastery had lost the inner thread and was following rote. It provided a society, but not techniques. If you got the content, you got it accidentally, but not systematically. Belief carries you from not-knowing to knowing, but if you never get to know, it erodes. It erodes. Sincerity is not enough. So little progress, only erosion, don't know there's anything significant. Died in his fifties because he was tired of not-dying. No hope. Doesn't care. No fear, no hope."

And after he died? "He was relieved that he was wrong. He had come to think he would die and that would be the end." He was fifty-four-plus when he decided to die. "He just quit. 'I've had it.' But there was sure a sense of relief that he was wrong—it was a great joke." I summed up the life by balancing it against the Roman diviner in fire. The Roman knew a lot, and really was in tune in what he could see, but not with his emotions. The Japanese monk knew his emotions but didn't know any effective techniques. The Roman was very little structure, all experience. The Japanese was all structure, little experience. It balanced.

Summing up his life, I said, "The sincerity was constructive. Maybe it fueled a hunger to know more next time." I added that it gave me a "distaste for taking people's word for it. I didn't fall into that trap again. He didn't have the concept of that kind of choice, or right to choose or anything."

So now we had a diviner in fire, who had happened to be Roman; a journalist and wanderer, an observer of people, who had happened to be Welsh; and a monk, who had happened to be Japanese. And at the MacLaine seminar, someone had come up to me, out of the blue, and asked if I was a priest. When I said no, he said he had the impression that I had been, at some time or other. I had that impression too.

– 5 –

The fourth lifetime was supposedly set in Atlantis. Of course, the word Atlantis suggests scenes of wholesale destruction, but I knew that this Atlantean life "doesn't have to do with catastrophe and destruction. It was *normal* life; the significance is, the lack of connection. The Roman had terrific psychic awareness. The Atlantean had terrific *lack* of psychic awareness. The Japanese was always striving, the Atlantean was just putting in his time."

I described the Atlantean society as "stronger on noticing the world as something to be manipulated than as something to be enjoyed"—which sounds like America, only more so. But the Atlanteans were more mechanical than we in another sense: I got a sense that the people thought of machines as somehow an ideal to be striven for, *because* they were not organic.

And on the Atlantean's final day, what did he feel? "Regret. Just regret." And after his death? "It's not like coming out of Japan [like Senji-san] and saying 'phew!'" So what was the moral of the story? "There's still a tendency to overlook the world a little. Too much theory, too little enjoyment." Also, "the whole people were fascinated by machines, as we are but worse. Mesmerized by an idea, to the point that they couldn't see the world. They couldn't see anything else."

– 6 –

Several things should be said about all this. First, How do you know you aren't making it all up? The most productive response I have yet come up with is this: Say I am. Why am I making up this particular thing rather than something else?

In the absence of chance and accident, *everything has meaning.* So even this doesn't have to do with past lives, but with, say, psychological tendencies—still, if we are willing, it will teach us something. All those supposed past (or, I would say now, other) lives: Are any of them historically real? Or are they just embodiments of psychological tendencies on my part? Though I have opinions on the subject, I still don't *know.*

Second, concerning the nature of facts and impressions in trying to do this kind of recall. In light of what I learned five and six years later, I became convinced that Owen—the life I eventually came to think of as David—couldn't possibly have lived as early as the early 1800s. And for years I floundered around trying to pin down even his name, and also the title and location of his book. In May 1987 a psychic friend suggested the book's title might be *Waterborne Reflections.* She said if not *Reflections*, then *Memories.* In my journal I wrote, "But I think *Reflections* myself: it would suit his quiet sense of humor and his civility." The fact that I had a sense of "his quiet sense of humor and his civility" should demonstrate how David's reality was growing on me.

Years later, editing Joseph McMoneagle's book *Mind Trek*, I realized from his discussion of remote viewing that incorrect details don't necessarily discredit the whole picture. They may indicate not that the whole story was made up out of whole cloth, but that one's left brain, hurrying to make sense of things, jumped to incorrect conclusions. The possibility of such subjective overlays requires that we keep going back, checking as best we can to assure that we caught them all.

First we come up with impressions, then we try to weave a coherent story around them, incorporating each new fact as it arises. But what happens when a "fact" is really an incorrect assumption? Then the more you try to make the story cohere with that "fact," the farther afield you get, and your story can become a confusing mixture of fact and fiction. When you discover that at least parts of what you thought were true memories had to be fiction, you are tempted to throw out the whole thing as an exercise in fantasy. But then you find something that *really* rings true and you are back to wondering. Once you realize that analytical overlays can confuse the issue, you are spared the necessity of saying it's *all* true or *all* false. You are back to using your judgment, and doing more investigating.

Note, too, that sometimes I got an impression—a "knowing" with great definiteness—only to find later that the knowing changed, or I changed my mind about it, or it didn't fit in with what later looked more persuasive. Reckless generalization: The strength of your conviction is not an infallible indicator of the truth of the perception.

As I think of the past-life stories that surfaced in 1968 and 1987, and from 1992 on, I know now why the subject of past lives matters. In dealing with other lives, we are not just looking at old scrapbooks in the attic. It is true that in talking about past lives, we probably don't have our concepts straight. But it is equally true, and in a practical sense more important, that we are dealing with parts of ourselves that may be vitally affecting our *present* lives, as I will show. For there came a time, described in due course, when I discovered another lifetime in which a little girl died, disoriented and tormented, at age eight. That motherless child lived within me, affecting me—here, now—from the time I was a child until I was able to retrieve her and bring her to a place of safety. She had left this life disoriented and lost, and until I was able to rescue her, a part of me— a part of the individual living out this lifetime—was disoriented and lost as well. I had a motherless child crying within me all those years, though I was never consciously aware of her, and certainly never considered that this might be a past life resonating within me. After I rescued her, that motherless-child feeling ceased to exist. In rescuing her, I had rescued myself.

I am well aware of the conundrum this poses, when we look at reincarnation from the conventional point of view. How could various lives interact on an ongoing basis? How could one rescue one's own past self? I will deal with these questions as best I can as we go along, but I repeat that here I am concerned primarily with telling what I have experienced, even when I have no theory with which to support it. From various experiences in the years since 1992, when I did my Gateway Voyage at The Monroe Institute, I have become very aware that each life affects others. This is true not only between individuals ("no man is an island") but between the individuals who coexist within us.

FOUR

Guidance

Many things in my life—and yours—suddenly make more sense when we look at ourselves as intimately connected to one another. It manifests in the ways we as individuals are inexplicably attracted to one another, in the massive unlooked-for blessings we receive from one another, in the way we as strands are woven into the tapestries of each other's lives. As I look at my life I see person after person who functioned on my behalf as local agent for the universe.

Case in point, Suni Dunbar. About a month after the Higher Self Seminar, I met seven others who had attended. We arranged our chairs in a circle and introduced ourselves. Directly across from me was a striking, slim, redheaded woman in her sixties. She totally captured my attention, and I was aware that I had caught her interest too, though I thought it might be because I was the only man there, or perhaps the only person there she didn't already know. It wasn't that; it was recognition. We were old friends who were just meeting.

After the group broke up, Suni invited two other women and me to her house nearby. Her husband Jack showed up shortly, an outgoing, cheerful man I liked instantly. We decompressed from the meeting till midnight, and I got home charged with energy, not quite knowing why.

I was having problems that have no place in this narrative. As usual, I had no one to talk with to discuss them until, a couple of weeks after that first meeting, I was able to record in my journal "a wonderful lunchtime conversation with Suni" at the office she maintained for her business, not far from the newspaper. Our little group continued to meet once a month for a while longer, but its part in my story had been fulfilled in its serving as an excuse for me to meet Suni.

I got into the habit of having lunch with her about once a week. Funny lunches, really. We rarely ate. Mostly we'd sit and talk about weird stuff and life and dozens of things—emotions, problems, feelings, perplexities—that I could discuss with no one else. Driving over to see her one noontime, I realized that I very much *needed* to talk to her about such things—and was humiliated and downcast and ashamed to have to admit to feelings of dependency or pain. It wasn't manly. Once I did, that day, force myself to tell her what I was feeling, I felt much better. She neither mocked nor criticized nor expressed skepticism. She listened, and let me know that she had heard, and said she trusted my judgment. It helped so much! It was all I (or probably anybody) needed. It was the beginning of the most effective stretch of mothering I ever received.

Dear Suni. I had no idea how much I needed her mothering until I got it. (And I was more than forty years old!) Suni, who ate only healthful foods (no chocolate!) and lived right; Suni, who painted beautiful ethereal paintings to have a healing effect (but she used no dark colors; she wanted everything light). Suni, who was clear-eyed, openhearted, intellectually curious, and open to exploration. She was an angel in my life, and in the lives of others.

I see that we are often angels to each other, and I suspect that this is the right hand helping the left, so to speak. Suni brought me to her friend Fran, and thereby to dream analysis, and thus (not very indirectly) to a closer connection to The Boss (not God, as will become obvious) and ultimately to The Gentlemen Upstairs, and thence to the larger being of which we are a part—though I didn't then think of it in those terms.

– 2 –

In September 1987, a few months after we met ("again," as we put it), Suni told me of her friend Fran, who had become a Jungian analyst. I met her, and liked her, and on Thursday, October 1, I awoke to record a dream in three parts.

1. *My father and my son and my older brother and I were sitting in an apartment where in real life my wife and I had lived for a few months when she was pregnant with our first child. We went downstairs and outside. My elder brother had brought me a whole truckload of stuff and unloaded it. It was a gift, but piled high all over the place, and I had a sort of dismay as to what I would do with it.*

2. *My brother and my father hadn't been getting along; Dad came out somewhat wistfully to see if they could. My brother refused, and I silently started to cry (I, who never cried) because they couldn't—and it actually felt good to cry.*

3. *From nowhere Fran's face appeared, and smiled.*

I woke up realizing that the thousand dollars my mother had recently sent me—out of the blue—would pay for at least some sessions of analysis with Fran. Within a few days we had begun analysis, and as soon as I began to pay attention to my dreams, I gave myself access to the larger being's greater knowledge, and thus its foresight and wisdom. Immediately, dreams came. Dozens. Scores. At first I often found them mystifying, often seemingly meaningless—but upon careful examination they revealed much.

The mind seems to take advantage of whatever comes by: an event, a thought, or an external dream (that is, a story in print, or on the screen, or from another person). It takes these as suggestions, remolds them to suit its needs, and presents them in dreams, reveries, and fantasies to make its report. And although it took me a good while to figure it out, when I finally did learn to examine dreams *in the context of the preceding day's events,* another world of meaning emerged. Dreams, it turns out, don't appear at random, disconnected from everyday life. The dreams I busily recorded and analyzed were trying hard to bring me messages that I often didn't get. At first I had to depend on Fran, as outside observer, to show me the unnoticed bent of my thoughts, dreams, and life. But what I then called my "Higher Self" showed itself ready and willing to communicate whenever I was ready to pay attention. Later I would discard the term "Higher Self," but it served as a useful intermediate model while I learned to experience new inner depths.

My friend (not yet my business partner) Bob Friedman listened with interest to my description of the process (though not the content) of Jungian analysis, and suggested that I try directed dreaming, telling myself before going to sleep, "You will have a significant dream, you will remember it, you will understand it." I tried it and it worked. As is so typical of me, I then forgot about the technique for a long time. But can there be much doubt who was responding to the request for a significant dream?

It is not my intent to recapitulate a year and a half's experience of Jungian analysis. But from my record of the dreams that came to me during that process, here are a few examples of messages communicated to me in dreams by the larger being. If you have never worked with your dreams, maybe this will give you an idea of what may be learned by doing so.

A dream that says I am almost out of time is followed by one that has me as an officer, bent, hunched forward, with a briefcase with a book or books. My boss in the dream asks why I still have the books, and am still hunched over, like an enlisted man. I say I need to for a while; he accepts that and says some people can't straighten up right away.

"Straightening up" refers to independence and self-sufficiency. The dream points out to me that: a) I am not functioning as I should—I am not as independent and in command as I should be—but, b) I need not beat myself up over it; it is recognized that I am living my own internal possibilities as best I can.

A dream, the fifty-ninth since I began analysis, from February 1988:

I am in Russia. Someone I know well—sympathetic, though in authority—has put me under arrest again. He starts driving me to the police station. We stop, I forget why, and we are in the countryside among people. I start talking to them. It's so strange, I tell them, Stalin has stunned (or I may have said numbed) the whole country. Some are still stunned, some are waking up, and some are free. I start to sing, "We're going to have a dance! We're going to have a dance!" I grab people one by one and start dancing around, trying to wake them up. Some respond. I grab people's arms, one by one, shake them side to side to measure how loose they are or how rigid. I get somebody to do it for me, and I turn out to be very tight. . . . More police cars materialize but they don't seem to change anything. People aren't any more or less afraid or numb than before.

Which I take to mean roughly this: My inner thought police—or perhaps I should say emotion police—who work for the great dictator are losing control. The benumbed inner populace are beginning to come out of their long trance, and I can see there will be joy. "We're going to have a dance! We're going to have a dance!" Description of my inner change, and reassuring prophecy that a day will come when I will want to, and be able to, dance. You see how clearly the message is embedded in a simple but vivid image? Of course there is much more, including the very feeling that filled me as I awoke. In my experience, the more careful my analysis, the more I got out of the dream.

Repeatedly, as the process went on, Fran said I needed to honor the feminine within, to restore her vitality. (For as I begin that process, I was a mess, unable to feel, unable to cry.) I begin to realize that my anima—my inner feminine—manifested as a carping bitch telling me I don't measure up. Finally it occurred to me that maybe this is how she responds to life-long neglect. As we continue working with dreams, I gradually realize that I am in little touch with my emotions, my feelings. I touch them, then flee. But a well-balanced person develops four facets equally—feelings, intuition, sensation, thinking—and I realize that I am grossly overdeveloped in thinking (versus feeling) and intuition (versus sensation). I learn that I must pay attention to my body and the world, and must get in touch with my feelings. But it takes a while to learn how to do it.

One day I awakened from a few minutes' daydreaming, realizing that I had been envisioning a woman without eyes, or without a well-defined face, riding in a car on a course that ran parallel to mine but was going to diverge soon. Then we weren't so much driving as walking, yet in cars. I stopped and she stopped and I told her I wanted us to go together. First I said I'd go with her wherever she wanted to go, but then I reconsidered and said I wanted us to go as partners, neither following the other but both going together, now to one's destination, now to the other's. She agreed and we were one: that was the feeling. We're going to go off on the less-defined road—more track than road—that was somewhere to the right, and heads further to the right, of the major highway I was on. "I and my anima have been getting acquainted," I said to myself, "and have now apparently formed a partnership, belatedly."

A few nights earlier, I had awakened from a dream hearing the sentence, "Where there is no vision, the people flourish." I hadn't been able to figure out the misquotation. After my day-dream of the anima, I realized that if one's life is not dominated by a vision—an ideology, religion, political idea, whatever—one has room to breathe, to grow, to re-create oneself. In that sense, where there is no vision, the people flourish—as I had been told.

Dream # 154, July 1, 1988, deftly used images to show me where my emotional state had become stuck:

I go down into the library stacks at the university where I'd gone to school. To my astonishment I find that they're still holding a study carrel for my friend David, who died in 1970. His books were still there, so obviously it hadn't been used in all that time. I laugh, it's so stupid.

David walks in! It is so real! We shake hands and I tell him how glad I am that he could be there. Marvel that after eighteen years, they're still holding a place for him. Some people never get the word.

Then I'm looking up at the sky. Snow is coming down, looking black as it does against the light. (Frozen tears, I thought later.) Then the snow is white, at night, and I am crossing the street where the Catholic Church was in my hometown. I was going somewhere, but I hadn't gotten far.

Boy, I thought at the time, *that's* true enough! Some people never get the word—and I haven't gotten very far from where I was as a child.

Once I dreamed that I was sitting with two attractive young ladies I was on good terms with, listening to them talking about some series of books they read when they were kids. One mentioned a book in which the young girl who was the heroine wanted to own a dirigible. I started laughing. "Everybody else in the world," I said, "wants a pony. She wants a dirigible." They laughed too, and I couldn't stop laughing. I took the dream to be smiling at my unrealistic expectations of life, and leading me to join in that smile.

And I dreamed that several of us were in a boat, and suddenly folk singer Judy Collins began to sing. We were surprised, and pleased, for she had been singing propaganda songs— "cause" songs—for so long, and now she was singing a song of life. I knew what this dream meant: I am coming back to life.

– 3 –

In late October 1988 (being inspired by my friend Bob Smith's book *Hugh Lynn Cayce: About My Father's Business*) I tell myself that "I want nothing more than to open myself to the levels of life that have become blocked." I note my life's pattern of knowing and forgetting, and tell myself it is time to be moving again. I say, "God, your will, not mine. But if you will it, let me be whole: remove the barriers that close me off from you, from me, from others. Let me be of service. Show me the way and keep me on the path."

What you pray for, you will surely get. This need not be read as a threat.

A few days later, a dream ushered in an important healing. On the morning of Saturday, November 19, 1988, I awakened half remembering a dream prominently featuring a rendition of "roll out the barrel, we'll have a barrel of fun." A National Public Radio piece the previous week (on the occasion of the song composer's death) had put it into my consciousness. But I awakened convinced that the dream was using the song in connection to the upcoming twenty-fifth anniversary of the murder of John F. Kennedy and the maiming of a good part of a generation of Americans.

Kennedy's reputation had been systematically tarnished over the years by a series of revelations and allegations. But in this twenty-fifth anniversary year, I as editorial writer and occasional columnist had had my say on the editorial page about his many excellences, and others too had poured out their hearts, reminding me that millions shared that intense loss. That political crime had done great psychological damage to many unknown individuals of all ages, harm that was not recognized or dealt with at the time. Many years later, when the space shuttle *Challenger* blew up, schools knew to send psychologists into the classrooms to talk about what had happened. Back in 1963 dealing with one's emotions was a private matter, hit or miss.

The boy that I was then had had his hero shot out of his life, more or less before his eyes. He couldn't express what he felt in front of anyone, particularly his father, for fear of unspoken contempt. So when he wanted to cry, he wouldn't, and then couldn't. He pretended. And paid and paid and paid for it.

But in this fall of 1988, with Fran's help, it finally came *real* to me that that was a long time ago. In response to that dream, I wrote it all out, the whole ghastly weekend and the blank weeks that followed, and I knew that all things come to an end, even torture and deformation. "Roll out the barrel," I wrote, "and we'll have a barrel of fun. Finally." My next meeting with Fran took place, appropriately enough, on November twenty-second, the date of JFK's assassination in 1963. When I made it clear to her that I had relived the old emotions and convinced them that I was forty-two now, not seventeen still—that I had come to grips with it, finally—she seemed very pleased.

Dreams and the habit of paying attention to dreams; benefit of: Case study.

– 4 –

Dream # 216, on Saturday, December 17, 1988, seems to me to have implications for many people besides myself. Please don't skip over it.

I am walking down a road and come to a place where the road turns into a driveway. As it is by a large, well-kept house to my left, I enter, looking for somebody to give me directions or assistance. I look through several rooms. Nobody is there. A strange feeling, no one there.

I go back to the street and try to hitch rides. A car speeds past. A bus-like car, loaded with people, many seats, stops a little beyond me. But there is something unwholesome about the people. I start looking around this town, looking for a job.

The town is strange in many ways. I try to get a job and am finally directed to a store across a crossroads. I go in, and work, and at the end of the day the family tries something connected with my shoelaces.

"What are you doing to me?" I ask several times, but get no answer. I get a slow-motion evil, a somehow uncoordinated or almost unconscious evil. I break away, bolt out of a door in the room, let it slam behind me. Down a few steps, I push open the door to outside and leave it open, then silently, in about three bounds, run down to the cellar, hoping they'll find me inexplicably vanished because I will be nowhere in sight outdoors. I'll have refuge in the cellar; somehow I don't think the outside would be any safer.

They had been intending to tie me up by my shoelaces, sort of. The father was the leader, though he had the boy (a teenager) take the lead. A strong sense of reluctance in the boy, and of strangeness in them all.

My road was giving out. When I looked in a well-kept house for direction or assistance, I found nobody home. When I tried to find a ride, individual cars didn't stop, and the *group* who did stop were somehow unwholesome. Worse, when I gave up moving on, and I got a job, "they" tried to eliminate my ability to move independently, not so much from evil intent as from their own unconsciousness. I hid in the cellar.

Moral of the story (perhaps): Neither "respectability" nor the company of others can lead you or help you to find your way. Don't let people tie your feet. And, Mr. Introvert, don't hide in the cellar just because you're afraid of the wide world. Fran said this was a serious warning, so I paid attention to it. That warning sounds pretty clear to me now, yet I could not have come to it consciously. It was a gift from within. A gift from the larger being, that sees us so intimately, and so much more clearly than we see ourselves. And this is an example of how we can learn from dreams, partly by analysis, partly merely by restating the dream in outline, to make the symbols clearer.

– 5 –

Late in December 1988 came an example of how unconsciously I still lived, even knowing better. I had been reading the first four books of writer Mary Summer Rain, with an eye to doing a group book review, and had felt compelled (though I didn't know why) to interrupt that project to read Laurens van der Post's *A Mantis Carol*. As I did so, something within kept saying, "Call van der Post. Call van der Post." But I kept responding, "What will I *say*? Why should he talk to me?" I could get no answer to the question, but still the urging came. I even wrote (but did not really hear, I am ashamed to say), "Is it possible that *I* could give *him* anything? The woman in *A Mantis Carol* did." Still I did not act on the impulse. Then one night when I was in the living room, on the couch reading, one of my kids said, "What is *that*?" and I turned and looked out the window, and saw, crawling up the frame, a praying mantis.

And thought nothing of it!

I had been reading *A Mantis Carol*; I was being urged to contact van der Post. A mantis came—never saw a mantis on the window before or since—and I thought nothing of it! It took about a week before it finally struck me: "Oh! This is exactly the synchronicity between outer and inner that van der Post and Jung talked about. Maybe it *means* something!" God, what a slow boat I am sometimes. In *A Mantis Carol*, van der Post says that the balance between farmer and hunter has never been fairly struck because the wild man has been undervalued. This is part of Mary Summer Rain's message, as well. So, I concluded, maybe it is telling me to preserve the inner wild man (don't be tamed) and maybe it is also a reminder to be a bridge between the hunter and the farmer.

But when I tell Fran my brilliant analysis, she asks, why haven't I called van der Post?

But I never do follow that inner—and even *outer!*—prompting, for I could never get it to "make sense" to me. Sir Laurens lived nearly nine years after the mantis that appeared on my window was intellectualized away. If I had followed my internal guidance, I might have met him. Perhaps I might have gotten to know him, and something would have opened up in my life. Certainly he would have encouraged me to live with ever more integrity and consciousness. But I didn't follow the prompting, so now I will never know. And what hurts much more is the thought that perhaps I had something for him, a gift he never received.

– 6 –

A final example of dreams commenting on real life, deepening our insight into ourselves. In mid-January 1989 I was invited to what was billed as a "New Age Party." Within seconds of my arrival I realized that coming was a mistake. I had brought a bottle of Virginia Gentleman whiskey. The hostess was incredulous. "Whiskey?" She made it very plain she didn't think it at all appropriate. Was everybody there too spiritually advanced to drink whiskey? Finally I decided doubtfully to put it out, in case anybody should want some. (Bob Friedman, when he saw it, said I had good taste. And I noticed that by the time I left, the bottle was one-third empty.) So was she too spiritually advanced to be gracious and thank me for bringing something? I felt I had made a faux pas, but not nearly as big a one as hers in not smoothly receiving it. As I said, I knew instantly that I didn't belong among these people.

Two friends of mine were the only people of substance there whom I could find—other than me, of course! The others struck me as Hollywood-on-the-Atlantic: the hugs, the posing. I sure didn't seem to have much in common with them. For one thing, they were so scruffy! Then there was the guy who showed up in blue jeans, an unzipped leather jacket, and scarf down to his waist—and no shirt or undershirt. On a cold night in January. In the course of the evening he walked around without jacket and scarf. Did this demonstrate that he was spiritual? Or even conscious? And there was the jewelry maker who showed us two pieces of her work, which, she assured us, were pushing other people's work out of a store where they were being exhibited. Not one, but *two* pieces she showed us broke. Two pieces, two breakages. Wonderful jeweler.

Finally I found myself in the kitchen, sipping a white wine that tasted terrible, watching people I had no interest in, while a row of people sat on the stairway giving each other back rubs. Suddenly I realized that it reminded me of the kids in my wife's law school class years ago, the same lostness and phoniness. But this time I was way beyond thinking they may be right and I wrong. I slipped out rather rudely, not saying good-bye to my gracious hostess (or even to my friends). I thought to myself, if this is New Age, I prefer old age.

However, that night, I had a dream in three scenes:

I had stayed at the party and finally had found a quiet place (somebody's bedroom or study) and looked at their pictures or books and was unimpressed by both. But it was quiet and solitary. After a while, my wife was on the phone. I got on intending to say merely that I'd be home soon, but she, not knowing how much I hated the place and the people, went on and on, until I was embarrassed to be on the phone so long when everyone was obviously leaving. As I was on my way out, some of the women started telling me about one of the men, who told them he was the greatest artist in the world. His stuff was the best, nobody else's was any good. After being silent a long while, finally I made a sly or sarcastic reference to the difference between his opinion of himself and the evidence of his art.

The dream left me with uncomfortable questions. Since every character in our dreams is generally ourselves, maybe my dream was saying that: I consider myself a better artist than I have demonstrated myself to be, and neither my reading nor my creative activity is distinguished; my lack of knowledge of my feelings is holding me longer than I would stay otherwise; and I am beginning to become aware of, and comment on, the discrepancy between my opinion of myself and the external reality.

Today I would take it even further. I believe that external reality is a mirror of internal reality, and we attract to ourselves what we *are*. And what I *noticed* that night was people who were scruffy and mostly without manners or consciousness, full of pretense and shallowness and conformist nonconformity. What did that say about *me*?

Well, nobody ever said dream analysis is supposed to make you feel good. It does open your eyes, sometimes, though—if only long after the fact, and against your best efforts. And it is available every day, every night.

– 7 –

By 1989 I was getting bored with writing editorials at the *Virginian-Pilot*, but as the job was the most cushy I had ever had, probably I never would have left voluntarily. Life took care of that for me. The newspaper downsized the editorial office from five people to four, and I was tapped as the one to go. After weeks of discussion, management and I agreed that at the end of June I would take my two weeks' vacation, and would come back to the newsroom where I would spend half my week editing the Sunday "Commentary" section, and the other half working for a news editor, coming up with my own story ideas. I *told* myself, this was okay and should be a big relief. But why didn't I feel anything? The reason surfaced *two days later*; suddenly I realized with great violence that I didn't want to do it. "But what can I do? Where can I go?"

Now, as it happened, I did have an option. Bob Friedman was asking me if I wanted to come in with him in starting a new book publishing company. And looking at my finances, I realized to my surprise that my wife and I had money available that I could invest in a likely enterprise. The idea scared me. If we lost this money, I couldn't imagine ever being able to replace it. And I had neither extensive savings nor an assured career, nor an accumulated pension. On the other hand, sometimes it's best to just jump and trust.

I dithered for a while, consulting with my level-headed, practical brother Paul, meditating on it, thinking about it. I told him that my horoscope indicates that my task is to try to hold together within me every influence, every tendency, however centrifugal. I felt that if I could make of them a unity, somehow I would help others to do the same. As a result, I had been led from one thing to another, trying to reconcile, to assimilate, to give each its due weight. I could see *some* fruits of this effort. I hadn't confined myself to one way of looking at the world. I hadn't become trapped in ideology or politics or religion or irreligion. Nor in science nor mysticism nor technology or art or whatever. Not even in ideas or daydreams. I had forced myself to move into the very practical world around me, relatively successfully. But what it would ultimately come to, I couldn't tell.

I returned to Virginia, and wound up in the *Virginian-Pilot* newsroom, and hated it. My family took off for three weeks with my wife's family in the Midwest, and I found myself alone with just my affectionate cats. I had time to ponder some more. Did I dare to leave a secure job (no matter how unsatisfying) for the thrills and terrors of what I called *"real* private enterprise"? I wasn't drawing up balance sheets or even weighing pros and cons; I was trying to get a feel for the situation, and I badly needed sage advice. Dreams continued to come, and many were recorded, and they continued to be an important source of insight, as I hope they always will be. But dreams come like the wind, at their own bidding. Now came another resource, more accessible than dreams, more versatile, and seemingly inexhaustible. Enter the personage I affectionately began to call The Boss.

– 8 –

I had made some experiments in automatic writing, my first in many years. I would write a question and wait for an answer to surface. Sometimes it came a word at a time, sometimes in entire sentences or paragraphs. This was less like channeling (I did not lose consciousness or bring in another personality) than listening to the still small voice that the Bible, and particularly the Quakers, talk about. Yet the personality that came through was clear enough.

I have lost the first stumbling steps, which must have been recorded on stray scraps of paper rather than written in my journal or typed out. The earliest thing I have left is this transcript from Saturday, July 22, 1989, before I had any idea how important the day would be in retrospect. A pity we must begin *in media res,* but I no longer remember what preceded this day's work. I do know that somehow I already had a sense that this voice belonged to a woman. For a while, I thought it represented a young woman. There follows a long excerpt, with omissions indicated by ellipses.

– 9 –

Frank: So. Are you mad at me?
> You know I am.

Frank: I guessed. But I don't know why.
> Because you aren't working/writing.

Frank: Which?
> Either. Both.

Frank: Why am I not?
> Inertia.

Frank: Is it only that? I deny it.
> Laziness.

Frank: Oh come—as the *mismo* used to say.
> Do you want to blame it on self-doubt still?

Frank: Well—something.
> Yes.

[Pause.]

Frank: But why do I go blank when I sit in front of a pad, or typewriter, or whatever?
> You don't think you have to work. Do you not see that a lifetime of menial, degrading, useless underemployment stems from nothing but this habit of not working unless and until kicked?

Frank: *Messenger*?
> *Messenger* could yet be a fine book—and could be your ticket. Why are you not fixing it?

Frank: I don't know how to do it.
> You do. Or you could learn how, by doing it.

Frank: You think I'm using meditation to escape the need to work?

Not exactly. But you're not occupying it with effective efforts externally.

Frank: Like what?

Well, before you can do something, you have to want to do it. But life's prizes aren't forced into your hands. You have to struggle for them. It is the struggle that creates them, creates the possibility of attaining them.

[A pause, during which a thought raced through my mind.]

Yes, that is very true, what you just realized. This is precisely how you need to write your books: Not out of logic or as a chore but as a conversation. . . . Well, do you see now what has been blocking the writing of . . . everything you've tried to write since at least 1969?

Frank: Yes, perhaps I do. I let the logical maniac set the stage and push off you—my beloved. Gadfly. Conscience. Irritant.

Flattery. . . .

Frank: It's really true, isn't it?

About not working unless kicked? You know it's true. With exceptions, but trivial ones. . . . You read so much because it's easier than writing, and you, like Conway [in James Hilton's *Lost Horizon*], are naturally rather lazy. But it is only laziness in doing stupid things that can be a great virtue. Laziness in doing virtuous things can be a great stupidity.

Frank: Nice phrasing.

I could be—have been—very valuable to you.

[We went down a list of career possibilities, which she ruthlessly demolished.]

Frank: So it comes down to Bob.

You tell me. Is it not the opportunity you hoped for
soon after you met him? Haven't you been saying books
are all you know? Doesn't he believe as you do?

Frank: But the terms aren't right.

No, they aren't. So what should you do?

Frank: Fix them, my beloved.

Exactly. So why won't you? . . .

Frank: [But] wouldn't I be being kicked by monetary necessities
if I went in with Bob?

Yes. And at least you're used to it. You'd be getting
kicked into doing what you wanted to do—or would you?

Frank: Writing, again.

Look, friend, you don't have to be a writer. You can do
anything you want to do. But that's what you keep saying
you want to do.

Frank: I take your point.

Well—sharply put—what do you want to do? If it is read
books, what do you think you'd be doing with Bob Friedman?

Frank: I guess I never looked at it that way. . . . I'm awfully
grateful for this. Couldn't we work together all the time?

A flush of pleasure. Do you know how long I've waited
for you to ask?

Frank: I wanted—but I had to ask, didn't I?

A woman wants to be asked.

Frank: I'm asking. Stay with me. Be my partner. Let's wake people up.

So you do want to write, after all.

Frank: Yes. I always have. But by myself it always dries up.

You have me now, if you remember.

Frank: If I remember! Well, I may forget—I usually do—but I
remember again. And can't you prod me, remind me,
poke at me?

My dear boy, what do you think I have been doing, and
for so long.

Frank: Like Joan Grant. Is this what she did?
> Sort of. She was hypnotized and talked. But we could do it this way. . . .

Frank: Will you give me the story of my past lives?
> Don't get distracted. How about some money first?

Frank: Practical, just like a woman.
> An insult? A complaint?

Frank: Just a comparison.

And that was the beginning, or near enough to the beginning anyway, of one of the most important relationships of my life. But perhaps I should say, the beginning of *my consciousness of* the relationship.

– 10 –

The Boss's feedback (not detailed here) gave me Bob's point of view, that he saw me as a combination of intelligence and inexperience. Till then I had never had much insight into how others thought, certainly not into how they saw me. And so I had a couple of talks with Bob, and we worked out equitable terms, under which we would go in fifty-fifty, each equally responsible for raising capital, each owning fifty percent. But for her assistance, I never could have done it. I called my brother Paul, who thought it a good idea, but said he would ask his psychic friend Joe Holzer to meditate on it. I spent several days waiting to hear Joe's reading on the situation, during which time, I had a dream.

– 11 –

A dream, in three parts:

1. I am standing on the shore with my hands full of sails, laughing at myself that I had been thinking of sailing in the America's Cup or some similar race.

2. I see a rigid, tightly disciplined friend of mine take up sailing. He is so determined to master the art that he gets no fun out of it.

3. I see laser lights against a clump of trees, and know it is signs of a new game, a sort of tennis played with laser-emitting rackets. It looks like fun, and I want to learn to play it sometime.

With feedback from The Boss, I analyzed the dream easily enough:

1. Now that I had started to see what was involved in going into business, I was smiling that I had thought I could do it alone, with a few materials gathered but no structure.

2. Sailing is more to be enjoyed than it is a race to be run. Restrain the inner fanatic.

3. There is something creative, re-creative, about games, and the beautiful scenery of the world reflects some of the light of the game. But I do have some question as to how the new game is played.

My experience with analysis had begun to teach me how to read the strange, rich language of symbols as they well up in dreams. My new contact with The Boss would teach me more about how that language expresses in our lives in other ways.

– 12 –

Sometime in August I put together for my own sake a piece describing the surprising thing that was going on. I called it "Shaping," not quite knowing why. An excerpt:

All summer, she has approached nearer. I on my part have tried to remain receptive, have concentrated on giving her welcome. I have swept and made a place, and she has come to fill it.

When I ceased to see my Jungian analyst, some months ago, I told her that something within told me it was time to stop, if only for the moment. For at least a while, I needed to be on my own. Why? I couldn't say. Still, I did not doubt that what I was being urged was for my own good. . . .

Well, first came weeks of quiet exhilaration of sailing without a pilot. And then, again in quiet, with these beautiful weeks came a sense of an inner pilot, equally sure-footed, equally well-intentioned, and wiser and older and more intimate with me than the one I had left.

Jungian psychology, until I experienced the reality it described, was only words, only theory. But I knew, in theory, what was the anima and its function. The difference between theory and practice is the difference between thinking of the anima as "it" and thinking of the anima as "her." This is not poetry or metaphor, but strict fact.

I knew it was important to give her a chance to speak, and I was determined to pass up no chance to listen. As best I could, I practiced meditation. Yet when I had been working with my analyst, I was continually dreaming, and remembering those dreams and recording them. Now, my dreams fled from me, or I awoke without the ambition to rise and record them. Yet, oddly, I did not feel that I had taken a wrong turning, nor did I feel depressed nor even impatient. And I was born a *very* impatient individual.

– 13 –

If these sessions hadn't been conducted by pen and ink in my journal, probably I would have long since forgotten some of the questions raised. Very early on, The Boss challenged me:

Do you notice that every time the question is one of immediate importance to you, one like yesterday, that calls for information you don't have, rather than opinion, which you devalue, you get all tense, choke up, try to impose the right answer? Just so, you were tempted to hold me to the point in answering what you just asked. A mistake; subjugating one brain to the other.

Was she saying that in fact she represented, or lived in, or was, the half of my brain opposite the half my conscious self lives in? I had no idea. Later that day:

Frank: I see, rereading, that I did ask about last night's dream, but I feel like I have spent all day avoiding it, and you.
> And so you have.
Frank: What am I afraid of?
> You don't know what I know and are afraid the answer will be: nothing, or will be that I don't exist.
Frank: In which case I lose my guide.
> Yes. And you know you need one.
Frank: But I'm hooked on other states too, aren't I? Like the other New Agers.
> At least know what you are.

Later that same long Saturday, this:

Frank: I'm beginning to see how it happens that psychics become fakers. If I had to do this in public—if I had to come up with a usable record here—I'd start faking it. When I genuinely let go and let you talk—difficult to do anyway—I don't have any idea what's going to come out.
> Just like the world. That's why a certain type of person retreats into fantasy, be it reading, TV, daydreams, science—whatever. Anything for the predictable. . . . You

can't make the world predictable without losing something. Let what happens happen with you where you are at
that time. Be here now, there later. . . . Try to exert control
only when and where you should work; remove control, to
the extent possible, in perception and—

Frank: And?

You're clutching.

Frank: Yes. Well, "perception" is interesting. That's why we—
I—don't see fairies, et cetera.

You've got it. If you can remove the habit of control
from perception . . . you will enter different worlds and,
more important, will then return to this world with your
understanding enhanced.

– 14 –

Another time, I lost part of an interesting dream, and
asked her for any part of what I had forgotten.

Frank: Can you tell me? Will you tell me?

I might, if your anxiety didn't block me. You know that
hypnotism could elicit the dream. Why doubt that I could
give it to you?

Frank: Emotional investment.

I know. Can't you let it go?

Frank: I don't know. Interpretation doesn't threaten nearly as
much as information.

A reflection of why you wrote editorials off-handedly
yet choke at reporting. Facts overawe you even as you
devalue them.

Frank: Meaning that if I could change, the necessity for reporting would go away.

Yes.

Frank: Too little respect for external facts, too great awe of
them. How can this be? And, I suppose—corresponding

too little awe of internal facts and too great respect? You might say that. It's one world. Why be overawed by geography, say? Or physics? Rather than biology, or criminology, or history? Take the world as it is, it is all sacred, all profane. Don't (and certainly this isn't only you!) don't split it up—don't split up your attitude—so much. Look at it with one eye.

Frank: Surely with two eyes?

Very funny. Look at it with two eyes to get stereo, to get perspective and depth perception. But look at it with one attitude.

– 15 –

On Tuesday, August 1, at Bob Friedman's invitation, I drove up with him to meet Bob Monroe and his stepdaughter and her husband at The Monroe Institute. He and I drove up to Charlottesville on I-64, then down 29 to Nelson County. Our directions said turn west on Route 6, but as we traveled south on Route 29 from Charlottesville, a sign for Faber—which was the Institute's mailing address—pointed east. And there was Route 6, heading that way. I was driving by then, so I suggested we turn east and see if our directions were wrong. We went for a mile or two until it became obvious that we weren't getting anywhere. We turned back to 29, and after a few minutes there was Route 6 west, and from there we got to the institute without incident, not missing the turn at the intersection with the dumpsters (Nelson County is rural, and gives rural directions). I mention this insignificant detour only because it *became* significant three and a half years later, when I did the Gateway program at Monroe.

And so I got to meet Bob Monroe. Over a long lunch, he told us some of the fascinating things that had happened to him, and explained what they were doing at the institute. Bob Friedman and I got a tour of the place. Of particular interest to me was the lab, especially the chamber (I came to call it the black box) they had built in such a way as to isolate an individual from light, sound, vibration, and electrical interference, while feeding him special Hemi-Sync tones via headphones to bring him to unusual states of consciousness, while leaving him still in communication with the control room via a microphone.

A way to get to specific desired mental states *at will!* I bought some of their tapes, hoping that they would provide a controlled way of doing what in the past had been possible only with the assistance of chemicals or other individuals. I found this very exciting. For most of my life—at least since reading *The Mind Parasites*—I had longed to develop psychic powers, if only so I would know. The tapes at least promised a way to pursue the matter.

To anticipate a bit, over the next three years I spent quite a bit of time practicing with the tapes, lying on a bed in the spare room, using earphones to listen to the tapes, trying with great intensity to help something to happen, trying (as probably most people do) to have an out-of-body experience, not knowing there were better things to do with the tools provided. I wanted to have an OBE primarily so that I would know (rather than have to believe) that it was possible to do so. As to what good it would do me, and what came after that, I didn't give it any thought at all.

And although I never did succeed in going consciously out of body before I did Gateway in December 1992, it is clear to me now that working at home with the tapes familiarized me with them and with the basic Monroe terminology and concepts, and helped get me past many of the expectations and fears that often hold back the beginner.

But that was all in the future. What I wouldn't have given, at that moment in 1989, to have a session in the black box!

– 16 –

The next day, Wednesday, I was back in the newsroom, doing things I didn't want to do, depressed at the contrast between the way I was spending my day and the way we had spent the day before. Perhaps significantly, on Thursday the newspaper management came up with an assignment for me that looked actually interesting. I asked The Boss:

Frank: Does this mean the paper really could come to something?

    It could. Do you want it to?

Frank: No. I want to work with Bob.

    Why?

Frank: Because it will be fun, exciting, profitable, and perhaps important—and the *Pilot* will be none of these.

    So now you know.

Frank: I do, indeed.

    Monroe.

Frank: Yes, largely. And talks with Bob. We discussed possible funding tonight. . . .

    And you learned that Bob would prefer you as a partner to any of the others.

Frank: Junior partners are easier to live with, at least initially.

    Yes, if they share your vision.

But in a way, this consultation was only theoretical. The day before, I had told Bob I'd go in with him. And the next night, my brother called. First, he wanted to know if I had experienced anything. (He was hoping I would tell him what he already knew from his friend. Like me, he wasn't above looking for reassurance.) But I hadn't consciously experienced anything.

His friend Joe, it seems, had gone looking to see what the new company's psychic surroundings would be. He saw four balls—one white, three black—which he took to mean that one of four people we would meet in business would be good, and the other three would be—if not bad, at least self-centered. As he put it, they had psychic ability, but they used it to get what they wanted. In some fashion that Paul could not explain, Joe had "called in some angels" to change the pattern, turning the black balls to clear, neutralizing them. From that point, I was told, it would be up to me to see clearly—consciously—what I already saw unconsciously: what people are. And then, Paul said, Joe said he felt *my* energy helping him with something, as a way of thanking him. (And this, of course, is what Paul was wondering if I would mention when he called.)

I found it curious to think that I could be doing everyday things at one level, and other, more significant, things at another level. I have since realized that that wasn't the half of it. Our lives are vastly more interesting than what we Downstairs usually experience consciously.

I also liked being pictured as a wise old soul, which was Joe's description. But the next day, in a different mood, I said, "I sure don't feel like a wise old soul today." The Boss said, "Good. If it were good for you to feel that way on a regular basis, you would have, long ago. You're in greater need of balance, groundedness, rootedness. You can't fly till you take off, and that implies pushing off from the ground. But you have to be firmly grounded first."

– 17 –

On the night of August seventh, a little dialogue with The Boss resulted in my being able to give her a name. I had modeled a woman's head in clay, and realized (though I won't go into *how* I realized) that The Boss had quite a bit to do with the way it came out.

Frank: It's a nice head, that Indian lady, that grandmother. How about her name, can you give me that?
  Gave you the head, what more do you want?
Frank: Simply this. Until you gave me the head, I was thinking of you as a young woman, a woman to have a romance

with, a sexy young thing. And now I see you as an old, wise, introverted, withdrawn woman who has seen and understood much, who has been there and back again. The image, the physical image of you changed my ideas, you see?

Nice that *you* see.

Frank: So how about a name? . . .

What about "Hey, you"?

Frank: Not respectful enough, in all seriousness.

Don't make an idol of me, I warn you.

Frank: I won't. I haven't. But I take you seriously.

Then take me seriously enough to name me.

I finally decided upon "Evangeline" for reasons that are too long to go into here, after The Boss said that "I was not, am not, a minority in my own country, it is more that I am an exile, never *in* my own country." And she told me not to keep working on the statue, even when I objected that the nose was crooked. "So do another, but don't fool with that one. That's Evangeline, and it is a gift of love and I don't want you fooling with it and wrecking it and then not having it."

"Okay, okay," I said. "Anyway, I think you're beautiful."

– 18 –

So Bob Friedman and I began setting the company into motion. He and I and one employee, trying to put out an 1,100-page free-verse poem by astrologer Linda Goodman called *Gooberz*. Clearly, it was going to be a monumental job to produce, and expensive too. Since we didn't have anywhere near the amount of money we needed to put it out, we made up a flyer describing the book, and mailed it to her list of people who had asked for the book over the years. I spent a certain amount of time one weekend in October trying to visualize ten thousand people writing to Hampton Roads, enclosing $22 checks ordering

Gooberz in advance in response to the flyer we had sent out. I didn't quite know why or how I was doing it, but I mentally called up a map of the United States and went from section to section, visualizing people writing checks to us. The Friday before I started doing it, we had received about $2,800. On Monday $15,000 came in. Coincidence, maybe—but I didn't stop visualizing. It was only while writing this book that I came across a biography of British occultist and writer Dion Fortune that describes her doing the same thing. It appears to be an essential ingredient of magic, unsuspected at the time by my conscious mind.

– 19 –

The next two and a half years totally transformed my life externally, and then gradually, internally. And if that period of time had a theme song, the chorus would go like this: "Work, work, work." The externals of my life from late 1989 to August 1992 were these: I went from working at the newspaper to working for Hampton Roads, and I got pulled into the innumerable problems of building and maintaining a publishing business. To my surprise I realized that I had a talent for business, and even a liking for it, even if the process was often depressing and even frightening.

The Boss quickly proved to be an invaluable partner in every aspect of my life, the "mundane" quite as much as the "spiritual." Indeed, if I could teach (by my example) only one lesson, perhaps I would choose to quote Thomas Merton (*Merton's Palace of Nowhere*, p. 21):

> The spiritual life is to be earnestly pursued as though no spiritual life existed. This is the only safe and sane way to travel in the deep waters of the Spirit. Indeed, such childlike simplicity in the face of God expresses a realization that there is, in fact, no spiritual life as such separate from life itself. There is only one life, and that is God's life

which he gives to us from moment to moment, drawing us
to himself with every holy breath we take.

– 20 –

I was able to leave the newspaper primarily because of
Living Is Forever, a manuscript by one J. Edwin Carter, sent us
in the fall of 1989 by Eleanor Friede, an agent who was a friend
of Bob Monroe's and who knew Bob Friedman as well. I read it,
and saw that it had good scenes, an interesting story, and an
important message, but needed rewriting. As much out of the
goodness of my heart (or so I thought, not yet recognizing what
economists call enlightened self-interest) as for any business
reason, I wrote Mr. Carter a three-page letter saying why I
thought the manuscript not publishable in its present form, and
giving an extensive analysis of the changes that I thought would
make it work.

I noted this in my journal, adding, "Not that any of this
helps deal with my personal life." Proof once again (as if more
proof were needed) how little I know.

– 21 –

Ed Carter was the son of Georgia schoolteachers, who
grew up to be CEO of Inco, Ltd., the Canadian parent company
of International Nickel. In 1984, four years after he retired, he
broke his hip in a mysterious fall that landed him in the hospital and led him to spend several years trying to write a book he
didn't want to write, as he describes in his prologue to *Living Is
Forever*.

In December 1989 Mr. Carter responded to my letter,
agreeing with my criticisms, but saying he could not himself do
the work needed to fix it. The most pressing of the reasons was
his wife's sudden critical illness. He said that he would be willing to pay a professional editor to do the job, and at Bob
Friedman's suggestion, I offered to do it and also guarantee

publication by Hampton Roads—for I did believe in the value and appeal of the story, and knew I could put it into publishable shape. In due course we came to agreement. I arranged it so that he paid the money to the company rather than to me personally (out of some fuzzy concern about being fair to HRPC) and the company in turn would put me on the payroll part-time. This meant that I could begin to leave the newspaper! Before the end of January 1990 I was working half-time at the paper as "Commentary" editor and half-time at Hampton Roads.

Soon he and I were conferring over the phone and sending each other disks in the course of the rewrite. And since he had specified in the contract that I should confer with him in person at least once a month, I two or three times flew down to Jekyll Island, Georgia, where he and his wife, Meredith, were wintering, and spent weekends with them. In short order Mr. and Mrs. Carter had become Ed and Meredith, and he and I had become friends.

Then, between the book project and our developing habit of telephone conferences "just to check in," he became ad hoc financial advisor, then investor, and finally full partner in our publishing enterprise. In the seven years we knew each other, he and I went down several surprising roads together, Hampton Roads not the least of them.

– 22 –

I wasn't working part-time for long before I saw a lot of things I could do to help our company grow. In mid-March 1990 I got up my nerve and quit the *The Virginian-Pilot* on two weeks' notice. My first day full-time at Hampton Roads was, I was happy to see, the day of a new moon in Aries. Good start for a new beginning, I thought.

In June, Bob and I went back to The Monroe Institute (TMI), still pursuing the possibility of distributing TMI tapes. But the significance of the trip for me is that I bought the first two volumes of Gateway tapes, despite inner qualms about spending the money, which at the time seemed a lot.

One of the tapes helps identify and dissipate specific fears. As I began to work with it, I found three very quickly, and bubbled away my fears and their associated emotions. The Boss said, "You *felt* it do good. You *felt* the resultant lightness. The laughter bubbled up at you as you waved it on its way away from you."

Before the end of the month, still using the TMI tapes, I found another three fears, and found where they had come from, and bubbled them away. Felt like I was flying, particularly after releasing the third fear and having all that weight gone. The third fear had been symbolized by a huge lead weight, holding me down, and I watched it become buoyant and float off. I thought, *"This stuff is working!"*

– 23 –

I am omitting, of necessity, mounds of material I received from The Boss in response to my continual questioning about business matters. In this period probably ninety-five percent of my consultations had to do with business ideas, finance, worry about the future of the company, and in general how to work effectively with Bob and with our employees. But there's no reason to repeat those conversations except to remind you that in fact this advice turned out to be invaluable. It would have been invaluable if it had given nothing more than perspective on my own thinking and my own areas of ignorance and blindness. But in fact I received much more. If I don't repeat it here, it is only because there are other things to report that I think would prove more helpful to more people. After all, not everyone has the fortune (whether good or bad I'm not always sure) to own or build or have to run a business.

Speaking of which, I can't resist mentioning that one day The Boss said, "You need to consider that many of the things you see front and center are only peripheral from the large scheme of things, and vice versa. We don't care who pays the rent or collects it. You and Bob tend to worry about such things—but is it important who delivers your newspaper, just so you get it? The pattern is for you to succeed. The details don't much matter."

There was much more in this particular consultation, which began by my stubbornly trying to steer it one way. When I finally realized what had happened, I said, "It requires a lot of mutual patience, this talking between worlds, doesn't it?"

The Boss said, "You get the idea. You were determined to hear about your physical office situation. I could talk about that or be blocked. Because I have come to trust in your trust, I chose to go along, and sure enough you recognized that you were stepping on my lines and then listened."

– 24 –

On Friday, September 28, 1990, a strange thing happened to me. At five that evening, as on every Friday for the previous three years, I had joined my friend Frank at a restaurant in downtown Norfolk for a couple of beers and a general debriefing on our week. Our ritual was hardly riotous; I don't think we ever had as much as three beers apiece; usually two; sometimes just one.

On that night, we were walking back to the newspaper office to pick up our cars. About to walk across a small deserted street, I turned my ankle on the curb and fell full length in the street. For a moment I lay there stunned, then slowly picked myself up, taking inventory. My left arm and leg had gotten scraped; my ankle swelled a little, then went back to normal (which in retrospect is peculiar). I wasn't really hurt, but I thought it strange. There was no obvious *reason* for the fall.

That night, talking to The Boss, in the course of my usual angst I said I really wanted to be a writer, and asked to be given a plot for a novel. I promptly was given *ten* journal pages of plot, characters, motivation, et cetera. Saturday morning I wrote another nine pages, working out problems, then asked The Boss how I should tell it. She gave me the answer in three short paragraphs, and there was my novel, just waiting for me to do the work of writing it out.

Now, by Sunday I began to smell a fish, or a rat, or something. First I fell, then came a burst of writing and a seemingly new attitude, a new start. I wondered, "Is there a direct connection?" For there was something strange in it, like Ed Carter's fall. Then I went back to another three pages of plotting. On Sunday, October 7, I asked, "Well, Boss, *was* there a connection between my fall nine days ago and a change in perspective?"

> You fell and jolted yourself awake. As when you fell at age seven and jolted yourself asleep. Then it was important to preserve something. Now it is important to *use* that something.

Frank: It was a cue, then?

> More like an activation. The next part of your life will be very unlike anything that came before, but the long delay and enforced inactivity was necessary. You had to be kept in the ranks, as you once put it. You were preserved from premature success.

Frank: A part of me was paralyzed.

> Tranquilized, would be a better way to put it. It did you no damage, merely deferred your career until that career would do your character and insight and influence no damage.

I accepted the explanation and went on with my life. It would be only in the course of actually writing this book that I would obtain further word on what had gone on, and why.

In the few days between my fall and consulting The Boss, several things happened. I quit a men's group I had attended for some time, which had become somewhat stale; I told a literary agent to return the manuscript of my novel *Messenger*, as it was suddenly obvious to me that she could not well represent it; and I went back up to The Monroe Institute and bought more tapes, using them to help me resume my internal exploration.

– 25 –

Meanwhile a local author named Danny Lliteras and I had become friends, encouraging each other in our careers, sharing our enthusiasms, our reading, our thoughts. By contagion from working with Danny's *In A Warrior's Romance* manuscript, which we later published, I began writing haiku poetry, finding it very much to my liking. Danny, having read the *Messenger* manuscript and other things I'd written, continually told me I didn't take myself seriously enough as a writer. The Boss started chiming in, playing the same old tune, saying at one point that Danny had been sent to me (as I to him) to encourage me. And then she brought out the big gun, using information that had come to me about the Myers-Briggs Type Indicator, a measurement tool psychologists use to type people in Jungian terms:

> You feel alone and unacknowledged, because nobody can really see you. . . . Your primary process goes to internal matters and only your secondary process is spent on externals. You are therefore unknowable, as are all introverts except through your self-expression. But if you don't express yourself in writing or painting, you won't at all. Even then, prepare to be entirely alone. Is that so bad? It has served you well to date. Now it hurts because you are more alive than before, but don't worry about it. You're doing better than Conrad's father in *Ordinary People* [who was entirely out of touch with his feelings].

– 26 –

All through this time, I repeat, I was asking for and obtaining endless advice and analysis on very practical matters from

The Boss, as I learned how to do what needed to be done if the business were to survive and prosper. Always the same themes: Do what is closest to hand; don't worry; do what is worthwhile; do it as best you can, and the money will come. True enough. But not all my life was business. On March 12, 1991, I realized that I was filled with blind rage, and The Boss told me why. I was running away from myself, and it stemmed from worrying about money, thinking (unconsciously, where it couldn't be seen and therefore fought) that if I didn't do it, it wouldn't get done. "And," The Boss added, "you are at the brink of a new life and a new way of living. You sense it and you're very nervous."

To uncover the rhythms underlying our lives, usually unsuspected by us, I can think of nothing as useful as a journal. Only four days later, I wrote, "Dr. George Ritchie's book is great, a great book by a great man, and I am honored and privileged to read the manuscript and help make it become real." And this was before I met the man.

George Ritchie's near-death experience had years ago inspired Dr. Raymond Moody's research into NDEs. His book *Return From Tomorrow*, published by a Christian publisher, had sold in six figures. But this second manuscript, which he called *Ordered to Return*, didn't pass the Christian publisher's litmus test. George demonstrated that the medieval Church's condemnation of reincarnation was a political decision, and stated on the basis of his professional career as doctor and psychiatrist that homosexuality was one of a range of sexual orientations occurring naturally.

I hadn't known of his first book, but this manuscript I *knew* was important.

I consulted The Boss, who said in part:

> You were put into place to serve. You are willing to serve. This is good. . . . The other press might have had him but could not stomach his views—which is your opportunity. You can edit his prose and make it well. Do. Don't

trust anyone else to do it. Think it, live it, spread the word about it.

Well, we agreed to do the book. After the usual conferences and cogitations the title became *My Life After Dying: Becoming Alive to Universal Love* (which we later reissued in a new edition titled *Ordered to Return: My Life After Dying*).

As I read George's manuscript, and still more as I worked with him, I experienced the extraordinary warmth of this man. I began making conscious efforts to open myself more to all aspects of my being, known and unknown, including not only other individuals but also the transcendent force I was calling God. I did not instantly transform my life. I was still short-tempered, irritable, and frequently depressed. But gradually I felt some progress. And I came to realize that essential to psychic abilities was the ability to feel and express love. I had known this first ten years before, reading Harmon Bro's *Edgar Cayce on Religion and Psychic Experience*. Now I decided to live it.

– 27 –

"Joy is in life," The Boss said, "not in withdrawing from life. In giving, not in withdrawing from giving." And when I objected that "everything is so unsatisfactory," The Boss said, "So is life, but you can make of it a dance and get along okay. Help people; rewards come, so it isn't as if you're giving yourself away. Relate. You can learn to relate *partway* as most people do. . . . Then you have some openness but you can always close or slam the door."

Another unnoticed or scarcely noticed turning point came in June, 1991:

Frank: I'm fasting more or less—with the gluttonous exception of all those peanuts.

Don't be too hard on yourself, you saw it and changed. You've persevered since Saturday, nine days. Pretty good. . . . If you want to live only on fruit—why not try and see what happens? If it proves to be not possible, still you may learn something. Already you can see it has its benefits. By putting all nonfruits off-limits, you eliminate temptations and decision-making. And you *have* lost weight.

I did change to a fruit diet, and after a while, for the first time in eight years, I was lean again. When I went off my fruit diet, I didn't go back to eating meat, and so became vegetarian almost absentmindedly. Though I didn't know it, this was all preparation for something that wouldn't occur for another sixteen months, when I did the Gateway Voyage at The Monroe Institute. Abstaining from meat, I am convinced, significantly raised my vibrations and allowed me to get the most out of that incredible week-long experience.

– 28 –

On August 8, 1991, I said in my journal, "I want to do better as a person. I want to express love."

The Boss replied:

Then do it. There is no shortcut, because there are no obstacles. Love is. Express it. Feel it. Have you considered? God *loves* you. Loves *you*. As you are, as you are trying. He loves you not a bit less than he loves everyone. He knows your sincerity as he knows your temper! Your strengths and weaknesses. And what are they to him? You are good enough for him, if not for yourself. Love and be loved. There's nothing to it. And everything to it. . . .

You lose sight of yourself. Don't worry so much. Life is serious, but not important, or important but not tragic, or—better—serious but not *only* serious. It's dancing too. Dance.

– 29 –

So we stumbled along. When I'd ask The Boss, in some anxiety, the refrain was always the same: Work hard, don't worry, do what is at hand, trust. Using feedback from The Boss, Bob and I—after long discussions with Ed Carter—devised an investment program that we called "STPs" (Single Title Partnerships). In the next couple of years, STPs would raise enough money for the company to keep us in business and finance growth that was not only rapid but often seemingly out of our control. Worthwhile to have such information on tap.

On the other hand, one Sunday at 2 A.M. I asked, "Why did you wake me?" and got this:

You are not focused properly. Forget receivables and loans and continuing in business, and concentrate on the spirit. Nothing is the same, nothing will last much longer. The spirit first is your way out. It is the *practical* path out of difficulties. Pray.

– 30 –

These conversations turned out to be invaluable. They would have been invaluable if they had given nothing more than perspective on my own thinking and my own areas of ignorance and blindness. But in fact I received much more. As I said, The Boss quickly proved to be an invaluable partner in every aspect of my life, the "mundane" quite as much as the "spiritual." And you, reader, are—or *can be*—in intimate touch with your own internal guides, so there is no point in giving you secondhand reports. On the day before Thanksgiving 1991, the word really got through. I wrote in my journal:

I decided—I've trusted God ever since I learned to; I'm not going to stop now. He can do what he wants to do; it's okay with me. Succeed or fail, up or down—something will happen, and it's all okay with me. Hidden supposition—

that life is meaning, pattern, richness. That we aren't orphans in the desert.

My New Year's resolutions were to try harder; to be more of a perfectionist for myself and less for others except legitimately; to demand more of myself—and deliver.

I'm still after greater openness—to God, to myself, to others.

And then it was 1992, the year in which the way suddenly opened.

FIVE

A Matter of Focus

The Upstairs conversation must have gone something like this: "It's time! Let's do it," followed by: "Ready if you are. *This* will shake things up some."

The Downstairs conversation consisted of a phone call, in the summer of 1992, from a woman I will call "Mary Johnson," a prospective author in California wanting to know if Hampton Roads might be interested in looking at a thousand-page manuscript novel on the lives of Martha and Thomas Jefferson.

I explained that we mostly did metaphysical books, but that I had a deep interest in history, and I'd at least give her my opinion of it, if that was worth her time and postage. Then Downstairs-I went off on vacation. When I returned, the manuscript was on my desk.

I picked it up with no special expectations, but it was so good! I started it, and—necessary interruptions notwithstanding—read it right through in a week, reading it at the office by day and at home by night. I had read a good deal about Jefferson, but never anything that brought him, let alone Martha Jefferson, so vividly to life.

I sent Mary a long letter telling her how good I thought that manuscript was. I still couldn't see how Hampton Roads could ever publish it, so I thought I was just being helpful. I suggested that she try a mass-market house, made a few suggestions as to format, and then—still in kindly editor mode—asked if she would consider deleting its many intimate (though hardly X-rated) scenes and conversations, as we in the twentieth century couldn't know the inner lives of these people from the eighteenth century. By return mail she came clean, though it took me two rereadings to clearly understand what she was saying. She wrote:

> I speak not as an outside observer, but as one who lived with and amid Thomas and Patty. [Martha was known as Patty]. You might understand that I have been very cautious about going public with such information, for I have no desire to be taken for a nut, or to have my credibility as a scholar questioned. What I *know* does not invalidate my ability to sleuth out validations of it, but I doubt the public at large is ready to hear the truth. I am only telling you to assuage your qualms. . . . You are free to think of me as a nut if you wish.

She thought she had been Martha Jefferson! What was I to make of that? She didn't strike me as crazy, and I was confident that she was reporting what she thought was true. Certainly it would explain the vivid, sure-footed description. But was it possible that she really had been Martha Jefferson? However in the world could I judge?

I was willing to leave the question open. After my rejection letter, we continued a correspondence (mostly on her part, for she was a prodigious letter writer) throughout September and part of October. For some reason that looks extremely suspicious to me now, I wasn't thinking of her as a psychic. I thought of her primarily in terms of Jefferson, and of writing, and of scholarship. This although she had told me she was accessing past-life memories!

Now, although I didn't know it at the time, Mary had established something of a reputation as a Jefferson researcher. She had been invited (she told me one day) to come to Monticello in October for a conference on Jefferson. The only problem was that in order to get the lowest airfare she would have to stay the weekend after the conference ended. No problem, I told her; come stay in the DeMarco hotel. (This was something we often did. My wife and I enjoyed getting to know authors, who were generally interesting people.)

Mary accepted, and on October 14 she called from Charlottesville to say she had arrived and to be sure it was still convenient that she stay with us. I no sooner got off the phone than my mother called from New Jersey. My uncle had just died, and the funeral would be Saturday. My wife and daughter were tied up with a school activity that weekend, so I drove up alone, and didn't get back till late Sunday afternoon.

When I first met Mary, she was all aglow. Over the weekend, by combining her anthropological training and her inner guidance, she had found the foundations of Martha Jefferson's childhood home! Naturally, she wanted to tell me all about it. I found it mildly interesting, but I remember standing there in my hallway wondering, do we talk about Jefferson all night? Then as she told *how* she had found the place, I suddenly realized: She was in the habit of talking to what she called "the guys upstairs." She was psychic! She had done her own past-life research! She could help others do the same!

It's all highly suspicious. It seems clear to me that Upstairs wanted the connection made in a certain way, at a certain time, and had made sure that Downstairs didn't make the mental leap beforehand. And thus Mary and I wound up sitting at my dining room table from 8 P.M. to 2 A.M.

– 2 –

I asked, "I'm helping you with your manuscript even though my company probably won't publish it. Why is that?" She sighed and closed her eyes, and for a second I thought she was offended, or weary of people asking her such questions. But it was just her way of going Upstairs. (A few years later, after I'd been doing it a while, I noticed with amusement that I was doing the same thing; the closing of eyes to reduce sensory input, the brief sigh as I got centered. In this I wasn't copying her, at least not consciously; I was doing what seemed most natural.)

My present help was a reversal of form, she said. We had been together in an English monastery in the twelfth century. (Later she decided it was the thirteenth century.) She had been a monk, the head of the scriptorium, responsible for recopying books. I was a young man from a wealthy family, a second son, whose family wanted him to rise in the world. "He could have bought his way to a bishopric or an abbot's seat," she said, but the head of the scriptorium urged that he be fostered and trained in secret ways. (What *that* was all about we didn't find out right away.)

Right then, and very naturally, she and I started to work together. Something she would say would spark a knowing in me; something I would say would bring forth further detail from her. Because this isn't a book on how to learn to discover your other lives, I won't detail how we fumbled around for information, getting a word or a name or a "knowing" and sometimes later modifying it. I took notes, but I didn't think to tape-record the session. In my journal next day I said that she "turned out to be a *big* surprise."

On that first night, we came up with material that matched what I had been told by a psychic earlier. And in the course of that long session we came up with parts of two stories (put it that way) that seemed important. And perhaps it is as well to say in advance that in both cases, neither the names nor the dates were quite right, yet those stories took us far.

The first man's name I at first thought was David Peterson, or Paterson. He had lived in America, roughly in the years 1823 to 1867. He had met Emerson, had been inspired by the thought of the transcontinental journey of Lewis and Clark, had crossed the continent in the 1840s or 1850s, and among other things had written a monograph or dissertation called "The Etymological Derivations of Plant and Animal Names of the Northwest Indians." We didn't get the entire title that first night; the words "of Plant and Animal Names" were missing, but we had the general idea. And there he rested until my Gateway Voyage a few weeks later, at which time I thought I heard him called "Dr. Atwood." A year or more later, in a semi-sleep vision one night, I *saw* a hand write on a blackboard the name "Josiah (or maybe "Joseph"; the certainty faded quickly) Smallwood," and Smallwood is how I've thought of him since.

The second lifetime was even more interesting. It was more of the story of the man whose life outline had come to me in that unsatisfactory hypnotic session five years earlier. I knew he was British and thought that his years were 1887 to 1939, though later I decided (still tentatively) on 1871 to 1932. At first I got his name as David Cornwall, then David Cornwell. Later I would remember the British author David Cornwell, master of the spy story, whose pen name is John LeCarré. In light of what I later learned about the inner nature of David's life, the fact that his life was introduced under John LeCarré's real name seemed symbolic and significant. But only three years later, during a Lifeline program at the institute, was I given what purported to be his real name, David Poynter. For whatever reason, when I try to get names, I often pull in the name David.

About names. "Names are *hard*!" Mary would say nearly a year later, and something sardonic within me says that it figures that the thing that would be easiest to verify is often hardest to dredge up reliably, like your phone number ten years and three moves later. For all I know, it is hardest *because* a name would be so helpful. By implication it would be the most potentially devastating if wrong, and fear of being wrong is a major barrier to developing psychic ability, which requires that one be willing to rush in ahead of the angels.

At any rate, the next day, full of hope, I went to a university library looking for evidence. Nothing to be found, perhaps because I was deficient in research skills, but perhaps because the information was just wrong.

Frank: Boss, I am wondering—worried—that all this may be just a pleasant daydream, which is why I can't find anything to corroborate Cornwell or Peterson. The drawings [of two men] came to me—but do they really mean anything? And is Mary really as incredible as I thought she was Sunday night?

You are afraid that your dreams could come true. They *are* coming true. . . . You are not the one you were. But you can access these memories and convince yourself of their veracity and reality. The idea of keeping a record of your search is okay but not essential. What you become will be more impressive than how you got there. David Cornwell can be found. David Peterson can be found.

Frank: But are the names accurate?

Seek and find. All you need do is go within and listen. And yes, you do best with pen in hand, so why not?

There followed a long attempt to get more, which I duly recorded without much hope of it being true. What came clear was that the names weren't David.

Frank: "Then why did David come?"

"Much attachment to that name. Colors things."

I asked again if I was fooling myself and wasting my time. "No. You know better than that. But you're driving with the brakes on. Fantasize first, criticize—that is, verify—later." Looking back, I see now how hard I found this to do. I was very fearful of fooling myself.

– 3 –

Mary's visit occurred in mid-October 1992. In the next six or seven weeks, her presence in my life transformed my sense of possibilities. For the first time I had a partner, a partner experienced in the methods of research. In a flood of letters and phone calls (Internet access would have saved us a fortune), she reported where she had looked and what she had found. A particular academic friend, she said, "is convinced that more biographical information would yield results, so get working on those details! Let it go, let it flow. Don't be afraid to see what you see. The question of 'validity' or 'historical truth' . . . comes later."

I sent her sketches of the two men that had come to me in a mildly altered state. Her reply:

Dear Frank—
About the sketches:
YES YES YES YES YES YES YES
YES YES YES YES YES YES YES
YES YES YES YES YES YES YES
YES YES YES
I am not surprised that you could only write "Cornwell"; I've had that myself the last couple of days. He surely looks like a Welshman. . . .
As per Mr. Peterson . . . were he and Emerson related anyhow? Cousins, maybe? . . . One gets the feeling that he felt like a failure, esp. in comparison to his learned colleague (Emerson). But he *wasn't*. He has a legacy, especially out here, that has lasted down to this very day. . . . He had vision. Maybe visions!

At just this time, out of nowhere, Bob Friedman—acting I have no doubt as Authorized Agent of the Universe, or put another way, as Upstairs-directed facilitator—said to me that maybe if we did the Gateway Voyage, The Monroe Institute's six-day residential program, Monroe would feel more comfortable about us distributing his Hemi-Sync tapes to bookstores—a proposal that was still hanging fire more than three years after we had first proposed it. Bob suggested that he and I do it together and have the company pay for it. Yes! That way, I could afford it! I was on the phone within minutes, inquiring as to which Gateway had the next openings. November was booked up, it turned out, but there were two openings in the first week of December. I signed us up, and began waiting impatiently, meanwhile working with Mary, trying to do the things she insisted I knew how to do if I would only let myself do them.

Of course, ordinary life continued. But in the living, as now in the telling, my main interest was elsewhere. (I don't propose it as a model way to live; I only describe the way I am.) Mary continued to encourage and exhort me by every post.

Letter from Mary, October 31, expressing her frustration at my caution and self-doubt:

> . . . My dear old one, don't you ever read anything you publish? You know all of this! What is holding you back from it manifesting in your life? Why do you question where your knowing of past incidences and all comes from ("How do I know that?") This is not meant as a criticism!!! But it anguishes me to see you ground-bound, when I know you can *fly*. The other part says, "have patience, he has chosen this unremembering for its lessons, its experience."

She pointed out that if I would do the work of obtaining the information, we could validate it afterward, but the hardest work would have been done.

> Also, we are bound to have some confusions in this matter (instance the names of the two gentlemen). . . . These little confusions invalidate neither the information nor the process. . . . So do not be discouraged! In the refinement of your fine-tuning, all will become clear.

One day that fall, I noted that I was quietly restless, that money was extremely low, "yet I am not worried; hardly touched. It is something within saying, there's always more, don't worry about it. And I do not. . . ."

And *why* did I not? Because Mary "has turned my life upside down, or rather has opened it into wider channels. Between her and [certain others] and the prospect of going to TMI for Gateway, and the opening up of communications with people in so many places, physical and psychic, I am ready to burst out into new levels of awareness. Or so it feels. . . . If only I could have the little bit—that giant bit—of external reinforcement that would be breakthrough into direct memory—and into direct powers of perception and management—"

Boss?

> The way to know is to know. An important part of knowing is already there before you begin, or how could you know *what* you know? If you want direct access to what you were—are—you need only integrate it with the part of you that is active now. . . .

I want to grow into whatever I was and can become.

> Work! It takes work, not merely desire and longing.

I began to follow my perceptions more, spending less time wondering if I was on a fool's chase. This soon led me into strange territory.

Throughout November, Mary rummaged among her scholarly resources, looking for information on my behalf. And we pursued other clues as well. One day I wrote her asking if I could have been Martha Jefferson's first husband, Batt Skelton. For he had gotten killed in Williamsburg by crossing the street while reading, which is exactly the kind of thing I would have done, and do yet. It (and my feelings for her) felt right. She wrote back:

Your remark about Batt Skelton made me stop and
consider. Honestly, had I not known who he is/was, it
would have been easy to say "yes," for we have had that
relation before, and Scotland keeps coming up for me. . . .
I would put money on the Isle of Skye (1570s–1620s).

She said that one Margaret MacDonald and one Robert
MacLean had been lovers. *That* ratcheted up the tension! The matter
was more complicated than I had ever thought, and not just in terms
of relationships between individuals in this life. I began to realize that
we don't deal with each other on the basis of just this life, or even this
life and any one other. Relationships are folded one atop another.
Mary, responding to my feeling that Paterson had known Thoreau (a
great influence on me in this lifetime), said she thought that he

Affected Thoreau more than Thoreau affected him, or
it was mutual. At any rate it was a not a relationship where
you were the low man on the totem pole. He's a person you
have a "past" with. He was in Salisbury (12th C), but I had-
n't much truck with him. He was a cell mate of yours.
(Things are never as simple as they seem. He couldn't just
be Thoreau, y'know?)

– 4 –

In mid-November Mary sent me, among other things, a map
of the Lewis and Clark expedition and a copy of Jefferson's letter of
carte blanche to Meriwether Lewis. She thought the man we were
calling Peterson (who I later learned was named Smallwood)
made two or three trips cross-country emulating Lewis and Clark.
On one of these journeys, she felt, he encountered young John
Muir. "You'll know better than me if this resonates at all." I went
to the library and found a book on Lewis and Clark as well as one
editing (summarizing) their journals. I found it fascinating. I
made particular note that John Bakeless, in his introduction to

the Journals of Lewis and Clarke, said: "The Indian vocabularies collected by the expedition have largely, if not entirely, disappeared, though they may eventually turn up in some missing legal or governmental file." I thought of his lost monograph.

That night, most atypically, for some reason I had coffee and doughnuts (caffeine and sugar) at about 7:30 P.M. I read about Lewis and Clark till late, went to bed, and got up at 11:15 P.M. in an altered state, though of course not in a trance. I sat down with my journal and wrote four and a half pages.

It began from my point of view, then abruptly changed to the viewpoint of this man of the nineteenth century:

> Always, since I was a boy—as far as I can remember; when I read that book about Daniel Boone, with the one picture of the land spread out before him—I have pictured America as an empty land, an unspoiled, unoccupied land. The interruption of an airplane or the sight of a house or road or any sign of human habitation has always spoiled it for me. I wanted at least to pretend I was again in the West, among no one.
>
> Yes, I went west, and I traveled alone and I loved that land and the time. I saw God in everything I saw, and there were no invidious comparisons to be made. All was one, and if mankind was sort of contemptible, sort of hopelessly backward—it was only a stage, a phase, and would pass. I criticized Thoreau as a rustic, and that he was. He had the rustic, provincial habit of thinking his home everywhere, and everything else the less because it was elsewhere. He'd have made a natural Virginian!
>
> But Emerson—Emerson was intimidatingly superb. For one thing he was half a generation older than I was, and that lent a certain aura. Was famous—soon to be lionized throughout England—and *in a way* that was appealing and lent authority, in a way not, for he was growing a little too

comfortable, as who would not who had conquered one world and hadn't ambition to conquer more? Put another way, he had invented a place for himself. The world acceded, therefore he had no need—almost no possibility—of reinventing himself and becoming something perhaps frighteningly different. In some respects he was seemingly so audacious, because he *saw* so differently. Yet he was timid and sluggish and cold, always well aware of his interest and his position, fearing poverty and more than that, fearing that [giving] the last ounce of trust might leave him open to betrayal. So he ventured only so far, and after he was forty, he had nothing new for any young man *who had been inspired by him more than a few years—maybe months—previously.*

This is not to say a word against him. He was sincere and honest and well-meaning and put himself to immense trouble to spread his gospel—if not The Gospel—far and across the American Midwest and West. And would have the South, if it had not been a waste of time.

Still, there it was. The man was an immense, intimidating success—yet I would see the flaws, the hesitancies, the cracks. And could nonetheless do no comparable or better work. Of what use to criticize, if there is no improvement to be made?

So—go off quietly into the wilderness. Be your own man, much as Henry Thoreau did, I realized later, only our paths were so different exteriorly. Mine was wandering. He never traveled far save in his mind. Maybe I did too much of my wandering inside my mind, not seeing where I was, or maybe I moved my body around, always seeing the same thing, but only that. It's the same in the end.

So what is a man's life worth, seen from outside? Lewis and Clark filled me with wild desire to *see*. I met John Muir and set him on fire. He is still arsonating [!] men's minds today, as [for example, author] Richard Fleck.

But—failure! Failure! That's the inner gnawing, an inability to understand the disparity between inner and outer measurement. I was not what I appeared. Neither was Emerson. But he was taken for more, I for less. So he *did* more, accomplished more—externally. But maybe lived far less.

In other words, this life, too, rang true. And the next day, driving, I was still half in another consciousness, seeing the buildings and roads and all as sitting heavily on the land, sitting as the late additions they are. I sent this information to Mary, but didn't get her response until after I returned from a Gateway Voyage at The Monroe Institute, by which time, as she noted, masses of water had flowed under the bridge.

– 5 –

In 1987 had come the Higher Self Seminar, Suni, and Jungian analysis. From 1989 on, I had been in continual, ever more intimate internal communication with The Boss. In mid-1990 I had begun using the Monroe tapes regularly, and had consciously worked to open myself up to God and others. In mid-1991 I had rather absentmindedly (having no idea why) become a vegetarian. In the fall of 1992 had come several weeks of work and intense communication with Mary, which had given me more growth than I had gotten in my entire life with the exception of my time twenty years earlier working with Louis Meinhardt. Mary and I, working together, swapping insights and questions and knowings by mail and telephone, had helped each other immensely. From me she got acceptance and eager cooperation. From her I got direction and encouragement. And now suddenly Bob Friedman and I were on our way to do a Gateway.

Monroe had written in *Far Journeys* that Gateway was designed to lead people from normal consciousness—what he called "consciousness one," or "C1"—to less usual states. He did it a little at a time, so as to dissolve what he called the fear barrier and unleash the formidable power of individual curiosity. He had said that in Gateway, many people learn for the first time, by personal experience (the only way possible), that they are more than their physical body. And now maybe I too would know, and before another Saturday came around. Was it too much to hope for?

– 6 –

To understand what happened to me at Gateway requires an elementary understanding of how Monroe came to see the world, and how his technology helps individuals to investigate for themselves. Monroe said in *Ultimate Journey* that it took a full year before he accepted the reality of the out-of-body experience, but that after forty trips fear began to be replaced by curiosity. He began to experiment and take notes, being careful to keep his experiences secret. (In the 1950s, science and mainstream religion more or less dismissed the idea of out-of-body travel as impossible. Fundamentalists and occultists—New Agers as such did not then exist in any numbers—thought it possible only for saints or enlightened beings. Nobody but nobody thought it was something for the common man.)

So far as Monroe knew, no one else had ever experienced what he was going through. That made it hard. Nor did his concepts allow for the possibility. That made it harder—and made him the perfect interpreter. He says in *Journeys Out of the Body* that he never gave much thought to God and religion, as the subject didn't interest him. I think that this lack of exposure and lack of interest provided him with protection from concepts. He had the advantage of knowing that he didn't know.

He investigated Western religions, and got no help. Tried Eastern religions and got more acceptance of what he was experiencing, but "no details, and no pragmatic explanation of what was meant by spiritual development." He discovered what he called the psychic underground—people who believed in the reality of psychic matters, but kept their beliefs to themselves, lest they be thought crazy. But nobody he met could help him find out what was happening to him and what it meant. He looked particularly closely into Edgar Cayce, finding that Cayce's readings confirmed the reality of what Monroe was experiencing, but did not explain it. He found that both "occult" literature and the Bible seemed to be referencing the same experience. But neither literature nor live people could answer his questions.

Monroe was a practical man, with little patience for conventional religion, or for metaphysical jargon, or for scientific blindness. He had curiosity, he had familiarity with technology, he had money enough to finance his investigations. He began to experiment with recording, and then with altering, brain-wave activity. Pouring his own money into research, he created the technology and the body of workers who became The Monroe Institute, which came to focus on expanding people's control over their own conscious states, gradually inventing a technology to teach people to achieve certain levels of consciousness *at will.*

They did it—they still do it—by monitoring the entire top portion of a person's skull by topographic analysis, producing a twenty-channel EEG—ten readings on each side of the brain—to establish a range of "normal" beta, alpha, theta, and delta brain-wave patterns. (Gamma waves, which are in the relatively high frequency above 30 hertz, were and are beyond the range of TMI's equipment.) Then they experiment until they find combinations that surface when people are in specific unusual mental states. When psychics are channeling, for instance. When healers are healing people.

As they identify the sound pattern that produces specific mental states in the majority of people, they produce tapes that consist of those sound patterns, with verbal instruction overlaid. This gives them a way to show people what these states "feel" like, so that they can learn to recognize them and return at will. These Hemi-Sync tapes—"Hemi-Sync" for hemispheric synchronization, because the frequencies lead both halves of the brain to work in tandem—can't *force* someone's brain into a given state of consciousness. Instead, they use what is called the frequency-following effect, hoping that the person's brain, not having any reason to resist, will move to the amplitude and frequency combinations of beta, alpha, theta, and delta waves played on the tape.

These mental states existed long before Bob Monroe, of course. Monroe's contribution was to create a system that allows people to go there systematically, repeatedly. He used to tell his Gateway groups, "You can't learn anything here that you couldn't learn using other techniques. But we can maybe save you twenty years." This mental biofeedback technique, as you might call it, is of enormous value for those who want to get control of what's going on between their ears.

In *Journeys Out of the Body*, which was published in 1971, and *Far Journeys*, in 1985, Monroe reported on the Second State, the reality beyond the world our senses commonly report. *Ultimate Journey*, which came out in 1994, when he was near the end of his life, is a summing-up—the World According to Monroe, clearly and logically laid out.

Herewith, a quick summary of Bob Monroe's implied cosmology, though I know he would shudder at the word—and perhaps at the prospect! I think this is the best way to illustrate how his implied cosmology explains various things that happened to me, and to friends of mine, and potentially, reader, to you. I think that his worldview and his technology open up a way for us to build a common understanding through firsthand experience.

– 7 –

Probably it is worth emphasizing that Monroe's experience *preceded* his description and analysis. He began his investigations without having an emotional vested interest in any outcome but his own health and sanity and the satisfaction of his curiosity. He was able to be an excellent explorer and reporter because he didn't come to this experience with an ax to grind. In giving you this fast description of the conclusions Monroe came to, I am reversing the process. Hindsight is unfair advantage. Looking back from where Monroe eventually found himself, we can see how little he understood when he began. The very organization of his three books tells us.

In *Journeys Out of the Body* he talked of Locale I, II, and III, and listed their respective properties as best he could, dividing them into what seemed natural logical divisions. Thus, Locale I was the world we are familiar with, seen from the unfamiliar out-of-body perspective. Locale III was a baffling sort of distorted-mirror-image of earth, apparently functioning with the same physical laws as ours, but with a very different historical and technological development pattern, and with different habits and customs. Monroe didn't deal all that much with Locale III, possibly because he wasn't able to discover much about it. Nor will I pursue it here, having no experience of it.

But Locale II he described as "a non-material environment with laws of motion and matter only remotely related to the physical world. It is an immensity whose bounds are unknown (to the experimenter), and has depth and dimension incomprehensible to the finite, conscious mind. In this vastness lie all of the aspects we attribute to heaven and hell. . . . It is inhabited, if that is the word, by entities with various degrees of intelligence with whom communication is possible."

About this, much more later. Most of this book deals with the interaction of Locale II with what we think of as "normal" life.

By the time Monroe wrote *Ultimate Journey*, the information and experiences that had so baffled him earlier had been placed, mostly, into a coherent and useful framework centered on Locale II. He came to believe that this was the natural home of a second body, which "seems to interpenetrate our physical world, yet spans limitless reaches beyond comprehension. Many theories have been offered in literature throughout the ages as to the 'where' of it, but few appeal to the scientific mind."

Monroe made sense of his experiences through a theory that depended on

the wave-vibration concept, which presumes the existence of an infinity of worlds all operating at different frequencies, one of which is this physical world. Just as various wave frequencies in the electromagnetic spectrum can simultaneously occupy space, with a minimum of interaction, so might the world or worlds of Locale II be interspersed in our physical-matter world. Except for rare or unusual conditions, our "natural" senses and our instruments which are extensions thereof are completely unable to perceive and report this potential. If we consider this premise, the "where" is answered neatly. "Where" is "here."

If you skipped that paragraph, or skimmed it, go back and absorb it. Mull it over. It is the key to Monroe's view of reality, and the basis of his labeling of focus levels.

This model says that your experience is determined by what you tune into. If your receiver is set only to the here-and-now world, that's all you will receive. If, accidentally or by training, you start picking up other wavelengths, you are going to be living at least to some extent in a different world, like it or not, prepared for it or not. I would argue that this is what happened to Bob Monroe. Something shifted the knob on his tuner, and he began to pick up another program, although up to that time it had never occurred to him that there might be more than one station. That was the basis of all that followed.

– 8 –

But no new worldview, offered on a take-it-or-leave-it basis, would change our lives. Probably we would accept what seems right (which may mean, in practice, what we are comfortable with) and discard the rest. And even if *we* were to buy it whole hog, others would dismiss it entirely, or would similarly pick and choose. How would this help bring order out of the chaos we are enmeshed in?

Fortunately, Monroe's Hemi-Sync technology lets us see for ourselves, and his aversion to using "spiritual" or "metaphysical" terminology led him to invent a neutral language that would describe a given mental "place" without dragging in time-honored associations that might or might not have anything to do with what he and his fellow explorers were experiencing. So came the terms Focus 10, Focus 12, and so on, reassuringly matter-of-fact tags for states of consciousness that could be investigated in reassuringly matter-of-fact technical, pragmatic American ways.

Let's take a brief look at the focus levels primarily used in Monroe's system, always remembering that this description of these focus levels is *as I understand them now*, subject to refinement and to later better understanding. Also, resist the temptation to think of the difference between one focus level and another as a spatial separation. To *say* that things exist "on different planes" is to use a spatial analogy to clarify a nonspatial phenomenon. The various focus levels aren't remote from us. They are right here in this only-place-there-is. They aren't in a different place; they are on a different vibratory level, somewhat like colors. (Do blue and red exist in different places? Or are they different vibratory levels of the same spectrum, coexisting in this only-place-there-is?) So as we examine the map, let's remember that these logical divisions are as useful, but as artificial, as the lines on any other map. The map is not the territory.

– 9 –

Monroe loved coining acronyms and using abbreviations and initials. He called ordinary consciousness "consciousness one" and then shortened it to "C1." You know what C1 is like, because you live much of your life there. It is less a single state of consciousness than a condition of sliding around among various mental states, usually not realizing that we are doing so. We tend to think of our normal consciousness as being more or less uniform, when in fact it is anything but uniform.

In C1, from moment to moment, you live in varying degrees of alertness, of intensity. Sometimes you daydream, sometimes you focus intently on accomplishing a single task, narrowing your concentration until it blots out everything but the task at hand. Sometimes, in fact, you aren't conscious at all. You *think* you are, but you aren't. You are floating. And sometimes you have quite unusual, quite inexplicable experiences. You see a ghost, even though you don't believe in ghosts, or you experience déjà vu: "I remember that quite clearly. Either it happened before or I've been to this moment before." Perhaps you take a lottery ticket and somehow—quite irrationally, but accurately, and beyond your ability to doubt it at that moment—you know it's the winning ticket. Or you change reservations to avoid an airplane flight that crashes. Or you know who's calling you the moment the telephone rings, even though you aren't expecting them to call.

On the other hand, maybe you hear music in your head and can't get it out, or, more fearfully, *voices* in your head. You hear *conversations* up there. You hear them talking about you! And you wonder if you're going nuts. Or you have momentary visions of strange places, strange faces, and you impatiently brush them away, hardly noticing them; or if you are of a dreamier or more artistic temperament, perhaps you encourage them. Maybe you have a direct encounter with God, or with demons, or with your dearly beloved dead grandmother. To return to a more mundane focus (for many would deny that any of these unusual states are normal, despite mountains of evidence that they happen every day) maybe for a charmed bit of time you're "on the beam," and you get more done in an hour than you usually do in two days.

C1 may contain anything and everything life contains, from the highest experience to the lowest. But few or none of these states are produced *at will*. Instead, we experience them as we experience the weather; we take what comes, because we assume we have no choice except perhaps to train ourselves, discipline our minds and emotions, cultivate our perceptions. But doing all this is a long, slow process. Monroe's technique provides a shortcut, teaching you in a matter of a few days how to move to a desired focus level. Herewith a brief sketch of the characteristics of the most commonly used TMI focus levels. (And by the way, don't think that the higher the focus number, the more valuable the mental state. A TMI joke calls that "focus envy." Which is better, a hammer or a screwdriver? The one that is right for the job, of course.)

Focus 10

Ever been in a very calm space where you were alert but not tense? Focus 10 gives what I might call a relaxed mental clarity. Monroe calls it "mind awake, body asleep," and it is true that in TMI's protected environment, some people do suddenly realize that they—mentally wide awake—are listening to their body snore. But it is also true that people deliberately use Focus 10 to do all sorts of things that require the body to be relaxed but not asleep. The first time I drove a rented twenty-six-foot truck through a tunnel, I used Focus 10 to keep me calm. I used it too when an oral surgeon was taking out a tooth that was so decayed that it was expected to split into two or three pieces as he did so; instead it came out intact, and I was out of the office in less than twenty minutes from the time I sat down. And to my surprise, the first time I was able to focus a "5D" picture, I recognized that certain sense of peace, of quiet. It felt to me like Focus 10.

Focus 12

If you have had to really, *really* concentrate, or if you have been actively making mental connections, you probably did it in Focus 12. Monroe calls this the state of expanded awareness. In Focus 12 we expand our mental web; we see deeper into situations and make wider connections; we see better the significance of things usually hidden or passed over. I can't prove it, but I think this is where we are when we are learning language, or following an intricate argument in a book, or are absorbing great art. We're making connections.

Focus 15

Monroe calls this "the land of no time." This one is perhaps the most unusual, the most fascinating, the least explored, and least easy to explore of all the mental states labeled by Monroe. Mary told me, after sensing these states secondhand (through my experience) when I did Gateway, that she had used Focus 15 intuitively to explore her past lives. She and other friends independently have told me they use Focus 15 to explore possible futures, to check out probabilities. And my very first experience of Focus 15 threw me back into a past-life experience that was as vivid and direct as watching a movie. I wouldn't be surprised if we access Focus 15 when we get lost in memories, but on this I'm reserving judgment.

Focus 21

Focus 21 is described as the interface between conscious selves (what I now call our Downstairs level) and other levels of awareness. It's more efficient than psychoanalysis (and cheaper) as a way to open diplomatic relations with other mental and spiritual levels that can tell us all we need to know about ourselves.

In Focus 21 we also may contact other human consciousness directly. It is the road to telepathy. Call it intuition, call it telepathy, call it being "in tune" with somebody else, probably we have all experienced it. What mother doesn't know better than anyone else what her baby is feeling at any given moment? What pair of lovers has never understood things in a glance? What is this but telepathy—literally "feeling at a distance"? As far as I can tell, it happens in Focus 21.

And the consciousnesses you can contact are not limited to other levels of yourself, and other humans. According to much testimony, this is where you contact intelligences (besides those Upstairs) who are not presently in human form. Before you dismiss that as impossible, consider: Are you, after all, so certain that the only consciousness in the universe is presently in human form? Are you certain that the only consciousnesses we could contact would be those presently in human form? Are you certain that we ourselves have not been or may not later be conscious but not in human form? I'm not. And the attractive thing about Monroe's system is that it encourages you to go see for yourself.

Beyond 21

There was a time when Monroe thought that Focus 21 was as far as you could go while still in a body. Later he refined that to mean (I take it) that it was as far as you could go while living normal life. You can walk around and function in any level up to 21, and we do routinely whether we experience these states consciously or not. But it is also useful to visit the focus levels that can't, or can't easily, be encountered in normal life.

Again, perhaps these different focus levels are separated by frequency, by vibratory rate if you will, rather than by space. But I've never figured out how to talk about them without making them sound like places, geographically separated. This temptation gets particularly strong in the levels after Focus 21, because they seem so specialized, and so remote from our everyday life. But it isn't hard to demonstrate that lots of us have visited these levels inadvertently—and maybe scared ourselves silly! Particularly Focus 22.

Focus 22

This is the realm of those who are still in the body, but are dreaming, or hallucinating, or are in a coma, or are dissociated by use or abuse of drugs. It is also the "place" of ghosts—earthbound spirits unable or unwilling to release their grip on life on earth. This is the "low rent" area beyond physical life in which it is possible to have quite nasty experiences.

Focus 23

Some people die suddenly, or while disoriented, and don't know they're dead; or die and have no beliefs, or negative beliefs, or contradictory beliefs about "what happens now." Many of them wind up in Focus 23, caught in their own scenarios, endlessly playing a looped tape, until other spirits (us!) come to assist. And my experiences suggest there is more going on in Focus 23 than this, as I will discuss in the context of my experiences during two Lifeline courses.

Focus 24–26

Those who die with a well-defined set of beliefs about the afterlife find themselves in the world that meets their expectations—at least until their expectations change. Souls of a feather flock together. If you are a European Jew, atheist, socialist scientist, you may be one of a particularly small population, but wherever there are others vibrating to the same frequency, there you'll be. If you're a Polish Catholic housewife and mother from midcentury, you'll get what your expectations set you up for. (If you haven't guessed, I or those I know have experienced each of these specific combinations. More on these later.)

Note that it is not your beliefs, exactly, that bring you to one of these areas, but *what you are,* what your vibratory frequency is. But what we are is expressed by what we believe, and so beliefs are a convenient way to classify people.

Focus 27

The vibratory level in Focus 27 in many ways is closest to what we're used to in physical-matter reality. I think this is where we dream; I know it is where we get much of our creativity. And here, by human hand, though in the far reaches of antiquity, was set up a way station to provide a safe and useful place for departed souls until they could plan their next sojourn, whether to earth or elsewhere. We'll look more at Focus 27 as we go along.

Focus 34–35

I will have little to say about these levels, having had almost no personal experience of them. The other focus levels give us more than enough to work with for the moment. Suffice it to say that Focus 34 to 35 seem to be more about group consciousness than individual consciousness. In any case, our Gateway course brought us only to Focus 21, leaving exploration of the higher numbers to other courses.

– 10 –

Of course, this quick sketch is only a beginning. But it should be obvious that I think Monroe is correct in seeing reality as "an infinity of worlds all operating at different frequencies, one of which is this physical world." And perhaps the tremendous appeal of all this is equally obvious. If our minds are tuning devices, we can learn how to tune into a given channel at will. Until we realize that we *are* tuning devices, we tend to think that we are forced to drift rather than choose. But if we had a channel selector . . .

If we had a channel selector, we could learn to move to various points on the dial consciously, *at will*, rather than as we presently do unconsciously, being more or less blown about by circumstance. And *if* we had a channel selector, we could perhaps *teach*—and *learn*—some of the nearly unbelievable "knacks" that some people have demonstrated throughout history: the healing touch, say; telepathy; the gift of prophecy; the ability to speak to beings who are not of this earth (call them angels or demons or aliens) and those who have been here but are not here presently (our dead, for instance) or other levels of our own selves (call it the Higher Self, or the Super-conscious, or your Guidance, or the larger being—whatever). This would in itself demonstrate that these knacks are real, which would remove one unknown from the list of opinions to fight over.

Really, *if* we had a channel selector, the possibilities would be breathtaking. Suddenly psychic experiences could be made replicable, and scientists could experience, test, and explore the phenomena reported through the ages by psychics and mystics. Of course, it wouldn't resolve all arguments. If we are fortunate, though, it would bring some of the arguments—and those doing the arguing—to a higher level.

If we had a channel selector. Such as, for example, Monroe's Hemi-Sync technology. . . . And if we could do our initial exploration in a protected environment, complete with experienced people, willing and able to guide us as we did our exploration of this new realm—such as the Gateway Voyage. . . .

Then it becomes a matter of personal experience.

– 11 –

The experience began on that Saturday in December 1992. As Bob and I drove the four hours to the institute, I was filled with conflicting emotions. I had great hopes for the program, and correspondingly great fears that nothing much would happen. Mixed with these was even a bit of dread which, Mary had told me, was because no matter how much we want change, a part of us is always kicking and screaming against it.

Bob was driving the initial stretch, so after a while I pulled out my journal. "I want so much for this week to take me to a new place," I wrote. "Is there anything special I should be aware of, should do?"

The Boss replied:

> Be open and relaxed. Nothing is accomplished by pushing. What you are and what you are to believe are decided by your *will*, not by your intensity of effort. You can't *force* the wind, and the spirit blows where it will.

I'm just so *anxious*, and a little afraid that the week will pass and leave me little changed, little improved, little empowered.

> The universe unfolds as it should.

I never will have the power and senses I want, will I?

> You couldn't paint, and took lessons, and learned. This is a lesson. Relax and have patience.

I did my best to follow that excellent advice. Past a certain point on our way westward, as always, we started to see turkey buzzards, whose soaring always delights me. I chose to take their presence as a sign saying, "Welcome, friends."

Then we were there, and Gateway began. It is particularly odd, now that I come to think of it, that in 1992 I came to Gateway thinking the important things would be the tapes and the abilities that using the tapes might bring me. It never occurred to me, even as speculation, that the important thing might be helping another person—*loving* another person—and doing so unselfishly. Nor would it have occurred to me that after less than a week at Gateway I would be so changed as to regard my original desires as trivial. I wanted to become a psychic. Instead, as a side effect of clearing my channel to and from the larger being of which I am a part, I was given the gift of being allowed to join the human race. And the psychic way was opened as well.

SIX

Gateway Voyage

When I first returned from Gateway, I told my family something of the unbelievable things that I had been doing and had been experiencing. I called people on the phone. I told my employees and associates at work. But even the first night, I found I didn't have energy enough to give even the highlights of highlights. So I wrote it out, knowing that every sentence left connections undrawn and perceptions undescribed and—most important—emotional intensity unconveyed. But the alternative was to say nothing at all, except to those who had already been to these places.

So much happened in so little time. I accessed past-life memories, acquired new mental powers, gave up my old pattern of hiding my light under a bushel, and excelled, effortlessly. Most important, I did the right thing instead of what would have seemed to be the prudent thing. I loved—really loved—and everything was added. For this book I have expanded and clarified references as best I could, in an attempt to let you see the setting as well as the end-result. As when I first wrote it out, I have phrased my description of my Gateway experience in the present tense, the better to convey the intensity of a central experience of my life.

Saturday

We arrive at Roberts Mountain at about 4 P.M. and are greeted by TMI registrar Helen Warring at the front door of the conference center. The center, which was renamed the Nancy Penn Center after Bob Monroe's wife died, is built into the slope on the south side of Roberts Mountain Road. Thus the door from the parking lot, the main entrance, enters at the level of the second floor. A corridor leads past rooms on either side to a tee intersection and a flight of stairs leading down to the first floor. To the right, and also around the railing surrounding the stairs, a corridor leads to bedrooms and bathrooms. To the left, a much longer corridor leads to the bathrooms and bedrooms of the new wing that had been under construction in 1989, when I saw the place first. Helen escorts us down that new wing and Bob and I drop our bags in our room.

The bedrooms are not only where we sleep, but where we do our work with tapes. Each room has one, two, or three enclosed spaces, something like Pullman bunks, which TMI jargon calls "CHEC" units, supposedly standing for Controlled Holistic Environmental Centers, but I think mostly as an excuse for Bob to come up with one of his acronyms. These spaces, which are unobtrusively but effectively air-conditioned, contain headphones, a tape recorder, a reading lamp, and three concealed lights—red, yellow, and blue—on rheostats, so that you can create your own environment each time. You climb in, onto a narrow but comfortable bed; you close the heavy curtain behind you—using the Velcro fasteners to join it to the walls—and you are in a lightproof space. You get under the covers and get comfortable, put on the stereo earphones, turn on your "ready" light, and wait for the tape exercise to begin.

From the rooms upstairs you go down the central stairs, which reverse direction at a landing, so you come down facing the conference room, a large, cozy, paneled room with no windows, which gets its only natural light through the open double doorway connecting it to the stairs and dining room. A sign at the entrance to the room says to spare the carpet, no shoes in this room. And, indeed, after Saturday night, this whole December week I never put on shoes and socks until the following Friday morning, except when walking outside—and not always then.

To the left of the stairs is a room which was then the participants' dining room, with five six-person tables and chairs, enough to seat the average program's two dozen participants and two trainers. (It has since been changed to a lounge area; participants now eat in what then was the staff dining room.) Doors on the west and south lead to the surrounding deck and to the red brick walk that leads to David Francis Hall. Around behind the stairs, to the east, are the kitchen and, on the other side of the kitchen, the staff dining room. This main floor also has one room with three CHEC units.

The ground floor, beneath the conference room level, contains a lounge area, staff facilities, and at the far eastern end, a large exercise room complete with a mirrored wall, dumbbells, sticks, and other exercise equipment. To complete the picture, a glassed tower at the east end of the building encloses circular stairs that connect all levels: exercise room, staff dining room, upper floor, and roof. The roof is decked, offering unmatched views of the mountains all around.

A few dozen feet west of the Penn Center is David Francis Hall, which has a large conference room on the bottom floor, and to the west of that is a building that contains the audio lab, other offices, and "the black box"—the isolation chamber, of which more later. Beyond the cluster of three buildings are wooded grounds and pasture, including Lake Miranon and Roberts Mountain Road, around all of which we are encouraged to ramble when we feel so inclined, though driving automobiles is discouraged. This is our world for those few days.

Now, as I said, I have entered this Gateway experience thinking that the important part is going to be the tapes and the chance (who knows?) that I will learn how to go out of body at will. It doesn't occur to me that the week will be about *people*. It certainly never occurs to me that what I am after can only be reached *through* people (though looking back from where I am today, it is clear that *any* progress I *ever* made came by working with people. All my reading, my intense and sometimes diligent striving, were valuable preparation. But substantial, startling, encouraging progress has always come in connection with well-loved individuals. I could count them off: my siblings, my friends, certain respected professionals, authors, and other friends I'd never met in the body. Our lives are intimately connected to others, in ways not half-suspected).

And it *doubly* certainly never occurs to me that what I am about to find will make what I came looking for seem trivial and peripheral, which it is. This should have been particularly obvious to me in light of the preceding six weeks' work with Mary. But that particular connection comes at the end of forty-six years of isolation, and I haven't yet adjusted. On this Saturday in December 1992, I am still massively uncomfortable among strangers. As we descend the stairs I see that several tables have been pulled together to make one long table, and a blur of strangers are sitting around trying to make themselves comfortable with one another. We introduce ourselves and in my nervousness I immediately forget every name. I sit there and make small talk, working really hard not to be (or seem) ill-at-ease. But I *am* nervous, instinctively defensive, and in my shell. Only recently The Boss has said to me, "Maybe you are tired of being solitary. Maybe you are ready to be gregarious, to coast. To be whatever comes easily." But by this Saturday I have forgotten that.

After a while Penny Holmes, one of our trainers (already known to Bob Friedman and me as one of Monroe's stepdaughters), takes me into the adjoining room for an entry interview, a brief questioning of why I am here and what I expect and hope for. She cautions me that the process seems to work best if approached with expectation, but without specific expectations.

At suppertime, an hour or two later, three trainers (three, because this is Penny's last Gateway as a trainer in probation) and twenty-three participants gather at five or six tables. I am still ill at ease, and working so hard to conceal it that I am carrying on conversations with scarcely a word registering. Across the table from me, a strikingly thin blond-haired woman about my age, very intense, describes how she makes her living. I ask questions, but later I remember nothing of what is said. Too nervous. Right there, at that first meal, life is giving me a forecast of coming attractions, but I as usual am looking elsewhere.

After supper we troop over to the bottom floor of David Francis Hall and sit in a big circle in comfortable swivel chairs, our backs to the tables that have been pushed against the walls. I get a first impression of how our trainers work together. Big, smiling, handsome Bob McCulloch; blond, quiet, comforting Ann Martin; dark, intense, wisecracking Penny Holmes.

As an icebreaker they have us team up with the person next to us; we interview each other for a few minutes, then introduce our partner to the others. I am thinking (I realize now) that dealing with people is only an ordeal standing between me and the tapes and the experience. To my surprise I realize as I talk to her that the elderly lady I have teamed up with is a lovely person. First lesson, maybe.

The trainers explain the structure of the week. Each morning we will have an optional exercise class, then breakfast and a series of tape exercises. After lunch and a long afternoon break, we will do tapes, have supper, do more tapes or see a film or listen to a talk, then a final tape and sleep. Before each tape, we will meet in the conference room to be briefed on what's coming up; then will go to our CHEC units and listen to the tape over headsets and return to the conference room for "debriefing."

"Oh," they say, "and we're going to liberate you from the tyranny of time. For the course of the week, no watches, no clocks." We will know when it is time for exercise class, meals, tapes, or programs because they will ring a bell by the stairs that can be heard throughout the building, and will ring another bell out on the deck that can be heard surprisingly far outdoors.

I find the prospect of living without a watch a little unsettling, and I ask whether it is really necessary. (I am *very* time-oriented!) They are smilingly adamant: Put your watch in the box. Penny brings the box around and humorously but emphatically stands in front of me first. And as it turns out, being deprived of my wristwatch for a few days demonstrates how much, and how subliminally, we structure our time according to mechanical measurements. With no way to know what time it is, I quickly discover that it isn't important to know. More to the point, I live more in the eternal Now and less in the time-to-come. (After Gateway it is some time before I go back to wearing my watch. For quite a while I carry it in a pocket so that it will be available when needed, but will not be continuously reminding me of the passing of another mechanical milestone.)

Okay, time for the first tape, an introduction to resonant tuning. (This is old stuff to me, after many months of practice on the home tapes.) The trainers tell us, "We know you're all tired, many of you traveled a long way today. And it often takes people two or even three days to relax from the stress of their normal lives. So we won't have a debriefing session after this tape. If you want to come down and socialize, we will be putting some snacks out in the dining room. If you want to just turn over and go to sleep, that's fine and we'll see you in the morning: We'll put on the sleep processor." (The sleep processor tape uses Monroe's technology to lead our brains through two ninety-minute sleep cycles, which will allow us to get a good night's sleep in less time than we would need if we drifted around, as normally.) "Oh, and if you fall asleep in the middle of the tape, don't worry about it. You won't miss anything. Your subconscious will absorb it anyway."

So back to the Nancy Penn Center, and I enter my CHEC unit, lie down on the bed, adjust the headphones, turn off the lights, and practice the technique. When the tape is over, I force myself to go down to the dining room, snacking and talking, trying to fit in. On the one hand I am nervous around strangers; on the other hand maybe if I talk to them long enough they will cease to be strangers! I stay up late. When I finally climb into bed—into my CHEC unit— I can hear the background hissing of the sleep processor tape through the speakers mounted on either side of the unit.

Sunday

It is odd, listening all night to the muted sounds of the sleep processor. I feel like I never get to sleep all night long. (Later I conclude that I spent the night in Focus 10—mind awake, body asleep—for though my mind was more or less awake all night, my body got its rest.) As soon as the sleep processor ceases and I know they're going to put on the wake-up tape, I say, with some relief, "Oh good, I can get up now." (I'm puzzled, now, why I felt I had to stay in bed past when I wanted to get up. Maybe I was thinking that if I didn't do exactly as expected I would miss part of the experience.) In the morning, to rouse us, the trainers play a piece of Metamusic (music with Hemi-Sync tones in the background) called "Cable Car Ride"; it starts off slow and quiet and finishes jazzy and loud. One way or another, you *are* going to get up! I hear lots of humorous complaints about Cable Car Ride during the program, but I never do hear it until later, after the program. At Gateway, as at later TMI programs, I stay up with the latest and arise before the earliest. Why, I don't know at the time.

This Sunday morning I am up early (I don't realize *how* early, not having my watch) looking for the optional exercise class. I note how strange it is that I should be so open to the class. Normally, I hate exercise. But something tells me it is important. After a while, exercise trainer Larry Lorence comes in, gets some coffee, rings the bell in the dining room, and leads us to the exercise room. He brings us through what I later learn to be half an hour of various stretching exercises. I am so out of shape, so unused to exercise, that many times when he gives an instruction ("now touch your toes") I laugh, thinking he's joking, and then realize that: a) he means it, and b) it can be done. By the time we're finished, I feel great.

Also, physical exercise turns out to be tremendously important as a grounding tool. At first I, like many others, think that being "grounded" is the last thing I want. But in time I realize that if you can't ground extraordinary experience, you can't retain it in "normal" life. (I am physically lazy, resisting exercise other than jumping to conclusions, but whenever circumstance nudges me into making an effort, I find that my ability to function Upstairs is enhanced. If I were industrious enough to carry what I know into how I live, I would exercise regularly. Do as I say, not as I do.)

After exercise class, we're off to breakfast, and then our first briefing of the day, a long one, is followed by our first tape, an introduction to Focus 10, which TMI describes as mind awake, body asleep. In Focus 10, you're still aware of the body (at least, I always was), but it takes far less of your attention than usual; it distracts you less from inner processes. And of course, the light-sealed CHEC unit is designed to reduce sensory input so that we can concentrate on subtle effects within our minds, effects initially easily overlooked or discounted if not specially marked.

I am familiar with Focus 10 from my use of the home tapes, which teach various applications of Focus 10 and Focus 12, and I come to it with some expectation. But my first experience is: Lots of drifting. Visual images pop up but are forgotten as soon as I come out of the tape. I use a trick they have just taught us, to bring back memories, and it works somewhat. But the images are nothing special, and as usual I wonder if they are "real" or "imagination." It doesn't occur to me to wonder what the difference between the two would be. I think I meant, did the images come autonomously or did I will them into existence subconsciously? From the viewpoint I have come to, this is a meaningless distinction, but at the time it seems important.

In this first exercise I see again something I first noticed more than a year before. One night while using the tapes at home, I became aware suddenly that images were appearing continuously, or at least frequently, as though from the side of my eye, and some internal mechanism was blotting them out. I had tried to stop the blotting-out process, and found it quite difficult to do. I don't know which was the more surprising realization: that this apparently had been going on for some time, perhaps for all my life, or that I had never noticed it. The images weren't well-developed or long-lasting: a fraction of a second, a flicker in the back of my mind, or the side of my eye. They lasted so short a time, in fact, that it was the blotting-out process I noticed first. I don't know where that mechanism came from, but surely it isn't innate. My guess is that somehow as a boy I "learned" that visions are "just imagination" and taught myself not to see them. But I don't know; it's just a guess. I mention this, reader, specifically to encourage you to stop and consider whether or not this is your own experience as well.

Well, receiving confirmation of the blotting-out process is worthwhile, but after all, it isn't an out-of-body experience, is it? We do a second tape, and in my impatience I remark in my journal that apparently nothing is happening. But it occurs to me that I may have acquired the ability to move between Focus 10 and C1 at will. Also, while lying in the CHEC unit listening to the music they play before they are ready to start the exercise, for the first time, I became aware that the recording required someone to play and someone to record it. In other words, it was *created* by *people*; it wasn't "just there." A simple insight, not earth-shaking; yet in retrospect maybe symbolic of a change that is beginning to transform me, unnoticed. I'm beginning to become aware of people as people, rather than merely as abstractions.

Also, by lunchtime I can see that our group is more self-contained. In a way that would be difficult to pin down, the energy of the group has changed. (One of our trainers smilingly tells us, "What we don't tell you before you begin is that you can't ever go back to the way you were." Already we can sense that; already, who would want to?)

And after lunch, during the long midday break, I ask The Boss if she has any words of advice.

> Words of wisdom. Be. Here. Now. You are. Stay here.
> One thing at a time, and let them do the guidance. Your job
> is to let yourself be guided as it happens. Don't anticipate.
> Don't drag your feet either, but that isn't your problem, is it?

But waiting to begin the third tape of the day, the first on Sunday afternoon, I write somewhat impatiently, "Maybe something different happens now?"

Well, yes. Maybe something different happens now that begins to reshape my view of life, and my experience of life. Maybe something different happens now that starts me on a better road than the long, hard, solitary road I have been plodding for more than four decades. Maybe this tape, only the fourth of the program, brings me a vision that starts me on a path that will lead me far, very quickly. Maybe this vision—not an OBE, "just" a vision—is the first external sign that Gateway is going to be a Big Deal for me.

In the briefing before this tape, our trainers tell us that at tape's end they will for the first time activate the tape recorders in our CHEC units so that we can record immediate impressions. This is because, when coming out of an altered state of consciousness, it can be quite difficult to immediately wrap your mind around ordinary language again. Just as with dreams, images and impressions from altered states are fragile. Too much physical movement too soon can cause you to lose them. Yet it's important to record them before they are lost in the return to normal consciousness. Once recorded, they are less likely to be lost, and can perhaps be expanded upon in a journal. So at the end of the tape, the trainers activate the tape recorders in our CHEC units. (We take the tapes home with us afterward.) Here is what I record this remarkable Sunday afternoon:

> *I was floating over the trees and there were trees on the hillside, and as I flowed off toward the left, I was gradually floating higher and higher, and got to the point where I saw a white house—big, white frame house, an old-fashioned one by the side of a tree—and it had been dammed or something to make a lake; I remember a right angle in the water and unless I'm very mistaken her name was Clara and I knew her there somehow. Looked like Virginia hills. Looked like these hills around here, like these trees around here. Not in the wintertime.*

I know that doesn't make a lot of sense when read cold, but it does give the flavor of the desperate shorthand descriptions we wind up speaking into the microphones hanging in front of our faces.

I could see, with my mind's eye, the terrain floating beneath me; hence I had the impression of floating over it. I "knew" the direction I was drifting in, and knew the scene was *quite* near the institute, off to the east and a little north. I saw an old house quite distinctly, and if I could have retained the clarity of the initial glimpse, I would have been able to sketch it in some detail. As it was, the picture became fuzzy, and I was able to bring back little of the original clarity. Most important, I "knew"—in the uncaused way of knowing that is one of the four nonsensory ways we receive information—that this vision concerned a woman who was then named Clara, and it somehow involved the career woman I had talked to at supper the night before.

After the tape I ask the woman (whom I will here call Emily to protect her privacy) if the name Clara rings any bells. It doesn't. But she does tell me that in the beginning of the tape, she had the strongest feeling that she was *with* somebody. Well! Mysterious but promising. Better, anyway, than drifting through another tape and coming back blank.

After supper we repair to the conference room in David Francis Hall, sitting behind tables in those very comfortable swivel chairs with padded arms. Bob McCulloch tells us how TMI developed, starting with Monroe's early OBE experiences and going through the early days of the institute. Monroe had thought, if he could run as many as five thousand people through here, he would be able to tabulate their experiences with Hemi-Sync patterns. Gateway is still going strong years after having run through its five thousandth participant, and this basically with no advertising but Bob's two books (his third book came out in 1994) and word-of-mouth mention by former participants.

(In retrospect it would have been interesting to have taken notes, and to have asked something about the dozen or so trainers who ran the programs, but at the time it didn't occur to me. I was thinking about the tapes and the abilities they promised, and I was wondering if anything would really happen.)

I don't think about taking notes even when McCulloch says that really Bob Monroe ought to tell the rest of the story, and says, gesturing with a flourish at the door behind us, "And here's Bob Monroe." We turn and see Monroe standing on the stairway. Of course, they've done this many times together. But it works nicely.

I am pretty sure that Bob Friedman and I are the only ones in our class who have met Monroe previously, and certainly we are the only ones there who have met him in a business context. To the others he is a famous name from books they have read and treasured. I am fascinated to see how deftly Monroe defuses—transforms—the hero worship people are prepared to offer.

This old, old man with white hair, wearing an old navy pea jacket, slowly walks the length of the conference nodding to this person, that person, as he passes. (I can almost hear people reassessing: "He's an old man!") He comes to the empty chair the trainers have placed for him in the middle of the room, facing us, and slowly takes off his coat. He reaches with it to his right side as if to put it onto a hook—and drops it onto the floor. He shrugs. "Sometimes it's there," he says. People laugh. ("So! A comedian.") Then he asks the group, one by one, where they have come from, nodding as if absorbing the information—and not adding one word of comment! (Reassessment continues: "Well, let's be nice to the old man.")

And *then*—having removed himself from superman status, and having thereby returned people's focus to the work at hand—he begins to talk, speaking easily and without pretension about what they have done and what they hope to do, and taking questions. His sheer skill in defusing all that tremendous tension of people's expectations reminds me of Shirley MacLaine at the first Higher Self Seminar nearly six years before.

I am told that many of Monroe's talks to Gateway and other classes exist on tape. They would make fascinating listening. Later I note in my journal merely that Monroe spoke, and add, "They promise us great abilities by the end of the week, and I am without skepticism about it." I do remember him saying that if there were those who came to the program strictly to have an out-of-body experience, we could still have a nice evening together, and in the morning the institute would refund their money and they could go their way with no hard feelings. I don't know whether anyone ever took him up on it, but I doubt it— and not merely because of what their transportation to the institute would have already cost them. I don't think people get into life-changing situations "by accident."

Perhaps this is the place to emphasize that even when Bob was alive, the Gateway experience did not center on him. It is true that wherever he sat was the head of the table, but participants typically saw him only three times: on Sunday and Wednesday nights, and Friday at breakfast, on the morning that so many newfound friends had to force themselves back into what I call the unreal world. For the vast majority of the program, individuals interacted with one another, and with the trainers, and—mostly—with unsuspected parts of themselves. Gateway wasn't about hobnobbing with a literary superstar or metaphysical legend, but about working on oneself. I think this is why, when Bob died in 1995, the Gateway programs continued without disruption. If anything, Bob removing his physical presence may have helped focus the program all the more by eliminating the superstar distraction.

In any case, after Bob's talk that Sunday night, we return to our CHEC units for our final exercise of the evening, free-flow Focus 10. They tell us to have something in mind and pursue it. So of course I go to see if I can get any more on the house, the water, the trees and hills, and Clara. Immediately on returning to C1, I record what I remember, as best I can:

I had been deeper in Focus 10 than ever before, and gradually I developed a sort of dual consciousness. At the time, I thought of it as a split between consciousness of the body lying in the CHEC unit (and I remained aware of it staying there) while at the same time I was aware of sending my awareness out the corridor, down the stairs, into the debriefing room, out the door.

In that body I looked up at the moon and thought, "Well hell, I can *go* there!" So I started to launch myself in that direction, then thought, "Well, let's go look at Mary's house," and saw a three-story row house, apparently facing west, apparently light blue. ["If you come visiting me while at the Monroe Institute," she had written a few days earlier, "does that mean I have to clean my house?"] Then I got the idea to go hang out at my brother Paul's house. But this being blown about by whim ("Let's go to the moon, let's go to Mary's, let's go to Paul's!") lasted only a few instants.

I went looking for that house I'd seen in the previous vision. I saw it in several forms. I saw ruins, saw a modern house, saw an old house, saw a buggy drive down a path through woods and then a field. In my journal when I came back, I drew a sketch showing how the path wound to the right, then to the left again. It was that definite; but it quickly faded. I went looking for other people. Did I find somebody? Unsure. I got a glimpse of the man from the prior vision—is his name John?—as a big, bearded bear kind of a man. Several times I had felt another presence, or more than one, as if in the CHEC unit. And yet when I came back to C1 I told myself in my journal that I was unconvinced that any of what I thought I had experienced was real; yet it was "sort of real."

Always that question, was it real? It's a question that deserves some thought. Is a movie real? Is a memory real? One is produced externally, the other internally (or so it seems) yet either could produce emotions; either, in fact, could change your life. If something can change your life, is it real? Of course, these aren't the questions I and others were asking. We wanted to know if, in thinking we saw or felt these things, were we only fooling ourselves. In the place I have come to, at the other end of these experiences, that question is the most foolish yet.

In any case, the experience was unprecedented. Wide awake, I took a walk while my body stayed where it was. And when I called Mary at the end of the week, for verification of the only element in the experience that could be verified or disproved, she said that her house was a flat rather than a row house, but might easily look like a row house. And yes, she said (somewhat startled), it is light blue. So, okay.

But—was it an OBE? I never lost awareness of my body. Instead, it was more that I, lying in my body, had sent a part of my awareness other places, and had watched over its shoulder. Later I decided it had been something like remote viewing, though without the scientific protocols that the term "remote viewing" implies. Later still I unmade my mind again and left the question open. Today I would say that I became aware of my second body and sent it traveling while still remaining aware of my first body, not an uncommon thing for me.

The longer I look into things, the more I realize how important it is to keep perception and interpretation separate, and how hard. Which is what Bob Monroe said, and what ace remote viewer Joe McMoneagle said. It's what OBE-researcher Charles Tart said made Bob Monroe such an unusually good reporter of experience. But it's hard to give up the quest for certainty (and right now!) even when you know better. Whether OBE or remote viewing or something else, though, clearly something is happening. And it is only Sunday night. We've only been through one full day.

After that tape, I stay up very late talking to Emily. We don't talk much about the vision I had, but instead, about her life. I have become very concerned about her, as though I am somehow partially responsible for her. I can see (though perhaps she does not) that she is quite as alone as I am. She tells me that it is important to her to lead an independent life, making it on her own all the way. She also tells me that she runs away from what she calls "spiritual" men. Both these facts, plus her underlying aloneness, will mean a lot more to me in due time.

So will her obvious immediate fondness for another one of our group, a friendly man whom I also instinctively like. I'll call him "Peter." Almost from the first, she is drawn to him; and he, as I, seems drawn to give her emotional support. But she is willing and able to receive it only from him, not from me. In light of what I soon discover, this makes perfect sense. Viewed from a strictly Downstairs perspective, particularly from a "one life is all you get" perspective, it makes no sense at all.

But then, consider how strange our life is in this respect. You meet someone and within seconds you are with an old friend, or you are coping with an old enemy, or no sparks are thrown and you remain indifferent. This universally encountered fact is explained by different people in different ways (including the all-purpose answers "coincidence" and "chance"). Few of the proposed explanations explain (rather than explain away) how such sudden meaningful reactions can precede interaction. Yet they do, all the time.

On this Sunday night Emily talks, among other things, about her cat who has just died. Maybe that reminds me to go looking? The same night, I see my old favorite cat Pancakes, who had died nearly a year before. I have since read that many people, including Bob Monroe, think we sometimes keep contact with animals with whom we have formed emotional ties. Maybe, or maybe my vision of old Pan—and other visions of other pets—were strictly nostalgia. It's something I would like to believe, but I don't know. Maybe someday I will.

Monday

Monday's first tape brings us to Focus 12, the state of expanded awareness. It produces several visions, including a picture of two facing chairs by a window with a very open, warm, inviting sunlit window. Back in C1, I draw a sketch of a love seat facing an upholstered chair across a tall window, almost a glass door. Somehow I know that this is somebody's favorite spot in the house. Mary's house? I'd bet on it. (This too she verifies at the end of the week. And when I tell her I saw what looked like a little glass-topped table, even though I'm pretty sure that nothing so modern would be to her taste, she says she is looking right at a little wooden table that is so highly polished that the reflection looks like glare off glass. In some ways I find a near miss more persuasive than a hit. It seems to demonstrate perception overlaid by interpretation.)

In that first Focus 12 tape I also get a sense of walking along a road, with a stone wall to my right as far as I could see. It "feels" like Scotland. I see a man walking up the road, the first time I see someone so definitely. But as I question who he is or could be, the vision shimmers and is gone. Of course, Mary's letters have been talking to me about a possible life in Scotland in the 1600s, so maybe that's my mind spinning tales. No telling yet.

Our next tape involves "asking questions of the universe," using a technique centered on Focus 12. Expanded awareness, again: the drawing of information from sources not always accessible in normal states of consciousness. Our trainers offer us a few pointers. Hold the situation in mind. *Desire* to know the answer. Ask questions with *clarity,* with *intensity,* and with *gratitude,* which implies that you are willing to receive and that you *did* receive. We write down the three questions we mean to ask, then do the tape, recording the answers we have received. I ask, "What is most important thing for me to be doing here? Who are the most important people I should be dealing with? Was there a relationship with [Emily] and if so, when and where?" The answers come, seemingly on their own.

What is the most important thing for me to be doing here? "Deal with people honestly and openly and lovingly and not try to force myself to go and meet each one, or let them come to me. Just, if something happens, deal with one on one."

Who are the most important people I should be dealing with? "In terms of making the experiences happen, just relax and allow it, you've got all Monday and all Tuesday and all Wednesday and all Thursday and then you have Friday and you have the rest of your life, and there's a LOT of time and a lot of experience ahead and plenty of time for it."

Was there a relationship with [Emily] and if so, when and where? I record this:

> *I can see the house—I can see more of the house—it has a modern, like a porch or a one-story structure added to it . . . it's been added to an older house; it's a white house, it seems like it has stone foundation, white boards on top. Clapboard or something, and when I asked how old, it said the house will tell you how old and the way to find it is to drive . . . the way Bob and I did accidentally the first time [when we came to TMI, three and a half years earlier, I driving that stretch]; accidentally, so called. . . . What I got was that she died young, they were married and she died young, which explains the concern and the—whatever.*

"Whatever" in this case means "love," love undeniable, but inexplicable and apparently uncaused. I am as yet too embarrassed to write it in my journal. I draw a sketch of the house, and write, "An older house—stone foundation, white clapboard, with a more modern structure attached to it—not a shed, more like a family room or breakfast room. Look where Bob and I wandered that first time two years ago—almost three. It can be found, and 'the house will tell you [when it was constructed].'"

With only a few moments before we gather to debrief, I write that Clara was my wife, and died young, perhaps in childbirth, "and I became a wanderer," as shorthand to describe a feeling that John (I "knew" his name was John as I "knew" her name was Clara) had never again felt any attachment to the house or the life he had delighted in. I get a feeling that he had left those surroundings and moved on physically in later years, and I know, without knowing how I know, that never again have *I* really sunk roots; never again have I really committed myself to a person, a place, or a way of life. In a very real sense, this is where I lost the ability to fit into a settled scheme of things.

Thus early—for it is still only Monday morning—I become convinced that these visions closely concern me, and in general can be relied upon, however inaccurate the detail might be. And already I can see myself changing as a result of what I have been experiencing. I ask The Boss how I can integrate all this into my life when I return home, and the answer comes: "Keep the mountains within you."

I ask, "Am I stressing Emily by all this? Should I be leaving her alone?" Meaning: a) am I making this up, and b) in any case, would she be better off dealing with other things, with her own priorities?

"It won't bother her if it doesn't concern her," The Boss replies. But when I show Emily that response, she reads it as, "If she isn't concerned, she won't be bothered," and finds it meaningless. I am unable to express to her the sense in which they were being used, which I read as, "If it isn't something she should be concerned about, it won't bother her." In retrospect I see that she was already irritated, almost definitely not knowing why.

By this time I am already paying so much attention to Emily, worrying about her, wondering if I can help her, that it sometimes interferes with my concentration on the Monroe material. We do two free-flow Focus 12 tapes designed to help us get out of body, and I do the exercises, but realize afterward that often I am not really paying attention.

At one point I do remember an image of two or three people in a doorway, one of them saying, "Katherine, stop that, stop telling him it can't be done." I still don't know who Katherine is or what was going on. (This was before I had quite so many Katherines in my life.) At the end of the second exercise, I see an image—a very clear image—of a pair of white low-top baby shoes. Baby shoes? And they (whoever "they" are, providing the scenarios; it doesn't occur to me, then, to ask) have to call my attention to the shoes, as I take them utterly for granted and would have forgotten them. Mary points out to me later that low-top shoes are for babies too young to walk. Maybe it is their way of telling me (what, again?!) that I am only at the beginning.

During the long midday break, Emily and I walk out to Lake Miranon and paddle around in a canoe. I enjoy being with her, but we are not easy with each other. Always there's an edge between us. Again, it is the kind of edge that sometimes arises between people without apparent cause. We say our vibrations don't match, or we say we're oil and water. Usually we don't think to ask why, and if we do, we don't have much of an answer.

After supper, Monday, something very interesting happens. We gather in David Francis Hall to hear Joe McMoneagle. This was two years before we published his first book, *Mind Trek*, and nearly three years before he became famous as the military's number one remote viewer in its twenty-year-long Stargate program. When the existence of that program became public, to predictable ridicule, Joe didn't run for cover, but said that it was a valuable project that had achieved worthwhile results. (The results were worthwhile enough that he was decorated by the Army.) He was quoted in news media here and abroad, receiving our culture's instant and transient celebrity treatment. But this was in the future as we sat in David Francis Hall. In 1992 Bob and I knew Joe mostly as Bob Monroe's stepson-in-law and Penny's brother-in-law.

Joe explains to the group that remote viewing involves his sending his mind to view whatever is at a given set of geographical coordinates and a specified time. He says it is a natural talent that can be developed, and answers questions. After a while he invites us to try our hand at it. On a blackboard is written a set of coordinates. We are told to go to Focus 12 and try to "view" what's there, writing down whatever impressions come to mind.

For me it's a frustrating exercise. The moment I look at the coordinates (38 degrees, 37 minutes, 28 seconds north; 90 degrees, 11 minutes, 74 seconds west; present time) I think, "The St. Louis Arch." But I *know* that my guess has to be wrong. I haven't done the exercise the way they said to do it, and besides, I'm pretty sure that 90 degrees west would be Kansas somewhere. Still, nothing I can do will shake my initial impression.

I quietly ask trainer Bob McCulloch to tell me this answer is wrong, so I can try to do the exercise, but he refuses to say anything till everyone has told what they saw. When the time is up, and they ask people what they think they saw, the answers vary widely, though some describe aspects that turn out to be correct. Some got impressions of water; some of combinations of elements. I say that I couldn't do the exercise; all I kept getting was the St. Louis Arch.

They turn on the slide projector: there is the St. Louis Arch. I am more pleased than I let myself show, but I don't know what to make of it. I didn't do the exercise the way they said, yet came to the right conclusion. You are welcome to explain away the experience. The word "coincidence," however, is not an explanation, but a refusal to look for one.

Monday's final tape brings us Focus 12. Bob Monroe's voice poses five questions, one after the other, and tells us to ask for the answers and remember them. I ask; the answers come very clearly; I remember them long enough to write them down in my journal. And after the passage of more than five years, as I write this, I find the answers I got to be ever more significant.

"Who am I?" I get, "Muddy footprints in the grass," which I understand to mean, I am a sign that someone has passed this way. When you see muddy footprints in the grass, you may not

know anything about who made the tracks; you may not know where they came from or where they're going; you may not even know if the person who made them knew where he or she was going. What you *do* know is that someone, at some time, for some reason, went that way. As the vision comes, I take it to mean that others will profit from my experience if I spread the word.

"When and who was I before I entered this physical body?" I get an image of a man sitting in a lumberyard, named John Denver. I try to alter the name, but can't. Well, who is John Denver to me? A spiritual man who enjoys his life (he was still alive at that time) and tries to wake people up. What is a lumberyard? A place where they stack up dead trees to put them to other uses, I suppose.

"What is the purpose for my existence in physical-matter reality?" Again, an image of muddy footprints in the grass—and also, marrying people, holding their hands and acting as the means of them coming together.

"What action can I now take to best serve the purpose?" The word "excel." Excel at Gateway, I take it.

"What is the content of the most important message I can receive and understand at this point?" There comes an image of a man rowing in a lake, a little lake surrounded by hills. The focus keeps expanding, and I see from a larger and larger focus, as if the camera were rising farther and farther into the air, until the very lake is lost amid the surrounding trees. In an expanse of what seems many square miles, no one else is in sight. Yet a voice says, "You are not alone," and repeats it time after time. "You are not alone," "you are not alone," "you are not alone," "you are not alone." Must have repeated fifty times.

The experience carries conviction, and I find it a very comforting message, and I later share the message with the group, even though (at the time) I have no concept to put around it.

One thing that makes our lives hard is the painful and persistent sense of being alone. Our lives seem to us inherently disconnected and solitary. All the better, then, to learn, in the months and years that follow, that this vision was a straightforward description of reality. The intimate connection with a larger, wiser being exists, and while the connection may be distorted or forgotten, or never discovered, still the larger being is there to be contacted, using prayer, meditation, automatic writing, et cetera—whatever works.

Tuesday

Tuesday begins with a tape bringing us for the first time to Focus 15, which TMI calls the "Land of No Time," but which I think of as the Land of Free Time: you can go where and when you want to. Impossible to describe it. (Think of how it felt, the last time you got lost in reverie; that will give you a faint sense of it.) In this first Focus 15 tape, I think of various people I've lost to death, and I realize that this is how I can find and re-create old memories.

Nothing too important happens in this first tape. But in the next one, a free-flow Focus 15 tape, for the first time I see scenes that I connect with the Welsh lifetime Mary and I have explored and discussed in the weeks immediately preceding. I start off looking for David, and first I get clear images such as I have never gotten before, but I don't understand what is going on. There is a room of people eating, and then it is four or five women eating around a cafeteria serving-table kind of thing. Then at about the time I am asking to see his funeral or when he was dead or whenever, I see an old-fashioned English house, a room with two sets of stairs, very dark wood. The room is packed with people. There is a lady, there is a woman standing under an arch, in front of a doorway or something. When I ask her which one is David Peterson (forgetting, and not noticing for years, that his name is supposed to be Cornwell!), I see pale images of faces superimposed over her face, and after a while I realize I am watching her thoughts! I am watching what she is thinking. (Not that I could prove it, of course.)

A few words about this part of the experience:

- Though I had little enough information about David, the Welsh journalist who had traveled and had written a book, I did have a clear sense of who he was. A good Ident, as Monroe would say.

- The women were eating around a cafeteria serving-table like the one used at TMI. I had no idea what the symbolism might mean until, in the course of writing this, I asked The Gentlemen Upstairs for their take on that vision. They said:
  You have remarkable faith that we know things, given that you also have remarkable doubt that we are real. You understand the cafeteria symbolism in light of your later experience in other programs. You know that women have been particularly important in your TMI experiences. What's to explain? The women were choosing their nutrition in a common meal, a shared ritual. It had overtones of people eating at a wake, which tied in to the next part of your scenario—you thinking it was you who "thought" to ask to see his day of death. In actual fact, the vision of the women helped put you in mind of wakes and funerals.

- The details about the old-fashioned English house packed with people didn't make any sense from what little I knew of his life, but in a way details that don't make sense are almost comforting, in that they suggest that one isn't making it up. My friends, what was this?

It puzzles you why David's funeral should attract a lot of people, because you have the idea that he was basically an unknown. That was a valid scene of the house after his funeral, when people converged to be together afterward. No, it was not his house. Yes, it was too grand for that. But it was the house of his patron's family. You are forgetting that you later learned that he had traveled extensively as that man's secretary.

So I had. And while I don't know if TGU are giving me the straight dope on the great house and the gathering, it is the first explanation I have had that seems plausible.

- Finally, I asked TGU about my jumping to the conclusion that I was watching the thoughts of the lady standing under an arch. They said it was an example of my "knowing" what I had no way to know.
  At the time, you had no mental bucket. [This is a metaphor I often use, meaning that the experience didn't fit into any of my mental concepts that existed at the time.] Now you can see, easily enough, that what you in bodies take for your own thought are more often promptings from the wings [off-stage, in other words]. The experience itself—seeing her thoughts as images—isn't nearly as important as the realization, now, that much of what you think is your property is actually on loan from others.

But all this is only a forerunner to the big experience of the day.
Immediately after trying to see the last day of David's life, or his funeral, or his wake (and the lack of clarity of intention did nothing to make it any easier to get what I wanted) I decide to "go" to Emerson's house in Concord, Massachusetts, for two reasons. First, Mary and I had gotten that I had been a man who

had visited Emerson in the early 1840s. Second, I had been to that house two or three times in this lifetime, and so I thought (correctly) that at least I'll have no trouble visualizing the house. The time comes to me; it will be 1843. (Note—as I did not in 1992—that the idea of watching that visit to Emerson's house in 1843 "comes to me." At the time it seemed natural. Today it looks like guidance at work.)

What a difference this time! As soon as I make the decision, it is as if I am watching a movie. Rather than vague impressions, I see a scene, including dialogue, though I don't get that perfectly. In reconstructing it at the time, I used the word "I" to describe the man, not because I am confused between the version of me that is here/now and the version that is there/then, but merely for convenience. Looking back at it, I am not so sure about my ideas on reincarnation as I was then, but it will be less confusing to say "I" in describing how I experience the scene.

It goes like this:

I come to the front door, introduce myself to the maid. She goes away, comes back, lets me in. Emerson comes to the door. He says, "Mr. [or maybe Dr.] Atwood?" (I heard it clearly enough at the time, but it had already become vague when I recorded it a few minutes later. I would be undecided what his name was for months, until one night I had a vision in which I saw a hand writing on a blackboard the name "Josiah Smallwood," or it may have been "Joseph Smallwood.")

I say, "Brattleboro," meaning, I take it, "from Brattleboro."

Emerson leads me down the hall, introduces me in the dining room to Mrs. Emerson. She shakes hands, expecting me (I intuitively know) not to really see her, being focused on her husband. A sort of hooded look in her eyes says, "Oh God, another one"—another earnest young man come to sit at the feet of her husband, ignoring her. She is pleasantly surprised—gratified, in a guarded way—that this newest earnest young man is concerned with her as a person, as interested in her as in her husband. She is equally surprised and gratified that I have arranged to spend the night at the inn rather than quartering myself on them. Emerson offers to let me stay overnight with them—but she is the one who would have the work and the responsibility.

Emerson introduces me to "Mr. Henry Thoreau, like yourself a scholar from Harvard," and I shake hands with him. A sharp, instinctive guardedness between us, a sort of instant potential rivalry, a wariness. Henry Thoreau, like Emerson's wife Lidian, is used to people seeing him through Emerson, and is defensive and touchy about it, though he works on it. Yet there is also an immediate, inexplicable guarded comrade-in-arms feeling between us. (He and I had prior history, Mary had said. "He couldn't just be Thoreau, y'know?")

At some point Emerson suggests that he and Thoreau and I go for a walk down to Walden Pond. He asks "Lidian, my dear" if we will have time to walk to the pond and be back by dinner. There is something proprietorial, almost patronizing, about his attitude toward her that I dislike, not knowing why. She says yes. And I, in 1992, looking at her through the eyes of her visitor in 1843, see something familiar in her eyes and in the expression on her face. I say (from 1992), "Hold it. Freeze the film. I *know* that person." I start to really look at Lidian Emerson to see if I can figure out if I'd met her in this life—and at *exactly* that time, Monroe's voice comes over the headphones calling us out of 15 back to 12. I know who it is. Something about Lidian reminds me of Emily.

When the tape is over, I record as much as I can, as fast as I can, and then I lie there and say, "Hot shit! It works!" I realize that I just wasn't ever in the right mental place before. It's just that simple. "Till now I have been trying to be receptive to subtle perceptions—did I see it, did I invent it, did I this and that. And now that I have been there (and God knows what remains to be seen) it is so clear that I have never been there before." What a promise: that from now on I will *know!*

If this tape experience had stood alone, maybe I wouldn't have made so much of it. Maybe I would have said it was a fantasy. But coming as it did less than two months after Mary had found it (if you want to put it that way), it made a significant impact. Did it prove anything to anyone else? Obviously not. Did it prove *to me* that I could do my own exploring, just as Mary had insisted? It did that.

And I realize that if Emily was Lidian Emerson, naturally she would run away from "spiritual" men! Naturally she would want to lead a very independent life, making it on her own all the way. And suddenly I suspect that the man I am here calling Peter was Henry Thoreau. It certainly would fit, if indeed he had been Thoreau and she Lidian Emerson, that she should naturally turn to him for support. Lidian Emerson leaned on Thoreau, and he in turn repaid her with platonic devotion.

Of course, I am well aware that I have no objective reason for thinking Peter was Thoreau; the guess is based strictly on seeing the emotional tie between them, and reasoning that as she came to me in that context, perhaps he did too. But the tie between them could easily have been forged in a different lifetime. And it is not Peter I am primarily concerned with. He and I are both concerned about Emily, worried that she has not learned that she is lovable; concerned to find a way to educate her away from continuing to apply to herself the destructive self-criticism that seems to be her habit.

After the midday meal and the long break comes a "tapeless tape exercise," in which our trainers take away our training wheels, sending us to recapture the states without relying on a tape. (Obviously, if these new skills are to be of any use in the world, we will need to be able to access these states without tape recorders and CHEC units.) I try to return to the Thoreau-Emerson-Atwood conversation, try to persuade myself I could see them, et cetera. No go. I try various things that don't work out, then I think, almost sheepishly, to ask what the best purpose of the exercise is. And there is Emily, saying something like, "Why do I love him? I don't want to love him but I do. Why?" I ask if she means me, and the answer is yes. My body tells me (not that I need telling) that I am interested! Then our trainer's voice tells us to return.

Since Emily and I have so much trouble communicating Downstairs, I spend our next exercise trying, and failing, to communicate with her Upstairs. (Of course, it may be—seems likely, from this distance—that we communicated full well at the time, but not in any way that met the expectations of my Downstairs. It's hard to perceive reality if you have a really firm but incorrect idea of what to expect.)

I skip dinner and stay, "resting," in my CHEC unit. I am sick at heart, because I know that she is not going to respond to my efforts to break her out of her isolation. I know that she isn't going to understand why I should care about her, when a week earlier I didn't know she was alive. I know she isn't going to reciprocate the feeling. Indeed, why should she? Nonetheless, I am strongly concerned about her, and I feel unable to do anything to help matters. It makes me feel miserable. I am much more concerned about her than about myself.

In retrospect I realize that the situation threw me off-balance. If I had it to do over again, I would do some things differently, as will appear in due course. But you don't get to do things for the first time twice, so there's no use crying over spilled karma.

I hope it is obvious that this inexplicable attraction was not sexual. I was married, and if it was a fling I wanted, it would have been with Mary, with whom I was already happily engaged in what we were calling a "metaphysical affair" cross-continent. Nor did this attraction arise out of boredom. At Gateway, bored I was not! In fact, my concentration on Emily was actually interfering with my learning to do what I'd always wanted to do. It was inexplicable, save in the context of the visions I was having from the very first.

After dinner, I join the others in going over to David Francis Hall, even though I am feeling so miserable I don't want to do anything. But the program is for us to listen to what is called "The Patrick tape," and that snaps me out of myself.

The sound quality isn't always so good, but the content is—well, it's mind-boggling. Nobody on "this side" designed the Patrick tape. But in light of what it has led to, I expect that it was set up from "there." Bob Monroe was talking to a channeler (Rosie McKnight, called ROMC in his books) in the black box. She let a voice come in, and after a while he realized that he was hearing a frightened, discarnate individual who thought he was keeping afloat in the Irish Sea after his ship burned and sank in the middle of the night. In the mid-1800s!

At first Monroe attempted to gather facts by which the reality of what was being channeled could later be verified. But finally he gave up on that, and helped Patrick find the light. By the time someone who seemed to Patrick to be his mother came to him, we listeners were near tears. Monroe had done his first retrieval, and the first seed had been planted of what several years later became the Lifeline program.

Several of our class, Emily included, had already signed up to take Lifeline on the following week. I wonder if I would have believed anyone if they had told me that within three years I would be doing the same thing. As open as I was that week, maybe so. On the other hand, it's a lot to believe.

Think of it. Patrick had been floating in Focus 23 (to use TMI jargon for the place where disoriented discarnates wind up) for more than a century of our time. Because the dead, having no bodies, live outside of time, he had lived inside his own drama always in the present tense, thinking it a single long night. Only outside intervention was able to interrupt his drama and free him. "Since the dead have no time," we are told, "you can move through time to help them." Awesome thought for me, that night in 1992.

And sitting in the conference room afterward, waiting for our briefing on the last tape of the day, I suddenly realize that here I am, in the midst of everything I have wanted, acting like a lovesick schoolboy. I burst out laughing, bursting out of the melodrama without losing the importance of what has occurred and is occurring. Perspective is reimposed.

Wednesday

Wednesday morning we meet in David Francis Hall and are told that we will have a silent morning, doing three tapes in a row without meeting to brief or debrief. We are shown the brief movie *The Powers of Ten,* as a way of reminding us of the relative proportion of things in the universe. Then we return to our CHEC units for the first exercise.

Before the first tape begins, I send love in all directions, particularly telling Emily I love her, that people she hasn't even met yet love her. I meet Mary watching this and see her laughing/smiling at this form of polygamy. Great state! I send love to Mary. Send it to my wife and my daughter, to everybody I can think of. Since we are spending the morning in silence, I never leave my unit.

The first tape bids us expand and prepare to meet alien life forms. I envision myself in the depths of outer space, and suddenly I see a horrible-looking face against the blackness. But immediately I realize it is a mask, and behind it is my dead cousin Bub, laughing at his joke. That's as close as I come to experiencing an alien presence.

The second tape directs us to retrieve the five most important messages we can understand at the moment. The messages come, and at the time, the fact that I see distinct images and hear words surprises me, even after months of practice with the tapes. This surprise is the difference between believing and knowing.

I find the messages profound, and find them equally so now, after the lapse of years.

They come in increasing order of importance.

Number five begins as a sketch of a figure turned to stone, like those found in the streets of Pompeii. Then it shows a table with many chairs, all empty. People appear. I'm at the head of the table, the host. More people appear and there is room for them—the table and chairs expand as more people arrive. (All right, I can understand *that* easily enough. I have been living as if turned to stone, but I need not; I can have a life filled with people, and with joy.)

Number four. I see a set of stairs viewed from above, descending into a room below. I am sitting on the second floor, listening to the party going on below, feeling sad and left out. The stairs become a ramp down into the same room. I descend, barefoot. They welcome me not as one coming from above, not as one who isn't or is properly dressed, but as me. (This seems to me self-evident, but perhaps it is worth underlining that I see it. I descend from cerebral, disembodied heights into the warmth of life among humans. And, it occurs to me much later, at TMI programs we—certainly I—spend much time barefoot.)

Number three. I see something mysterious floating in the water. It swims up to where I am standing on the dock. It is a mechanical dolphin, with a handle. I try to pull it out of the water, but it is far too heavy. So I get into the water and take the handle and it begins moving with me. It's phenomenally powerful, and moves swiftly and easily. I think, why a *mechanical* dolphin rather than a living one? The answer comes: *I* am the *living* part. If the dolphin had a life of its own, I would in justice have to consider its desires and needs. As things are, I need think only of what I want. (Again, self-evident, I think. I am in touch with phenomenal, nonhuman power that will bring me wherever I want to go.)

Number two. I seem to be looking out at the universe, but I notice it has a transverse wrinkle down the middle—it's not the universe at all, but a picture painted on a fabric. Some people roll it up for me, right to left, and I see that it is a hanging backdrop on a wall of our meeting room in David Francis Hall. But the wall behind it, and the other walls and the ceiling and floors are all of very heavy wood, very solid, with no doors or windows. No way out. I see this not as something sinister, but as a fact of life. I get the message: There's no way you can see or get beyond this universe, this reality system, at this point. Play *here* for now. That's okay with me. As soon as the fact registers, "they" roll the universe backdrop back into place.

Number one, the most important message, turns out to be a great beating heart floating in midair. I grow larger, to absorb it. The spoken message comes. "Wear it inside and outside." My father used to admonish me not to wear my heart on my sleeve, but this message says wear it on the inside *and* the outside. Okay, I can hear that. I think of the muddy tracks in the grass. Not only am I to wear my heart inside and out, but I am to live in such way as to encourage others to do so.

Wonderful messages, not only in the analysis of where I was at the time, but in the clear portrayal of where I could come to. I don't see how any psychiatrist or counselor could have improved on them, either in effectiveness or clarity. If this doesn't excite within you a sense of the possibilities offered by inner guidance, it can only be because you think your case is somehow different from mine. Of course it will be different in details. But essentially? Not at all. I am no psychic superman. *This guidance is available to all.* To receive the messages, we need only clear our channels.

The third tape of the morning directs us to change our vibrations several times. I feel the differences, and get a very clear visual description of four mental states in what I would see as ascending order:

1. Staring out the window in boredom as someone talks.

2. Walking across a wooden platform over a room, noting people relating. Our trainer kissing one of his children, for instance.
3. Seeing more and more deeply into the nature of the wood on a beam.
4. Being concerned only that a certain individual (Emily, in this case) know that she is loved not just by me but by others. I almost hear the words, as the thought occurs to me: "And the highest of these is love."

An alien presence that isn't alien. Five messages from Upstairs. Graphic descriptions in ascending order of different mental states. Some morning.

In midday Peter and Emily and I take a long walk up to see the llama farm, as it was then, at the top of a hill along the road. As we rest by the fence, I tell them who I think they were. Peter knows nothing of Thoreau; Emily, nothing about Lidian Emerson. And Emily is somewhat bewildered and irritated that sometimes I call her "Mary," sometimes "Clara," and sometimes I can't remember her real name. It's inexplicable to me too. I tell her finally that I'm not used to thinking of her by that name.

The first post-lunch-break tape (free-flow 15) is a disappointment. I get to Focus 15 easily enough, but can't go back to the Emerson-Thoreau-Atwood scene, can't go see Emily. Frustrating. We are supposed to go to Focus 21, which—because I want to go back to Focus 15, and see again!—doesn't interest me particularly at the moment. But finally I do get out of the body! I experience the sitting-on-nothing freedom I had felt occasionally as a child (in a dream, I'd thought) and know I am free, finally. I am floating around in San Francisco, though I don't remember seeing anything in particular. Toward the end of the tape, I go to Emily's CHEC unit.

During the debriefing, Emily tells the group that she had experienced me in this exercise saying to her that "I can't control myself with chemicals, heavy." It makes no sense to her—but it makes perfect sense to me. Altered states are best achieved without pharmaceuticals! When she tells them, with my permission, that I had said I had experienced her in my first astral travel, another participant, a young man named Len, in some embarrassment says that in one of the morning exercises he had suddenly appeared in a bathroom and saw Emily entering a shower, and had somehow known that I was already inside the shower, waiting for her—which certainly had *not* happened "in the physical."

He is more embarrassed about it than we are! Our trainer quickly points out that in these initial contacts frequently there is gross miscommunication, a mistranslation of symbols. Nonetheless, it is clear to me that Emily and I are dealing with each other on some level. And only when Len and I are in the Guidelines program together, three months later, will it occur to me that he, who provided the first outside testimony linking us, might be connected to both of us.

As I sit there during the debriefing, I experience great pain in my teeth, then in my back, alternately, intermittently. Later one of the trainers tells me privately that she thought the experience "blew out" a blockage I'd had. I wish I knew more about chakras as the interfaces between physical and nonphysical energies. It's an important subject.

Thursday

We wake up to see it snowing, a beautiful sight. The first morning exercise has us walking over the grounds, individually, in silence, practicing moving between different mental states without using tapes. We are told to alternate between 12, 15, and 21, but I mishear the instructions, and alternate between Focus 10, 12, and 15, evidently in order to experience 21 at the later time. I see some of the TMI employees out with their children. They're used to silent Thursday mornings, and they don't expect me even to say hello. But I break silence to say to one little boy,

"Want to ride *fast?*" I run with the sled until I'm out of breath, then go back to the exercise. A week before, I wouldn't have thought to interrupt "consciousness work" to give a kid a ride.

What else happened that long day between the morning and suppertime, I did not record, and have lost all memory of. In any case, the life-changing thing that happened was not a tape exercise, or in the program. By our evening meal on Thursday—the last day of the program—I am distressed. I had had concrete results, but psychic powers and all that no longer seem at all important. I am finally convinced that Emily will not accept my love and will not, either, be freed from her prison of self-criticism and loneliness. I see her at supper concentrating on Peter, whom I also am prepared to love, and I have just about as much as I can bear. My best efforts, it seems, have failed.

But then, after supper, she meets me in the hallway and asks me if I would massage her back, which bothers her from an injury years before. (I wondered then, and wonder now, was this a put-up job courtesy of Peter? Maybe he saw and correctly interpreted.) Anyway, I tell her I would be delighted.

First comes our group's last gathering. We stand in a circle and people say whatever they are moved to say. I (responding to The Boss's earlier prompting) read a poem I had written several months before that happened to be in the same journal book I have been using during the program. Although *I* know the imagery centers on Antarctica, only rereading it now do I realize that I nowhere state this, which perhaps confuses those who hear it. And although I know that TMI stands on ground they call the "New Land," when I wrote and titled the poem I wasn't thinking about that.

> ### New Land
> The older world we grew up in,
> grew old in, knew no additions
> save in tiny increments. Here
> and there, now and then, a Surtsey—

a dab, a morsel of volcanic rock—
hissed and shouldered its way
above the level of the vast sea
surrounding. But the sea was everywhere,
the island a pinpoint.

Now, ice melts,
poles move, oceans and lands change,
and two great parts of a buried whole
shrug off the ancient burden.

Ice melts,
hard-pinned rock recoils, and water flows.
From every interior gap, through every pass,
torrents spew outward to the sea,
sanding and battering ice mountains,
punching with bergs and floes, thundering
relentlessly toward the circling ocean.
Hours pass. Days. Weeks. Months.
Still this tremendous hemorrhage,
like water from a sack suddenly slit.
And the land appears. New land,
not buried land uncovered, but
land created in the uncovering.
Terminal moraines—deltas, peninsulas,
whole uncharted featureless countries,
dropped in the thundering, unresting,
violent hurrying. No people, yet.
No animals. No trees, or shrubs,
or even germs. But they will come.
It will be a harsh land, then a wild,
then a pleasant place, another new start.
The ice has gone. The rest will come.

—August 26, 1992

And this is what has been happening to me. The ice has been melting—in this past week, at a phenomenal rate—and I am beginning to see the outlines of the new land that is being formed as the ice melts.

After the group circle, the formal program is over. The trainers break out snacks and sodas, and everyone is in a state of relaxed exuberance. By this time I fully expect Emily to have changed her mind. But after a while I look at her—knowing, somehow—and say, "Ready?" and she is ready, and we walk out of the dining room into the conference room. She finds two overstuffed pillows and lies on them, sort of in a corner, but close enough that we can hear others talk.

She has a bad knot below her shoulder blade, so obvious that even then I could feel it. I start working on her, slowly, tentatively, carefully, well aware of the danger of making a careless move that might be misinterpreted. Gradually I feel my way into it. She guides me and I learn, seeing what is effective and carefully asking before trying anything that might cause pain. I am so careful! First I work over her undershirt, then directly on her bare skin.

There is some sexual pleasure in it, but so much more there is my gratitude to be able to pour out my love directly. I work on her for a long, long time, and every so often I lean forward and murmur that she is worthy of people's love and I don't want her to forget it, et cetera. I am constantly waiting for her to say, "Enough"; to my surprise and gratification she doesn't, and so it goes on and on, and so I learn to express love. I am very careful not to make an improper gesture or touch her in any way she or others might interpret as sexual. I know what I want, and it isn't sex, but to give, and give, and give. And so I learn to express my love, and it keeps growing as I express it. Finally we stop. I thank her for letting me do the massage, and she does not seem to understand that it is not that I have done her a favor, but that she has transported me from hell to heaven.

After I pour out all that love, I am quietly watching the fish in the aquarium when I spontaneously go into Focus 21. (Or so I assumed at the time. Now I am not so sure what focus level I "went" to, or that it matters.)

The fish are startled!

Startled, I am convinced, because they see me pop into view as a consciousness rather than as a background presence. Both of them are staring at me. Sounds ridiculous and unlikely, but they are. I call Emily over and she sees. We call others— a trainer among them—and they see. And then I realize I've broken through. I think of a John Denver song, sent me by dear Mary, about the man who talked to fish in the creek and tried to tell people that the animals could speak.

I am flying! Emily had let me pour out all that love (so small a part of what I feel) and I already have a little idea of what she had meant to me in past lives, and therefore why she means so much—otherwise inexplicably—now. But more than anything she meant before, this time she has been the occasion for me to learn the importance of living with an opened heart. It doesn't solve all your problems. In fact, it causes some even while it is solving others. But it keeps you on the path, and makes life worth living.

By now it is very late. I go to bed rejoicing.

Friday

Well before dawn I get up in my pajamas and go down to the exercise room, exercising just for the sake of moving. In the spotlights outside I see a fir tree tossing back and forth in the wind, looking like a great green cat getting its fur ruffled by a loving friend. Its bobbing and bowing is a form of calling to me, and for the moment I am not deaf, so I come, walking out there in my pajamas (again using a Monroe technique to protect myself from the cold), standing in the snow in my bare feet, in

Focus 21, engulfed in the fir tree, *so* aware of it. The experience is beyond words. I think to give it love; it gives me a tremendous outpouring of joy at being alive. I write later that this is the beginning of my life as a conscious being.

I write, "No wonder the one particular tree in my front yard has done so splendidly. It knows I love it, and it revels and thrives in that. So this is what I must do now. I must provide this atmosphere of love, I must wear my heart on the inside and on the outside. Oh God! How blind I have been, and how awake I am now. Of course we wake and sleep, wake and sleep, but now I will remain awake."

I go back upstairs after a while, dress, come down and spend all my time either drowning happily in the morning or immersing myself equally happily in the people. They are more than willing to be loved. There are so many people to deal with! Bob Monroe is there. He sits quietly eating an abstemious breakfast, smoking, drinking coffee, talking to anyone who wants to pull up a chair. I think I see a wistful look on his face, as if to say, "I wish I were that young again, with all this ahead of me." And I think I see pride there too: pride in his graduates and pride in what he has created.

One by one we say our good-byes as individuals leave. Back to the unreal world.

Bob Friedman and I leave in midmorning, Bob driving. He won't let me near the steering wheel! He thinks that, as high as I am that morning, I am not to be trusted with machinery. We take a small detour down the road we mistakenly took three years before, looking for the old cabin that my visions had said could be found there. I am about to give up quickly (perhaps not really believing it is there to be found) but Bob persists. One of us thinks to check a small side road, and as we roll slowly along, Bob points and says, "That looks like the sketch you made." I have been looking near the road, among the houses; Bob has looked behind a house to what appears at first glance to be an old tractor shed.

Second glance shows that the structure has a huge chimney made of fieldstone. Who builds tractor sheds with fieldstone chimneys? Bob stops the car and I walk up the driveway to the house, find no one home, and, trespassing, walk through the snow to the building, which I am already calling the cabin. Close up, it's bigger than it had looked. The central part is two-story, and very old. Lean-to wings were added to each side decades ago, evidently to shelter tractors, trucks, and farm equipment. The lean-to wings are dirt-floored and insubstantial, but the main structure is solid. Built on a stone foundation, as advertised. Large beams (maybe 12 by 12), hand-hewed. From outside (I don't go inside, this visit) it looks like it would have at least two rooms on each floor. There's enough room under the flooring beams for a person to stand nearly upright. That entire area is crammed with junk; the building radiates an almost tangible air of neglect.

Almost the only thing I know about psychometry is that for some reason stone retains psychic impressions better than wood. As high as I am at the moment, it is not difficult for me to get a sense of the story from the stone of the massive chimney. I go tumbling out to Bob's car saying, "This is it! Let's go get Emily," who I know is staying over for the next week's Lifeline course. But Bob doesn't think that's a good idea, so instead we turn toward Charlottesville.

After all these years, I still wonder what would have happened had we returned to the Institute and come back with Emily and perhaps some of the others. Who knows, maybe Bob Monroe would have come. A case of not following instinct and then wondering forevermore.

I found the cabin! Which means, maybe I haven't been making it all up. Which means, maybe the world is more the way I want it to be than the way I have feared it is.

As always, I am dancing the same old dance. Two steps forward and one back. ("Wow! What an experience! But was I making it all up?") Finding the cabin is important in helping to cement the impact of the entire Gateway experience.

I had run back to the car thinking we would go get others and return, and so I hadn't stayed beyond the time it took to realize that we had found the place my visions had showed me. But during the half-hour ride to Charlottesville Bob asks me questions as he drives. Although I would have expected to get visions or words, I get "knowings," feelings. With each question, chunk after shattering chunk of feelings come, tightening my throat, bringing tears to my eyes, leaving me for many seconds at a time staring out the window, unable to continue. Bob asks a question and I know the answer, or a part of the answer. What comes with overwhelming clarity is the *feeling* accompanying the fact. Appropriately enough, as it turns out.

The story I get that day is that in 1768 the young man's (John's) father had provided the money and some of the hired labor to build the cabin as a wedding gift for John and his bride. John had worked on it too. Emily and he had lived there an undetermined time when she died, tragically. Childbirth? That was my first assumption. As at TMI, I have a strong impression it was a tragic experience that turned the joy of life to bitterness for the young man, a bitterness that lasted the rest of his lifetime. More detail will come in the days and weeks ahead.

In a way that now seems symbolic, the ride from the Institute back to "normal" life does not provide a transition from the extraordinary to the ordinary. Instead, the two blend. We go into Charlottesville to pick up Bob's son, Matthew, who is in his senior year at the University of Virginia. Since we have to wait for a while, Bob, who is proud of being a UVA alumnus and always has a particular note of emotion in his voice as he talks of UVA, decides to show me the campus. It is special to him, in a way that my own alma mater is not special to me.

The day is bitter cold, and Bob is none too warm in his overcoat, but I walk around in a flannel shirt, protecting myself from the cold by the technique I had been using at TMI. Yes, you can use mental states to insulate yourself from the weather. And if I could *tell* you how to do it, I would. But how could I use words to bring you to a specific mental state? That's one prime value of Monroe's techniques, as I have said before. They bring you there, and then you know what it feels like, and you can go back there again.

Defending myself from the cold isn't the main point of using the technique that day, of course. The point is, we learned a technique; I intend to *use* it. What good is new power if you don't put it to use? In the process of using it, I realize two things: 1) The things we have just learned are the tip of the iceberg—an appropriately cold analogy this day—in terms of what we can learn to do *in the everyday world*. We aren't nearly the pawns of fate we think we are. 2) We invented overcoats and similar conveniences not because most people can't do what I was doing (whether or not they realize it) but because in ordinary circumstances doing it that way is unnecessary trouble. On this freezing day in December, I have to keep my mind on staying warm, and while it is nice to be able to protect oneself at will from the cold, it is also nice to be able to forget about the weather and do other things.

As we walk around the part of the university designed by Mr. Jefferson, I encourage Bob to go to Focus 15 to see if he can discover the roots of his lifetime love of UVA. He does (though he promptly enmeshes himself in the usual game of "did I make this up") but that's his story to tell. The point here is that I instinctively encourage him to use the tools in the real world, and they work for him as for me. As they would for you.

And when we go to get diesel fuel for his car, I, knowing nothing of Charlottesville, say, "Turn left up there at the bottom of the hill and go two blocks," not knowing why. We come to a street that I see is called Barracks Road, and I know why I have been moved to bring us here. Something tells me that in the Revolutionary War the prisoners of war from Cornwallis's army had been housed near there—and another chunk falls into place. John whatever-his-name-was had been a member of the militia and had guarded the convention soldiers. He had been befriended by an elderly German (a sergeant, I think) and although John was the guard and the German the prisoner, the older man had helped the boy, teaching him over a period of months that we can't just give up; we have to accept whatever life hands us, and go on.

Emotionally that rings true with the little I already know of what John became after his wife died. This new "knowing" rounds out what I learned earlier this morning after finding the cabin.

In hindsight, it is clear to me that my Gateway was orchestrated from Upstairs. At the first meal, I spoke mostly to Emily, though we didn't even particularly like each other. During the first tape exercise on Sunday, I had a vision of the old cabin. And the vision was able to give me a sense of where to look only because three years earlier I had taken a wrong turn when Bob Friedman and I had been on our way to see Bob Monroe about business.

Of all the things my Gateway might have centered on, the John-and-Clara lifetime took front and center. This enabled TGU to help me work on the emotional blockages that resulted from that lifetime. My coming to care about the well-being of Clara as expressed in Emily—if you wish to put it that way—served as catalyst to open up my heart. And it was my heart, not my head, that needed healing before I could make any progress. Beyond that, the past-life aspect of the experience reinforced my new confidence that in fact reincarnation was objectively true, not just something I wished were true. Working with Mary had brought me a long way toward this, but nothing substitutes for firsthand experience.

Externally, I had no proof whatever that any of it happened. I knew that the prisoners had been kept in or near

Charlottesville, but *were* they on or near what is now called Barracks Road? I didn't know until Mary later told me that indeed they had been. Also, every history I ever read calls the mercenaries "Hessians," and implies that this is what the colonials called them. Nonetheless, I have a strong, clear feeling that John and his fellow Americans called the captured mercenaries "Germans."

Surely the answers to these questions should be easily found? But I didn't go digging for validations, for several reasons: 1) I had plenty else to occupy my time. 2) I wasn't researcher enough to know how to pursue such an unanchored quest. 3) At least partly, I was afraid to find out that any of what I had gotten wasn't true. I knew that I was on the trail of something, and didn't want to be discouraged in the meantime. Something said that I must let nothing—least of all my own doubts, which were considerable—stand in the way of following this vague and shadowy path I was on.

My Gateway Voyage led me from experience to experience, transforming me as I went along. Some months later, in a moment of irritation, Bob will say to me, "You never came down from Gateway!" But it would be more accurate to say that the "I" he had known did not return from Gateway at all. Viewed one way, I had changed unrecognizably. Viewed another way, I returned to a very different world, with fewer rules and many more possibilities.

SEVEN
An Altered Reality

And so I returned to my family. Pray tell, how do you tell your family that in the week since you saw them last, you have accessed past-life memories and acquired new mental powers? How do you tell your wife that you had met an ex-wife (if you want to look at it that way) you never knew you had? How, I don't remember. But I did, and it worked out fine.

Of course, as soon as I got home, one of the first people I called was Mary in San Francisco. Starting to talk about my week, I asked if she knew anything about some detail of Monroe training. Focus 15, I think it was. She said, sort of humorously wearily, that yes, she had heard quite a bit about it lately. Turned out that all the time I was talking to her, she was hearing me. "It was like direct feed," she says.

As I mentioned earlier, she provided some immediate confirmation of details I had seen; and more confirmation came as I received her letters written while I was at Gateway. (And we laughed at the image I had gotten—which she remembered—of her smiling at my "transcontinental polygamy.") Interestingly, what I took to be a minor error—seeing her house facing west instead of east, proved in an odd way to be a verification. A few days later, looking at a map of the city, I realized that her house was north of Golden Gate Park, rather than south as I had assumed. So when I (visualizing myself approaching it from the park) had seen her house on my left, what I assumed had to be west was actually east. Thus I had seen correctly and interpreted incorrectly.

I told Mary some of what I had learned on the road between the old cabin and Charlottesville, that it had come to me that the inside of Clara's throat had swelled up, and that she had taken sixteen days to die. Mary, hearing it in my voice, was horrified. And when I told my wife's mother that I had had the impression that John's wife had died of bee stings, and had died painfully over several days, she told me that when people who are allergic to bee stings are stung, their throats swell up! I could all but see Clara gasping and turning blue from lack of breath, that long time, an appalling picture. My God, no wonder the strong emotions! *That* couldn't have failed to imprint its memory on them. And John's reaction included guilt as well as sorrow. He thought that the tragedy had been caused by something he had neglected to do. Perhaps she thought so too. That would explain certain things that were about to occur in *this* life, and pretty soon, as the edginess between Emily and me played out.

Thinking of John and Clara and that long aftermath, I began to be haunted by a line from one of the John Denver songs on the tape Mary had made for me: "Wind is the twister of anger and mourning." I wasn't anywhere near finished with all that.

It should be obvious that what I got from Gateway was not anything like what I expected. Neither was it necessarily what others got. TMI's saying, "People get what they need from Gateway," certainly makes sense if one assumes (as I do) that our lives are nudged from Upstairs at strategic moments. Our "intuition," our "knowing," stems from a place that knows better than our Downstairs selves what we need and how to obtain it. Upstairs knows us, and knows when, how, and where to nudge us. *This is a tremendously hopeful fact, as a moment's thought will make clear.* All the guidance we need is available for the asking. Right here, right now.

But Gateway was for me a radical change of direction—a quantum leap, rather than a one-time experience—because in Mary I had essentially immediate verification. I can't think of anything more important in helping me to integrate—and therefore retain—my new abilities after I went back to the so-called "real" world. The Gateway experience can leave its graduates gasping, somewhat. So much happens, so quickly. Sometimes it helps to have pointers, and not everyone's life provides them.

(Whether everyone's life *should* provide pointers is an unanswerable question, so far as I can see. One might argue that Upstairs guidance will provide the proper opportunities regardless of Downstairs beliefs, and in this I would concur. Yet one might also argue that we are here to choose, which implies the possibility of better or worse choices, which in turn implies the value of assistance from others, Downstairs as well as Upstairs. I would agree with this too. In a very real sense "all paths are good." But in the time that saw Hitler, can we really suggest that all paths are equally desirable? I have no answers to this dilemma, save to say that, regardless what reality may be like when seen from beyond time and space, down here in 3D Theater choices matter; injuries hurt; some paths are better than others.)

In getting to know Mary, an undoubted psychic, I had been freed from the doubt that such people (and thus such abilities) exist. This had allowed me to begin to find and develop those same abilities within myself. Processing her feedback after I returned, and working with her at an ever more intense level in the weeks and months that followed, I got a surer sense of what I could and couldn't do; what I could and couldn't trust. All that changed with time, of course, but as a means of speeding up my initial learning, the relationship was invaluable.

– 2 –

Meantime, carrying the Christmas tree to the living room and putting it up, I had hurt my back again—in the same place as always since I was nineteen. I wasn't particularly distressed about it, writing in my journal:

> I put a couple minutes into trying to make it okay again. Can't. Stopped trying because I realize it will help me get another piece of the puzzle—how John died. He was killed by Indians, I recognize that, but—where? when? how? Time to go look, given that my back is telling me quite clearly that it is time to know.

Now, at that time my wife did not believe in any of this. She was willing to let me explore, but "common sense" told her there was nothing to it. So I cherish the memory of the moment that first weekend when she, having misplaced a recipe and having spent quite a good while looking for it, concluded that she had lost it and would have to make something else instead. I said I'd go into Focus 12 to find it, and did, in less than two minutes. She didn't say anything, but she was so mad, I knew she would much rather have never found the recipe than to have it found that way.

A few minutes later my twelve-year-old son informed me that one string of lightbulbs had gone out on the Christmas tree. I looked at him and smiled (he knowing just how I was going to attempt to find the loose bulb) and put my fingers on two different bulbs, one of which was the culprit. Neat!

But then (still testing) he handed me a small wrapped Christmas present and said to tell him what was in it. I confidently told him. He said I was wrong. I maintained I was right. On Christmas day I found out that indeed I was wrong. This was an early lesson (to which I paid insufficient attention) on what I came to call psychic's disease: unwarranted certainty about anything that comes intuitively. It took a while for me to absorb this lesson. Many people using their psychic abilities never do absorb it. About which, more later.

– 3 –

As I said, reshaping my life after Gateway was made vastly easier by my interaction with Mary, who from the first provided crucial verifications that overcame my temptations to think it was "all in my head." I hadn't been back a week when I received a letter from her. She had begun it December third, and resumed four days later:

> 7 Dec. Monday 10:40 am.
> Masses of water under the bridge, I know, since the foregoing was writ. . . .
> You were here on Friday night, dunno if you're aware. I suspect not, as on Sunday, (yesterday) your presence was felt, but weaker, as if you were trying to get here, rather than just doing it. . . .
> [I can't answer for Friday night, but Sunday night I had done just that.]
> I'll say adieu. Or rather, Welcome Back, Lazarus!

And the next day, she had written:

> You were very far away yesterday, I felt. Some other solar system or high in the upper planes. What were you doing? You were talking to someone. A Pleideian? [Can't quite figure this out. She wrote this Tuesday, but Wednesday was the day we were sent to explore the solar system, the day I saw my dead cousin pretending to be a horrible face.] Today you're more or less back, I feel. You were *here* briefly—I heard you hear I got your letter—and I can hear you thinking at me even now. Slow down, you're

going to trip over your mind. [smiley] It's like being zapped with an electric current. It's *channeling*, listening to you. *You're doing it*, my friend! What *are* they feeding you? [smiley]

A brief word from my friend Cliff: He says that in Muir's *Boyhood and Youth*, there is a reference to some fellow M's father hired one season on the farm, who regaled the boy with the *native names for flora and fauna*. Well, I checked it out, and:

He was only hired for *one season* and he *is known only as the Yankee*.

"Checked it out," hell! I opened the book and there it was. . . . Thought that little piece of news might interest you.

– 4 –

By the Monday after Gateway, I realized that if the man I am calling "Peter" truly had been Henry Thoreau, and if Emily had been Lidian Emerson, then underlying their evident mutual attraction was Thoreau's twenty-five years of emotional care for Lidian then. And if Emily now had been first Clara, then Lidian Emerson, and John had become Smallwood (or "Atwood," as I then thought of him), then when Smallwood had gone to Concord in 1843 he had seen that she was physically okay but spiritually stifled. He left Emerson's feeling oppressed, probably not knowing why. This, even knowing that Thoreau was there to sustain her.

All this interaction would have taken place Upstairs with probably neither Thoreau nor Lidian nor Smallwood knowing anything about it on a Downstairs level, any more than I had in this lifetime until I had that vision in Focus 15. And of course, Emerson and Lidian would have been working something through between them. All these unsuspected resonances from other lifetimes make our existence a lot more complicated than we ordinarily realize.

But it took me a while to understand how all this worked through for us in *this* lifetime. On the Friday following Gateway, the end of the Lifeline that Emily and Peter had stayed for, I got up at 3 A.M. and drove to the institute to see them. I took them to see the cabin, and for the first time I really felt the oppressive atmosphere surrounding it. Emily, I noticed, did not seem to want to be there. She didn't have a whole lot to say to me either. We took some pictures, and then we had lunch and I carried them to the Charlottesville airport. The next day, somewhat depressed, I remarked on two things:

> I think I am beginning for the first time to *feel* things as others do, rather than from behind a plastic curtain. When I parted from [Emily and Peter], it hurt and I was depressed and sad for a long time, going home. Finally I realized that's what parting *feels* like. It's a little dying.
>
> I wonder, this morning: did Emily *not* want me to return? She wouldn't say so, but would she have preferred I stay away? I made an enormous effort — a great expenditure, thinking she would care; maybe she didn't, maybe she was humoring me, or rather, sort of going along....
>
> Net effect of that prodigious expenditure of effort was to reestablish balance. I will live my life *here, now,* and not worry.
>
> I asked, this morning, what message, and got me on a hill with the sun in my eyes, preventing me from seeing even the road signs, let alone the road. As I turn from the sun (put it behind me) I will be able to see better....
>
> Things are so difficult.

Clearly, Emily in this lifetime didn't know (Downstairs) if any of what I was talking about was anything more than delusion. What's more (as I should have realized, but didn't) she found the whole subject very upsetting, perhaps without quite knowing why. And it was only in writing this that I realized that of course Emily would be irritated and upset that I would be so happy at rediscovering a place inextricably connected in her unconscious mind with intense pain. I was still so new at feeling things. It's funny, really, thinking back at it. After I left Peter and Emily at the airport and began the long drive home, I was puzzled at what I was feeling, and why I should be feeling it. It took many miles before I worked out that "Oh! This is how people feel when they say good-bye to loved ones. It hurts!" If I hadn't gotten a thing from Gateway but the ability to feel and recognize feelings, it still would have ranked as the most important week of my life.

And I thought, and still think, that the image given when I asked for the message of the day—me on the road, but with the sun in my eyes, blinding me to what I needed to see—is nothing less than brilliant, if you'll pardon the play on words. *But I didn't really absorb it!* I went to Guidelines three months later with the sun in my eyes still, and didn't for the longest time suspect that this was so. In my defense, there was this: I was living in a new world, and hadn't yet gotten my sea legs. I didn't know how to act or react; didn't know how I should feel. This made it harder for me to adjust course. Yet on the other hand, I had asked for guidance, and it had been provided, and still I didn't really listen to it. I thought I heard the message, but really I had gotten it only at a rather superficial level. I never really pondered it, meditated over it, thought about day-to-day implications. And what good is it to get guidance if you don't use it?

– 5 –

On December fifteenth Mary sent, for my future research, a list of lives in which she thought we had interacted. On the twenty-second she sent a note suggesting that John's surname had been "Overton," and wondering if Clara's family came from

Orange. (For, of course, John was a contemporary of Martha Jefferson's, though they lived in far different social strata.) We talked about it over the phone; she suggested that his family were farmers, prosperous but small. I instantly, proudly—out of a smallholder perspective that seemed instinctive to me—said that "they did their own work." That is, they were not slave-holders and not idlers. When she asked me to describe the house as I saw it, I mentioned the "chim-i-ney"—and certainly I'd never said the word that way in my life. I asked if that's how they pronounced it then, and she said yes.

And when, over Christmas, I told my elder brother what Mary had at some time told me about the hidden cause of the death of my mother's brother during World War II, he did what I never would have thought to do: He called our mother—who verified every detail.

– 6 –

Christmas 1992—I having just learned the value of an opened heart—was wonderful. Just at the time that I (in Gateway) had thought to send love to my teenage daughter, she had suddenly said to her mother "let's get a Christmas tree and surprise Dad" (saving me the work of shopping for it). And when I came home, for the first time since she had become a teenager there was no tension between us. I could pat her head and she didn't bristle. And my wife's mother, who had seen my wife and me go through some very hard times, walked into the dining room one day and saw us embracing. She was embarrassed and started to withdraw, but I drew her in too. I had gone a long way toward getting the psychic abilities I wanted, but even if I hadn't, my week at the Monroe would have been among the most valuable things I had ever done. As I was to learn and learn again over the next few years, at deeper and deeper levels, psychic abilities are integrally connected with the ability to experience and express love. "Love is all there is" is not an abstract generalization, or a pious wish, but as close to a truly scientific statement about the nature of the world as I have yet seen.

If we are connected Upstairs—of course it would be!

And on the afternoon of Christmas Eve, I saw a beautiful example of this. My son's rabbit suddenly got sick, and my wife and I wound up traveling to an emergency vet's office an hour away. Not the kind of thing you want to do, necessarily, on Christmas Eve, but I, being still elevated from Gateway, knew to take it in stride: There might be a reason. Predictably, we had a long wait. A month before, I would have spent the time reading, or writing in my journal, or sitting blankly. Instead, I used the time to go around to every person there, talking to the people, cuddling their pets, until—saving them for last, not knowing why—I went over to a middle-aged couple. They were holding a beautiful ten-year-old cat which had become too weak to eat or drink. Clearly, it was about to die, and they knew that. A sad Christmas for them. I more than half believe that I had been called to that vet's office to comfort them, to make them feel less alone, if only for a few minutes.

I succeeded at that, and it occurred to me that the answer to our social problems lies not so much in reorganization or reform as in increased consciousness. If people were awake, they wouldn't be polluting the earth, and wouldn't be indifferent to it. They wouldn't be criminals or war-makers or profiteers. All our problems are a variation on the theme of stupidity, but the answer is not higher IQ; it is more *consciousness*, which is not nearly the same thing. Intelligent people are quite capable of doing evil. *Conscious* people would be less so. If people were aware of their connection, one to the other, and if they were functioning with opened hearts, everything would change. It is as Henry Thoreau knew long ago. He once wrote that he had never met anyone who was fully awake: "How could I have looked him in the eye?"

And on Christmas afternoon, I found myself watching the video of *Dances With Wolves* with tears in my eyes. Not primarily because of the man's personal story, which after all was fiction. Not even because of the underlying reality of the destruction of the unitary and sane Indian life by the fragmented but powerful insanity of white culture, though that was hard enough to bear. Primarily I was overwhelmed with loneliness. I ached for a wild free life "I"—Smallwood—had once lived, and had lost.

Dances With Wolves reminded me of my altered-state vision of November, when I had driven along twentieth century roads seeing the land with nineteenth century eyes. Someone within me dislikes twentieth century America, with its suburbs and its asphalt and its so-called progress. Several someones dislike it, in fact. Some of that crowd inside revel in technology and gadgets, but others want none of it. And observing this within myself, I wonder if this is not in fact the reason for our internal conflicts. In alternate moods, we may like or dislike something: the same something. Some moments we feel one way, only to contradict that feeling a moment later. Even more striking is the way our values change over time, so that what we value in youth we may despise with age. Maybe what is happening is that, at different moments, or at different times in our lives, different members of our internal community are dominant within us. Over the Christmas following Gateway, Smallwood—my inner transcendentalist, whatever his real name was—was active, probably because of the work I had done to reconnect with what I then called past lives.

In my journal I wrote, "I start to get back something of the loveliness of the life I led once. It's starting to come back. I know now what stops us from remembering. It hurts to remember. Nonetheless I want it *all*. I want it all back, good and bad and painful to remember." (Again, be careful what you ask for. Not that I'd trade.)

Early one day in January, I *saw* a hand write "Joseph Smallwood" as the name of the man who had visited Emerson. Reconsidering, I thought maybe it had been "Josiah" rather than "Joseph," but was quite clear about the surname. Where "Atwood" had come from, I don't know. Shortly thereafter I got a letter from Mary saying that she wrote her stories of her past lives in a sort of trance; "more properly, Focus 15." Showing the value of a common language.

– 7 –

The story gets ever harder to tell, for two reasons: It gets ever more personal; it gets ever more remote from what I take to be the average person's experience. For instance, astral sex. In *Journeys Out of the Body*, Bob Monroe discussed a form of energy exchange between people that happened in the out-of-body state. Not sex in the way we know it in this form of consciousness, of course, but still a definite exchange of energy, an exhilarating building and release of tension, a mutual gift of love.

On the last night of Gateway, as I had massaged Emily's back and shoulder in the conference room, she and I had half listened to several people nearby discussing the subject. I wasn't much interested, but when I came back a week later, I learned that she and Peter had been practicing. Peter told me how to go about it.

Naturally, Mary and I began to do the same thing, she in California and I in Virginia. As usual, she was way ahead of me in her perceptions, and in fact I wondered if she was exaggerating. But on December twenty-seventh I experienced it myself. The intensity was so great, I could scarcely stand up straight. I was literally quivering. It was a strange sensation, as if a circular object with raised bumps were rotating within my chest, grinding through. [I sketched a wheel with bumps on the side.] Weird description but I don't know how else to put it. I was exhausted, exhilarated, tranquil, shaken, wiped out. Ecstatic.

I tried to describe to someone the difference between this and sex, and he suggested that it made sex mundane. "No, not mundane," I said, thinking about it. "Localized." This is not the kind of experience one normally advertises, but how in honesty can I leave it out? And it happened not once, but often. It was only one of several kinds of unprecedented things I was experiencing, all in uncharted territory. I was back to making up the rules as I went along.

– 8 –

On the twenty-eighth of December I wrote Mary:

> ... Something you said ... reminded me that in 1968 when I spent quite a bit of time hypnotizing [a college roommate], repeatedly I wound up talking to the consciousness of a specific incarnation, and I wondered, how is he experiencing me? Who does he think I am? How is he still there as a separate personality?
>
> Never did come up with any satisfying or even tentative answers.
>
> But the memory sparked me, this morning, to go in to talk to John directly. Don't know what time I got him at; some time after Clara (if that was her name) died. Impressions of interest:
>
> (a) he wasn't surprised to hear from me; had evidently dealt with me or others before. My assumption is that later I will contact him earlier.
>
> (b) I recognize, so well, that attitude of hard, sullen, refusal to believe again in life or in hope. I recognize it from an earlier version of myself in this life. . . . Evidently I am a slow learner when it comes to emotions.
>
> (c) he seemed to say his name was Dunmore. . . . But I'm afraid this is bleed-through from a local history column that ran yesterday. . . .
>
> I think we can do some healing, here, in time. Healing my own past self? Interesting concept, but I propose to do just that. . . .

[By the way, I suspect he was killed in the Battle of
Fallen Timbers, August 20, 1794, under Anthony Wayne.]

Note the process. Still in unfamiliar territory, still trying to
decide what was real and what was imagination, I was nonetheless exploring rather than crippling myself with doubt. I was
beginning to *use* what I had experienced, to make sense of
things and open paths for further exploration. Nearly a quarter-
century earlier, I had had the *experience* of speaking to what
appeared to be someone's past lives, but it was only when I
began seeking out the *meaning* of the experience that meaning
appeared. And it was only during the initial writing of this book
that I read the disembodied being who calls himself "Seth," in
the books by Jane Roberts, saying that what seem to us past and
future lives are in fact all happening, when seen from outside
the space-time framework, in the same non-time.

Thus, I could begin to understand not only that I could
still contact other lifetimes, but that, in fact, they could contact
me. And this led me to suspect that each so-called individual is
a lot less individual than Downstairs logic would have us
believe.

Ultimately I came to believe that in fact each of us is a
community of Downstairs individuals, like beads strung along a
thread, except that the beads interact with each other, as noted
above in my letter to Mary (point a). Thus I came to see that my
Welsh journalist and psychic investigator (David Owen Poynter,
if that was his name) has done more to shape my adult life than
any other that I am aware of, but that my early years were
shaped more strongly by Smallwood, with his love of nature and
his transcendentalist way of experiencing the world. And judg-
ing from what I know of my own temperament and inclinations,
somewhere in there too are a politician, an aristocrat, a socialist (though that may be David), and probably several variants of
mystic, priest, shaman, and healer. And these are only what I

suspect! I have noticed that in my case, the lives that I remember most clearly are mostly British and American—that is, I seem to be most open to what is least foreign to my present existence. Perhaps it is merely a case of working from the most familiar to the least. Time will tell. Maybe.

The experiences of these others seem to shed light, too, on my experiences and psychological problems in this lifetime, as noted in (b) above. Since I wrote that in 1992, much more has been published on the subject of using so-called past-life memories to shed light on current psychological situations, but I am not sure that health-care professionals are right to treat those past lives (so called) as past, finished, done for. I think they and their clients might benefit from considering those other lives as active and functioning, interacting actively with the current personality. It seems to me that we are more than the passive sum of what happened to us "before." In a very real, if inexplicable, way, it's all happening now. Not that that makes sense from a 3D Theater viewpoint.

A final note on topics brought up by that letter: bleed-through does indeed seem to be a great problem in re-creating the record. As I suspected even then (c), Dunmore was a red herring. We—or anyway I, but I can't believe I am the only one—tend to jump in with logic, trying to fill every gap as soon as possible. If we aren't careful, we wind up making up logical, believable fairy tales that may or may not encompass much of what truly happened. As in everything else in life, a little elementary caution is in order. Not every bright idea that comes our way is true.

Yet some are. On the last day of the year, while I was driving home, it occurred to me (I can't remember now what brought up the notion) that my last previous lifetime—for I still thought in linear terms then—might have been, not the Welshman, but a very short, truncated life somewhere in Nazi-occupied territory. Instantly I knew, this might be the genesis of the attitude that had overshadowed my youth: "Don't fight back, keep your head down. Don't question authority." Maybe I could find that person, if I dared. But maybe, if I contacted a child who had died in the Holocaust, I would learn more than I wanted to know. I let this one lie for a while.

– 9 –

On December twenty-ninth I had gone Upstairs, trying to contact Emily—the twentieth-century woman, not her eighteenth-century counterpart—and half convinced myself that she responded with a gladness, an opening. I left open the possibility that I was merely deceiving myself, though I hoped not. A couple of days later I got back my photos from the roll taken at TMI and at the old house. They hit hard. I sent them to Mary, whose comments were illuminating:

> There's a *big* difference in the one at the Monroe and the one in front of the chimney [at the cabin]. As in vast. At the Monroe y'all [Emily, Peter, and I] are wearing your social, smiley faces. . . . But at the house! Bam! If you look closely, you see the personalities of John and Clara on (in) the faces of Frank and [Emily]. It's a much more *"real"* photograph. . . . Maybe [Emily] doesn't realize it consciously, but I'll bet that place got to her from the get-go, from the main road, even. No wonder she was out of sorts. The photo of her alone by the chimney . . . has a very "I hate this place" feel about it. The one with you there is, from her, an ambivalence, a tough shell over a soft heart. . . .
>
> And *you*. You look like every laconic upcountry farmer I've ever seen, then and/or now. "Yep. Set yourself down right cheer, and the missus'll fetch you up a buttermilk." There is also a pervasive air of sadness, which friend John probably *had*, when all was said and done. . . .

Bang on, as usual.

– 10 –

My transformation at Gateway didn't make my life all that much easier. I did tell my employees and associates at work something of what I had experienced (leaving Bob to tell his own stories). But there's only so much that can be told, and work itself—everyday life—was the true test. If you acquire new perceptions and new abilities and cannot apply them in what is called the real world (though I think that's a misnomer)—what good are they?

And life in "the real world," particularly in the business world, continued to be hard, particularly when I forgot what I had just learned. I remembered and forgot, remembered and forgot. While I remembered, I knew that my life was magical and was the miracle it really is. When I forgot, I fell into the delusion of meaninglessness, and conflict, and random activity. You think my employees found it easy? Or my family?

And at this point I find myself overwhelmed with material: my letters to Mary; hers to me; journal entries; consultations with The Boss, and beginning in mid-January, sessions with The Gentlemen Upstairs. Thousands of words. Page after page of valuable material. With Mary's irreplaceable assistance, I went working at relearning the ins and outs of mental communication, distant healing, past-life exploration, and other things I should not have known how to do but inexplicably did. All this great mass of material documents stages of the search. I had to ask myself not only, "What do readers most need to know?" but, "What do I *need* to quote and what can I just summarize?" Not that I necessarily always made the right decision. I have tried to be ruthless, but there was so much material!

A book could be (may be) written about my activities with Mary alone. We began to share an awareness of each other that is nearly impossible to describe. It isn't like I could see (or "know") what she was having for breakfast or what she was saying to someone on the telephone. And it wasn't Peeping

Tommery, either. (Sorry to disappoint.) It was knowing that the other person was (as Mary put it) "right there." Mary was far ahead of me in perceptions; she'd been doing this a lot longer than I, and perhaps she is wired differently anyway. But we both felt the connection, and perhaps the best way to describe it is to describe what we felt when suddenly that connection ceased.

All New Year's Day 1993 and all Saturday the second and part of Sunday (till I called her), I was outwardly going through my normal life while in sudden terror that we had lost contact. I said to my journal:

> Have been exhausted working hard trying to be *with* rather than merely *among* people. And periodically I lose contact with Mary and the loss of contact terrifies me. I forget about Emily repeatedly, and [my wife] and others I want to help—but to lose a feeling of contact with Mary is to return to the miserable life I had.

Then on Sunday, checking with her over what I was now calling "the Downstairs telephone," I found that she had been going through the same terror. I noted, "She says when her own emotions are most closely involved she is least able to see. Which would explain the unexpectedness of my own arrival in her life."

So what was the cause of the disconnect, and the terror? Simply that each of us, out of misguided courtesy, had decided to leave the other alone that weekend. I had refrained from contacting her Upstairs; she had refrained from contacting me. Misplaced mutual politeness. Result: a devastating sense of loneliness for each of us. When I figured that out, I vowed, "We'll never do *that* again."

To show how crazy things got, as the connection built, at about ten o'clock Sunday night, as I was going to bed, the phone rang. My wife picked it up. It was Mary, laughing. She wanted to know if I was responsible for the cat that had just walked across her house. My wife gave me the phone, thinking she was dealing with lunatics. A reasonable reaction. But a cat had walked in their front door, through the house, down Mary's side of the bed, and out the back door. Mary said her husband said to tell me, "Very funny."

Did I have anything to do with that? *Could* I have? Not consciously. I wouldn't know *how*, consciously. And yet I had to concede that perhaps I might be involved. I had been thinking about a poem I had written about the night Mary and I met (should I say, met again?), wondering whether to change the word "kitten." The timing was exact.

– 11 –

On January sixth I called Mary from work. Several psychics were predicting a major earthquake for California that spring, which matched my own premonition. I wanted to know if it rang true for her. It did. Either she and I had the feeling independently or we exchanged it somehow. Between us, each reaching for a "knowing" and receiving feedback from the other as we did so, we convinced ourselves that the great quake would happen while she was in the East in April. Before the conversation was over I got April 8 with great knowing, though I didn't know why. She looked at her ticket. She was scheduled to leave the West Coast on the seventh. Immediately she was in terror for her children.

And this was an example of Psychic's Disease. Both Mary and I knew full well, Downstairs, that prophecies of California's impending destruction have been made and proven wrong nearly continuously since Edgar Cayce began the trend before World War II. And we knew, equally surely, that if there's one category in which even the best psychics have a lousy track record, it is dates. Yet something in the situation that "felt" right led us to make decisions that could not be justified rationally. In all this I now see Upstairs manipulation, because although the rationale was incorrect—California is still there, last I checked—the results for Mary and me of her move East were far-reaching. The road we traveled while she lived in Virginia in 1993 and 1994 seems now like a necessary detour.

In the spring and summer of 1993, she and I worked together on retrieving past-life information. In 1994 we went up to TMI and had our brain waves measured as we communicated Upstairs together. Later she and I worked together for the first time in author-editor mode, as she wrote and we published *Everyday Life In Two Worlds*. Later still, *Dear Companion*, the manuscript that had brought her into my life, became one of the first three books in our "River Lethe" series of novelized past-life stories. None of this would have happened, probably, if she had been still in California. And these are only the communicable aspects of her effect on me. The most important effects, as I have indicated earlier, were that I had available a sympathetic, knowledgeable partner in many forms of mental and (oh well, might as well use the overworked word) psychic exploration.

Given the extent of the consequences, and working from the assumption that there are no coincidences, and assuming that the externals of our lives, no less than the internals, are subject to continuous benign manipulation from our Upstairs level, our earthquake-that-didn't-happen looks to me like an internal earthquake caused by the illusion of an external one.

Which is to say, Upstairs knows how to use anything that comes along. If we're acting rationally and consciously, it can use that; but even our unconscious acts, even foolish acts, are grist for its mill. This is not to say that we shouldn't do our best to act wisely and well; it is to say merely that there's no need to worry so much. When we make a mistake (whatever a mistake is), we don't ruin our lives, just our plans. That's why we can trust the universe. Upstairs does just fine.

However, life Downstairs can get pretty rocky. After that January sixth conversation, Mary and I lived the next three months in expectation of The Big One. She rearranged her entire life, betting on that prediction. I was more cautious, but I was fully prepared for the prediction to come true. After all, it wasn't just a vague "feeling" I had or she had. It was an intense *knowing,* passed and amplified from one to the other, and intensified as well by the fact that so many others were "knowing" the same thing. When the predicted catastrophe, like every other massive cataclysm that had been predicted from the time of Edgar Cayce onward, didn't occur, I learned a couple of lessons: humility and caution. I remembered that people can sometimes see the future, but often they see a future we don't go to.

I don't mean that as a joke. The very purpose of prophecy (in the Old Testament, say) was to point out what would occur *unless* people changed course. This implies that they *can* change course, and can therefore change the future that is foreseen. A major point of the Book of Jonah, perhaps my favorite book of the Bible, is that the prophet *knew* intuitively that God's message would be heeded, and the people of Ninevah would repent, and God would spare the city, and thus Jonah's own prophecy would appear to have been wrong. Why go to all the trouble just to make himself wrong? (So he took off for parts remote and wound up in the belly of the whale, which may seem to say that his own foresight wasn't all that great, but proverbially, psychics don't do all that well when dealing with matters closest to home.)

If nothing foreseen could be avoided, where is free will? And what would be the benefit in being able to see? I quite believe that Edgar Cayce's most dire prophecies will *not* occur, not because he was mistaken, but because enough people, reading those prophecies, changed. Not being what we would have been, not going where we would have gone, we're winding up in a different place. Well done, Mr. Cayce! And I mean that sincerely.

But at the time, I hadn't figured this out. At the time, I was entranced with the idea that I was developing the gift of prophecy.

– 12 –

Also, other things were happening. The day after my phone call that started that particular psychic earthquake, I got a letter from Mary thanking me for healing the congestion in her lungs. I thought, "What?" Then I remembered doing it! I had done it quite consciously, *sort of* feeling a response from her, *sort of* wondering if I was conducting an imaginary conversation—*and then had forgotten doing it!* And never would have remembered doing it if she hadn't mentioned it.

So encouraged, I then went to work on my twelve-year-old son, who was home with a sore throat and postnasal drainage. The next morning he reported being a little better, and *I* had a little bit of a sore throat, which I took as a sign that something was happening. The next day I worked on him again, and while in Focus 21, asked him (Upstairs) to take a nap, having been unable to get him to do so earlier. He did, and woke up feeling better. I can't recall, at this distance, but I think these were my first fumbling attempts at distant and near healing.

– 13 –

On the tenth of January, The Boss told me:

> You are pushing hard and making gains but now moving *too* fast, till just now. Slow down, smell the flowers. You don't *want* to get there a second beforehand, and stop worrying about it. It isn't "use it or lose it" but "use it and live with it normally."

I'm not much for slowing down anyway, and my life at this time kept spinning faster. Enter, on January 14, a woman I will call Elena.

She came to our offices with a short illustrated manuscript. I sat down beside her on the couch in our front waiting room and found myself reading the entire manuscript—in

Focus 12, as it seemed to demand. I then talked with her about it, pointing out its strengths and weaknesses, and somehow, very naturally and easily, we wound up talking about *how* I had been reading it: i.e., in Focus 12. From there we went of course to the Gateway experience, then to my self-description in one of my visions there as "muddy footprints in the grass," which I took to mean that I would be one whose experience would lead others to see that someone had been there before them, that they were not in a trackless wilderness. Then to the fact that she is a psychic, a channel, and a healer.

I took her into my office and showed her the photos I'd taken of Emily and me at that old house the week before Christmas. She scanned the photos and was able to tell me things I hadn't picked up—for instance, that the energy of the cabin was very dark and needed clearing—then spontaneously offered me what she called a "toning." I didn't really know what she was offering me, but something immediately told me to accept, and I did so immediately.

– 14 –

On the fifteenth Mary and I had a telephone conversation, the upshot of which was that we both knew that it would be a mistake to let our metaphysical affair become a physical affair when she came East. Sexual tensions had been building up between us, but an affair, I intuitively knew, could lead only to unhappiness, guilt, and a final disruption between us, let alone what it would do to the others involved. Relating it to myself in my journal, I wrote, "Somehow we managed to get the idea down through various levels—*all* levels, I hope—and at the end Mary said it was more relief than regret, which is true."

A few nights later, a dream:

Driving home, deep snow, slushy. Suspended. Stopped because I was wearing heavy snow boots that didn't give me any feel for the accelerator pedal. Got out, found some guys playing in the street, they helped push the car, got it started again. When I came to our turn into [the subdivision where I lived] it was a cemetery instead. . . .

I was wearing one boot and was barefoot on left foot. Walked all the way back to where the boys were, rather than first checking to see if the other boot was in the car.

If there was more (and I think there was) I've lost it.

Very aware of some complications coming. Nothing is as easy or simple as it first appeared. How can I go on, one foot in boots, one barefoot? That unexpected snow, melting as we slosh through it. A cemetery instead of where I thought I lived.

– 15 –

Meanwhile, on the morning of January 18, 1993, had come The Gentlemen Upstairs—TGU—who became a major, if sometimes baffling, influence in my life. It happened in the pages of my journal:

Frank: Is somebody trying to give me a message? Does that explain the slight persistent headache? Let me go to Focus 12 and see what happens.

You are for the first time in a position to begin hearing messages directly from other people. Mary is the first but only the first. Leave yourself open to more and more will come.
Frank: Who is talking?

You don't know me/us. The [*Messages from*] *Michael* book [given me by Mary a couple of months earlier] leaves you open to the possibility of this communication. Don't get carried away with the excitement and joy of the romance. Remember to work. If you want to learn through joy instead of suffering, fine—but—*learn.*

They suggest, and I hear, that I go to Focus 21.

Frank: Okay. 21. Now what? Who are you?

We are part of you. You are part of us. Together we function. . . .

Frank: You wanted me to become aware of you. What do you want from me specifically?

Awareness. Work. Growth. . . .

Frank: I feel a little sick.

Longing. The desire mingled with dread, as just before Monroe. A good sign, actually.

That night, I wrote:

> Tonight from 8 to 10 P.M. something happened . . . something profound but hidden from me. In fact, I retain a vague memory of knowing something happened and watching the memory fade as I watched—deliberately withdrawn from me.
>
> At any rate the result is that I am again changed. I am profoundly happy, satisfied—but [a moment before, I had been in bed] realizing that I am lying there ticking off items to be handled at work tomorrow. In other words, I'm ready to go to work again.

– 16 –

I continued to push. From my journal, January 24, 1993:

> *Into 15 to see what I can see. John, tell me something about your life. Were your people Quakers?*
>
> My father was a Friend, my mother an Episcopalian so-called who came to tolerate her husband's ways. Proud of her ancestors. Loyal to the old church, the old ways. No theological conviction but "that was good enough for my parents." My father John Cartwright was a Friend because he was converted at twenty-four by a wandering—not

preacher, but man who visited neighborhood. Friend families. There was one (house) nearby. You know this man today. Not a man today—Suni. Still a tie there. That man changed your father's life, your life. I was a friend without strong conviction but without rebellion. When Clara died and my child I didn't disbelieve in God—I hated him. Not following the voice was all I could do. Not cut out to be a sinner, no interest, but turned away from the world and God. Hard years. Bitter years. Empty purposeless waiting for the time to pass. You know. When the war came close enough, I joined when requested. Other Quakers dissented, didn't like my joining—but also knew it helped them that some did. Never saw a day's fight against the British. Never fired a shot except for food, until fighting Indians long time later, and that was just looking for trouble, which I found. My parents had my farm, but there wasn't anybody to pass it to, far as I know.

On the twenty-ninth I had an amazing night. I had fallen asleep while doing exercises without tapes. I awoke at 3 A.M. and went to bed and went astral traveling here, there, and everywhere, with great ease. Much earlier I had gone to Mary's, and sat in the love seat looking at her and her family. I had the impression they all saw me, and a certainty that she did. When I called Mary, she said she never saw me, but then with a start remembered knowing I was there.

That night I experienced what seemed to be two more breakthroughs:

I heard The Boss—or the committee, or whomever—plainly and clearly and at great length, without need of pen and paper. I lay there in [Focus] 21, having asked my question, and heard sentence after sentence come out as if being sent a line at a time. . . ."

To date this experience has not repeated, and I don't have any idea why it came then, what it meant, or why it happened no more.
  The second thing:

> Very late—or rather quite early this morning—I traveled again, but this time concentrated on Mary's yard and the material world rather than on contacting a person—though of course I did that too—and used her suggestion of calling for more light. [So that I could see clearly on these travels.] Don't know that I can communicate much of the difference in how I went about perceiving, but that was the important thing. Tried to heal her throat—and mine.

Unfortunately, the things recorded in a journal are not necessarily the things that would help one later to remember what one was talking about!

> "Finally . . . realized the next step — hardest yet — is to trust her not to say something to me merely to confirm my expectations. . . . And this I have resolved to do."

This deserves a word. Because I was so worried about fooling myself, I was equally worried that others were fooling me—even when I knew better. Thus, every so often, I would try to test Mary, to be sure she wasn't just stringing me along. I take it as a sign of her maturity (and perhaps our inner bond) that she confined herself to mild impatience, rather than being actively outraged and insulted, that I should thus periodically distrust her integrity. Probably she recognized that this recurring suspicion amounted to a suspicion that she was too good to be true. Anyway, over time I ceased to need reassurance. After a while I had amassed so many incidences that I would have had to equally distrust myself. Besides, after a while I could see that others, listening to my stories, would be equally entitled—if not nearly forced—to distrust me. Certain aspects of my new reality really are too strange to be believed, from a conventional viewpoint.

– 17 –

On January 30 Mary and I saw an interesting example of the strength of our connection. Although I had been sick, I went to a sitar concert (which I particularly love), and as I sat motionless, entranced, absorbing it, I tried to send the experience to Mary across the continent. I called her to tell her what I'd done, and she wrote me the next day:

Last night, while you were at the Indian concert, I was standing in my kitchen and got the weirdest, slow-spinning, I-have-to-sit-down, ear-ringing feeling. I heard you!!!!!! very strongly, and then it faded a little and I thought, "Oh maybe it's just I'm hypoglycemic," but some carbohydrates later, it still had not faded, and I spent most of the evening . . . in an altered state.

She also wrote:

If you've had a lingering headache for several days or weeks, it may well be a channelling headache, as we call it. Information coming through on circuits unused to it. You might also expect to experience extreme exhaustion, extreme energy, ravenous hunger, diarrhea, ringing in your ears, and what might be otherwise called faintness. All this calms down after a while . . . unless of course you've got somebody on the opposite coast way more powerful than he realizes sending you his experience of a sitar concert. . . .

This was of particular interest since on the night of February 1—before I received the letter—my lungs filled up with what seemed to be hardened phlegm, so much so that I felt like I was on the point of drowning. I called (mentally) for Mary to help me empty my lungs, and the lungs subsided but then my head and, in fact, my whole body ached. Very like the flu. When I talked to her on the telephone that afternoon, she said she had just written me a letter warning me of just that. And, she said, I might be overdoing it. Who, me?

– 18 –

On impulse one day, I called my brother in California and said, "What can I do for you?" Turned out he was having a lot of back pain. I said we'd see what we could do. On February 4, at about six Pacific time, Mary and I went in and worked on him. I got a sense that the physical cause of his problem was that he was sitting slumped over to one side whenever he commuted to the city via a one-hour bus ride. I asked him if this was so, and he confirmed it, and perhaps he ceased to sit that way; at any rate his back got better.

– 19 –

I went up to Elena's place on the weekend of February 5–7. Part of me was delighted and knew it would be important; part was fearful and wanted no part of it. With desire comes also dread. In the course of two nights and two days, she accomplished three things with me: counseling, which led to the uncovering and removal of blocks left from childhood; toning, which is the realigning of the dense and subtle bodies by use of precise sharp vocal tones (she has had operatic training at Juilliard, and the quality and volume of sound that she can produce is extraordinary); and what might be called redirection, or anyway reorientation, as a result of the messages we obtained when she channeled certain entities in both a preliminary and a "debriefing" session.

Naturally, throughout this time, we talked extensively about the connections between what she was doing and what I'd seen and learned at TMI. For it was apparent to me that psychics function spontaneously or through training by bringing themselves to certain unusual focus levels. Bob Monroe had often said that his techniques can't teach anything that people can't get elsewhere, but that elsewhere they get it slower and less reliably. This seemed particularly true in the area of psychic development. By the end of the weekend I realized (and was told by those she channeled) that the work there had been the culmination of changes begun long ago and focused during Gateway, something in the nature of a final adjustment: it seemed that I was becoming a psychic, a channel, and something of a healer.

She channeled a message at the end of the weekend, purportedly from the masters who had directed my realignment. (Who the masters are, I don't know. Not The Gentlemen Upstairs, anyway.) The greater part of the channeled material was recorded but is inaudible. Among what can be made out, however, are these excerpts:

> We would come forth at this time to . . . seal that which has been given here in this experience of vibrational alignment. That which has been brought forth and integrated carries with it the vibrations of those from our realms who vibrate to the energies beyond this solar system. That which your experience has been upon this planet, accelerated as it has been in recent months, represents only a minuscule fragment of that which is the totality of the consciousness which your awareness *now* considers your being. So we would have you know that from our realms we are grateful that a channel for communication has been established by the alignment and structuring of such vibrations into your vehicle.
>
> We would as well say to you that . . . the maintenance (we will call it) of such, lies in its responsibility in your own court, so to speak. Would this be understood?

[Me: Yes.]

As you are learning to experience that which you are, ponder not on that which is unfamiliar, and doubt that such experiences are truth, for all experiences bring some element of knowing, or of truth, and it is for you to discern whether your experiences are for learning and discernment, or for identification and integration, or for joy. And in all things there is choice to accept or reject.

I asked about Emily.

Indeed. This one comes forth to you now for your assistance in healing and releasing that which was experienced in this lifetime you have observed, and that which due to the sense of loss on the part of both of you has never been completely released. To hold on in any way to the hurt, the pain, to the grief, to the loss, only binds one to repeating it, whereas to hold on to the love and to the essence frees one to soar and to experience affection and joy in oneself and in one's relations.

After all this time I am still not sure what to make of it. But other things went on that weekend that would complicate my life and confuse my understandings. Turns out, I looked, sounded, and acted like a man Elena was once in love with. I took note of that but never considered that she might be tempted to transfer that love to me. I don't think this happened to her consciously, but so much the worse. Unconscious manifestations occur, of course, without the conscious buffers that might make such a transference more manageable. My self-confidence was then still impaired from a lifetime of being lost on a strange planet. That she might fall in love with me without my knowing it never occurred to me even as a remote possibility. If it had, I would have laughed the idea away.

This would create serious complications before any of us were very many months older.

– 20 –

My toning session certainly didn't make collaboration with Mary more difficult. If anything, it made it easier. Between telephone calls and letters and journeys together Upstairs, we made great strides in finding out things about our past connections. I got ever more confident about sitting down at the computer and talking to The Gentlemen Upstairs—and confidence was the key. With practice it got ever easier. In three days in February I got a good deal of information on the Welshman whom I was calling "David Peterson."

On February 11, going within, I asked about "David Peterson, if that was his name. What was the purpose of that lifetime?" Much of what I got, though, felt to me like myself trying desperately to invent something on demand. For instance TGU said David was born in Wales, "to a sheep farmer and his wife, Susan."

Frank: Sheep farmer had a name?

Wesley comes to mind.

Frank: Wesley Peterson?

Not right, but close W— something. Wescott? Something.

I couldn't make out if this was honesty or bluff. David, they said, was born in 1871, in Powys, an only child.

Alone in the world. That was the purpose. . . . To live a life free from emotional ties. He was born isolated from America and American memories. There had been the painful life as Overton in the 1700s, and the wandering life of Wood in the earlier 1800s. Where could he have been born that would not have brought him resonances of those two lifetimes? . . . Everything would have been memory-inducing, and he wanted rest from all that.

Frank: Because of the emotional pain?

This was to be a life of more aesthetic pursuits than the pursuit of the beauty of nature. Atwood had a lifetime of wandering around the mountains and plains in mind or body, seeing always the transcendental behind the scenery and delighting in the glory of God. But there are other glories to be delighted in than those of God; there is for example the glory of the creations of the mind of man. Technology, art, science, the world of the intellectual mind rather than the theological or mystical mind. David had planned out a lifetime of relaxation from the mystical tenseness of his previous existence. Yet in the background there was . . . Clara. In the light of that devastating experience he was not about to risk another emotional commitment. You might say he knew better, yet he also knew that there were other lives. You might say he said, maybe later, I need a rest this time.

Basically, they said, David's soul had overdosed on natural beauty the lifetime before, and needed something artificial and handiworked. The next day I continued my exploration, asking how he had gone to London, and in what year. They said that the year was 1893, he was twenty-two, and he took his first sea voyage to get there from Bath. "Took a couple of days and he learned that he was a good sailor, naturally at home on the sea. Liked the sea."

According to them, he wanted to paint, but did not have the money for art school, and so had no training, and so could only haunt the free museums in whatever spare time he could make. They said he had had a good education in fundamentals: grammar, spelling, writing, and he had a natural aptitude for writing, so he went into journalism, working on Fleet Street. "Fleet Street long after the time of Dickens, you understand. But that was his start. He had a good head, quick mind, active curiosity. Unencumbered by family or emotional ties, and infused with a love of wandering."

They told me that after five years with the paper, he was asked if he wanted to report from South Africa, and so was there when the Boer War broke out. I gather he was insufficiently pro-British for his editors or his public. "He had sense enough not to sound (or be) pro-Boer, but sense enough not to be whole-heartedly in favor of his country's subjugation of a small foreign country. Not that he exactly looked on Great Britain as 'his' country. He felt rather like you do, a native under occupation by an eccentric and in fact crazy foreign culture which had neither comprehension of him nor appreciation of him—mostly because it really couldn't see him at all."

So, they told me, he left the paper, and went wandering far into the interior, working his way around, doing odd jobs for those with clerical educations. "Not hard labor exactly—not in a land of kaffirs—but somewhat menial, and certainly nothing looking like prestige or success. But he had no one counting on him, no one to report to, no one to support or make proud of him, so he didn't care. He was free, and that was what he wanted."

They said he left the paper in 1901, wandered around for some months, and then got restless and thought he'd see India. Instead, he wound up going all the way to China. In Canton he saw a vision that reminded him of London: Standing on a stone bridge, looking down at the teeming people all around, he thought how similar it all was. Herds of people, like sheep, there as in London, as in all over the world. "Every herd thought itself unique; every herd rigidly excluded all customs but its own. Only a few people wandered around outside the limits; every-body else thought the limits were absolutes."

And thus he got the crucial central image for *Waterborne Reflections,* which, they said to my surprise, was a book of poetry. I pointed out that I had been unable to find it, and asked why it wasn't listed among standard sources. They said it had been privately printed, "and not necessarily listed exactly in that way. That was David's title, how he thought of it himself."

I said instantly, "It had another? What is it?" But here the information abruptly dried up. Because I had backed "them" into a corner? I more than half suspected so.

– 20 –

And just at this time Mary and I, working separately and verifying by phone, discovered that we had been brother and sister as half-Jewish, half-Polish children born in Poland in the 1930s. In short order we—Mary, mostly—pieced together a good few details of the lives of older brother Marcus (she then) and younger sister Katrina (I then). Their mother died of tuberculosis before the war. Their father was killed by the Nazis. The boy and girl were both killed in the camps. Since I now had access to TGU, I asked them in a computer session for some specific information, and got it.

Frank: Never mind the names of that particular lifetime. Why a girl, why a Jew, why in Poland, why brother and sister?

Brother and sister you already know. Reconnection in the only way possible in a life to be truncated so brutally and quickly. You solaced each other, suffered together, tried to protect each other (ineffectually, because nothing could be done) but loved each other constantly. You were Jews because this was an underclass that was yet cultured and cohesive. The father, she says, was an oculist. In other words, a cultured man making a living in a skilled trade in which only the results, not the social standing of the producer of results, counted. The mother died early. No mother love there for you, only a father's harassed love. And a little girl without a mother becomes a "little mother" for the family. You were that for your papa and your brother, he was your protector and took joy in you. Why in Poland? Central Europe was far enough away from America and the British Isles to have no resonances. This was to be the battleground, the charnel house, and where better than Poland? In Poland was no escape for Jews. In Italy, in

France, in Czechoslovakia, even, there was friendship and compassion to be found among the populace. Not in Poland.

As to why a girl? To prepare you, to balance you, for this lifetime in which you do not fit in among men and are very receptive to the love of women. You were a girl and did not partake in love and romance, because you were killed too soon. But you experienced a woman's love for the world and for other people, and it served you well here.

Frank: Where was she born?

Galicia. A little town near the border with Czechoslovakia. Not so far from Lidice, of which you read this lifetime as a young teenager.

Frank: What year?

Nineteen thirty-four.

Frank: Nineteen thirty-four for sure? Not later? [I didn't know why I asked that.]

December 1934, almost 1935. December 27.

Frank: Did the mother die in childbirth?

No. Not responsible for the death of the mother. She died of a fever, no one knew what. Combination of malnutrition and hard work. Died pretty young, in her thirties, in 1938.

Frank: When did the girl die?

Katherine, or the Polish equivalent of that name. She died in 1943. April eighth. [Note that in this life, I picked April 8 as the date for the major earthquake that didn't happen. Coincidence, maybe, except that I have never yet met a coincidence.]

Frank: And the boy?

Died in 1944, October twenty-fourth, though he didn't know the date.

Frank: Both died in concentration camps?

Yes. He was in a labor camp, but ultimately a death camp. Auschwitz. She was too. As a child, she was shielded by the older inmates to the extent possible, but ultimately was too little to be of use, and the Nazis and Kapos, of course, had no mercy.

Frank: In God's name, why these lifetimes?

As in this childhood, they toughened you up. Toughened, and gave sensitivity. You understood the reality of suffering and cruelty, after a lifetime perhaps a little too removed from human concerns. As for Mary, she had been sick, twice, mostly from self-induced guilt and feelings of unworthiness. This purged a lot of that: Real suffering induced by others for absolutely no reason purges imaginary or excessive guilt. It was harsh, but that very harshness helped her this time. She came back to the world knowing that she had paid her dues, to a large extent. The very vastness and senselessness of the calamity shielded her from her internal robots always blaming her for things. How—"in God's name"—could she blame herself for the Nazis? And it required almost that great a disproportion between her sufferings and any conceivable thing she might have done, in order for her to know without doubt that in fact she was blameless. As a boy then, she was removed from women's troubles; as a blameless boy, she did not yet know love nor romantic troubles, except in the ethereal way young David did from his vision of the girl in blue in Wales. So again, no distracting resonances. . . .

Frank: What else significant about that lifetime should I know?

This is already quite a lot. More will come in its due place. But look how much you have established, so quickly.

Frank DeMarco 1946–2023.

Katrina, the Polish Jewish girl, 1934–1943.

David Peterson 1871–1932.

Josiah Smallwood 1821–1867.

John Overton 1749–1793.

And after some blanks, Robin MacLean. And others, of course.

No, I haven't overlooked the fact that they supposedly told me the date of my death. But I don't invest in it either. I didn't know how to go about verifying the past, let alone the future. One thing I *had* learned was that just because someone sees a particular future doesn't mean we're going there. I was to get *that* lesson thoroughly rubbed in within a few weeks.

TGU's explanation gave me a believable line on how universal crimes and tragedies such as the Holocaust may also be used, in the universe's usual efficient fashion, to further individual growth. Knowing Mary and knowing myself, I could well believe that such an experience could have just the effects noted. And what is more, as I have found other returned Holocaust victims (perhaps I should say survivors), it seemed to me that one thing we have in common is anxiety about our basic worth, our lovableness, our right to be here. That the death camps and the preceding ugliness should have that effect on the individuals involved, doesn't seem to me surprising. I think the effects of trauma last even longer than people commonly suspect, extending life into life until overwritten by new internal programming.

Until I did the TMI Lifeline program, I was unable to provide any details of Katrina's short life but a sense of dread and bewilderment in her last days. I shelved the subject for the moment and went on to other things.

– 21 –

In working with Elena, I had seen David, as a boy, falling in love with a girl he probably never said a word to. He saw a beautiful young woman out in the country—using a spyglass, perhaps; at any rate it was from a distance—and in the romantic way some dreamy boys have, he seized that vision of loveliness as a model to himself of perfect feminine beauty. I had a sense that he kept that vision all his life, and I wondered if in fact this wasn't Mary and me (or rather what we are Upstairs) keeping in touch—holding the place—without the Downstairs components interfering with the plot.

Naturally I posed the question to Mary, and at first she and I were inclined to think that girl was Molly—a lifetime of hers she knew about. But as I began sitting at the computer in Focus 15 and quizzing somebody (myself, maybe), I'd get a knowing, and would contact Mary, to cross-check, and together we began to make rapid progress. For instance, I told Mary it couldn't have been Molly that David had seen in the early 1890s, for Molly was born in 1890, and the girl David saw was older than he. Besides, this girl had long flowing blond hair, and Molly's, Mary said, was black. She pondered that, went Upstairs, and realized that there was yet another lifetime truncated by tuberculosis or something.

– 22 –

From a talk with The Boss, Tuesday, February 2, 1993. I complained that each day seemed more than I could bear.

> You can bear it, though. Your days and nights are filled with strong emotion and anticipation, with work and longing. It is not surprising that this is a bit overwhelming. Remember, though, how you and Mary adjusted to a new level of intensity. You will adjust—you each will adjust—to this new level of intensity in everyday affairs, as well. Do not expect unprecedented levels of intensity, of complication, to be comfortable; expect only that they will be or will become significant.

In the event, this proved to be very true. Later, when I asked TGU to tell me something of what I would need to learn to do, they added:

You are doing it. Learn to connect with all levels of your own being. Learn to love, truly love, with all your strength. Learn to master the new and overwhelming emotions and forces in your life. The rest will follow in sequence. Master one step and the next step will be the thing nearest to hand. Always a safe thing to do: the thing nearest at hand. Only keep in mind that you have a real task to do and that you need to keep yourself as focused, as hard working and as altruistic as you can. . . . Lack of grounding does not enable you to fly; it cripples you. You know it. Live it.

Frank: What of past lives? I feel it is important, I seem to be making progress opening access, yet it is still so remote from me: me sensing feelings and giving voice to them, rather than seeing or hearing as I did in Focus 15 at Monroe that time with Josiah Smallwood. Is there something I can do besides more of the same to improve my ability to communicate with other parts of myself and at least find out the story?

Love drives the whole thing, as you are fond, now, of saying. The more you love, the deeper you will be in touch with your own emotions. The deeper with the emotions, the easier to get to other layers of being, which after all are more or less the same thing. A closed-off person cannot access other lives because he cannot even access his own life. The thing Elena did that was so critically important to you is that she lovingly corrected what had gone so wrong in your childhood: She acted for those who had done the damage; she acknowledged your integrity and honesty and valor, admitting that the world had been wrong. In turn you gave her love and validation and the score was even—but the important thing is that she thereby opened the path for you. If you can't go behind your own childhood because it is too painful, how can you go to other lives previous or future? You had glimpses, mostly when others helped you, but couldn't take it farther. Now you can.

– 23 –

I had asked Mary to look ahead to see what was coming. On the eighteenth I listed her pre-visions. In the event, none of the six came true. On the same day, I consulted extensively with TGU. As an example of the kind of misinformation psychics—and would-be psychics!—are prone to, I offer this communication:

Frank: What should I be asking, to get the best use of my time?

Where when how who what. As always.

Frank: All right, *where* will I be moving to? And why?

The Eastern Shore of Maryland is much closer to the heart of things and is somewhat protected from the ocean, as Norfolk is not. Closer to Philadelphia and inland closer to Washington, D.C. . . . Norfolk/V.B. is in a way a dead end, the E.S. is a corridor. Fast and easy communication there with the North and Midwest.

Frank: When will I be moving? Is it definite?

The time span isn't definite, as it depends on the decisions of many people, not just you. But two years isn't an unlikely estimate. Perhaps more. You are well aware of your two-and-a-half-year cycles, and have been in your present location several years— three cycles—already.

Frank: Why can't I stand in Virginia?

You won't want to, for good and sufficient reason. Don't worry about it.

Frank: How will it come about?

As an outgrowth of the work you will begin to become known for. Healing is a part of it but only a part—as Mary said.

Frank: Who is involved?

You will see. You don't know them yet but [they] will become instant friends.

Frank: And—what? What will I be doing? Why am I going to be so busy?

Marrying people. Muddy footprints.

Doesn't that message *sound* confident, believable? Yet it got a perfect score: all wrong. On the other hand, just two days later, this:

Frank: Last night Mary and I went in and helped heal Elena's two-year-old of a lifelong wound. Elena, Mary, and I think we did well. Comments on it, please? Observations that may have escaped our notice? Suggestions?

You are not hinting for praise? The praise is worthy, the deed was well done, the motives were correct, and the heart was available for the work needed. All this is good. To notice that you went not only after Mary but her own higher spirits, her spirit guides, her guardian angels—and yours, and Elena's. This was good. You see that way it involved all levels of all of your beings. As Elena pointed out, structure, guidelines, ground-rules, are important. You are moving fast; keep it up and you will indeed be learning from joy rather than from suffering. . . .

Frank: What is next?

The plot unfolds at its own pace. If you want previews, you know where to find them, and we can supplement if you feel it necessary.... There is such a thing as dependence on one's self, even overdependence. To rely on "the word" from spirit levels might tend to undermine your own confidence in your own undoubted abilities to perform on your own level in your own way. Doubt this not. You do fine.

Frank: Still, I can do fine *better* with some advance knowledge of where we might be going. It's true that it tends to steer me, but is that so bad? I won't be steered where I don't want to go.

That has been observed.

I waited—but nothing else came! So:

Frank: Elena—or rather her guides—say I'm likely to write a book on how to love, or something like that, based on my experience with Mary and Emily and [my wife] et cetera. As that hasn't played out yet, does this mean I can just proceed and wait and see?

How not? Why not? You respond well to hints: hence your letter to Bob Monroe which will bear fruit in its own time. [Never did, though.] But you may rush in a little too much sometimes, so it is often necessary to keep you in the dark, not so much "for your own good" as for the sake of the experience. What would you have gotten out of the struggles of your life so far if you had known consciously, emotionally, mentally, how it might work out? That from time to time you had inexplicable reinforcement was necessary, that you would not succumb to discouragement, which was a very real possibility. But that you should have had the blueprint would have been self-defeating. There is a difference between doing your best and going through the motions, as you well know. To know in advance might be to give less, to care less, to perform less well. And your effort is *necessary!* Doubt not that what you are doing is of great importance, as important as anything you ever dreamed of doing when such dreams were will-of-the-wisp wishing.

Frank: Very well, I'll soldier on. Again, you have my sincere and profound gratitude for your continuing assistance. I will do my best; I'm sure we all will.

The best is all that can be asked. Doubt not that your best, Mary's best, Elena's best, [my wife's] best, Emily's best, Bob's best, Bob Monroe's best, adds up. To reverse the famous saying, to assure the *defeat* of evil, or of what we would call bad times, all that is necessary is for the forces of good *not* to do nothing.

– 24 –

Exploring past-life reality continued to be among the most absorbing things in this new world I was exploring, but I haven't room to continue detailing it here. If you consider that I have *loose-leaf binders full* of information obtained either in my journals, or directly on the computer, or by transcription from audio tapes—not counting letters to and from Mary—perhaps you can see that it is impossible to recount the process. The point is, Mary and I searched, separately and together, helped each other, and our internal guidance gave us additional clues and nudged us in certain directions. But assuming that you came to this book looking for a sense of what is possible, rather than merely for tales that might or might not be true, a full recounting would be of little use even if it were possible to provide one.

EIGHT
Inner Connection

I had looked forward to doing the Guidelines program with Emily, but by the time March came around she had made it clear that she didn't believe anything I said about the "John and Clara" lifetime or about the abilities I had so rapidly acquired, and had insisted that I never contact her again. I complied, thinking, "Maybe some other lifetime."

Saturday, March 20, 1993, finally arrived, and I made my way back to The Monroe Institute again. On the way, I revisited the old house off Route 6, thinking—since it was Saturday, and my previous visits had been on Fridays—that maybe I would be able to see the old couple who lived there, see if they knew anything of its history, see if the cabin was built in 1768.

What made me think it was an old couple living there? But an elderly couple it was. The man was very friendly, let me climb up into the old house—climbed up with me, in fact. Two rooms on the bottom, two on top, just as I'd known. Filled with junk. General air of neglect, which somehow seemed appropriate. Over the next four years, I brought several people to see the house, and nearly all of them remarked that it gave off an oppressive air.

That oppressive atmosphere persisted until 1997, when it was cleared away as a result (I am convinced) of something I was led to do at a TMI program, as I shall relate in due course.

In 1993 all I could do was take down the lot and deed number, which the owner graciously supplied, and promise myself to investigate its history at some later time. Then I continued on to the institute.

– 2 –

At TMI, two of my buddies from Gateway, Len and Andrew, are there, and Bob McCulloch is training again. We begin comparing notes. Len tells me that in Gateway he patterned that he would achieve prosperity. In the following thirty days, he says, sales of a software program he wrote quadrupled, as a major vendor bundled his program. A powerful indicator of the strength of the tools we have been given. And a reminder—though I am as yet a long way from really absorbing the lesson—that we can lay down mental patterns that bring physical things, practical things, like, for instance, business cash flow. It reminds me that the circumstances of our lives are more within our control than we commonly realize.

When Bob Monroe talks to us after supper, one of the things he strongly suggests is that during the Guidelines course, we remember to use the left brain. As he puts it, "Wallow for a while, then let the worm in." That is, first wallow in sensation—go with the pattern, use the right brain for perception—then use the worm of left-brain logic to *analyze*.

I noted the suggestion, but the program was long over before I learned to follow it. My Guidelines was very productive, but I was enjoying the free use of the right brain so much, I neglected the left brain entirely. It would have been better if I had paid more attention. Or so I think now. Who knows? Maybe it was a necessary corrective, maybe an expensive (or inexpensive or invaluable) detour. In the long run this is more or less a meaningless distinction. The guys Upstairs really do seem to know what they are doing in guiding us—as I repeatedly realized over the next few years.

What I chiefly hear and remember of all Bob says to us this night is that in Guidelines we are going to discover who we really are; that we are going inside. This sounds perfect to me: This is just where I thought we *should* be going.

Participants at Guidelines each get a lab session, I find out—a session in the black box. And we determine who gets their session, and when, simply by "letting the universe decide." That is, we draw lots. The trainers put slips of paper containing times and dates into a box, and pass the box around, assuring us that we will each get the time we want. I want mine to be when I have gotten as much as possible out of the course, so I want it to be on the last day. Sure enough: Thursday morning, the next to last session. I am quite pleased about that.

– 3 –

All night the Hemi-Sync sleep processor has me lying there awake, trying to sleep, just as on Saturday night at Gateway, except this time there are intervals of unconsciousness. A dream comes:

> *Bob McCulloch and I among others are in a kitchen somewhere. I say something to one of the food workers and she replies in a way that makes me very aware of her perception of the difference between "them" and "us" in her mind. Later Bob and I pass each other and he says something to me and I say, "Yes sir," sort of just noting him, but he recognizes the air of sadness and queries it.*

Even in the dream, I didn't know where the sadness came from. I ask, "Gentlemen, what's going on in that dream?"

There are two worlds, one upper and one lower. You are now in a different part of the world than you have ever lived in, and part of you still identifies with the other part. This is good and is to be remembered, valued, and kept. You are not an officer among other ranks, though you *are*. Be both, be neither, be your unique self, as all ranks are external. You've all been called here, as last time, and all judgments cease.

Frank: I don't at all feel out of place.

No. All places are yours, which means though, no place is yours. The son of man, remember, had no place in which to lay his head. That is what that means. One whose place is everywhere has no one place.

Frank: How much did I do right or wrong (or well or badly, if that is preferred) last night.

You aren't being graded, but your meaning is taken. You were yourself, clumsy or smooth, in tune or wandering. That's all that is required: sincerity, honesty, caring. You listened to inner signals telling you to slow down, to become quiet, et cetera. Nothing wrong there.

Frank: Did Mary and I fix [my roommate's] lungs? [I had noticed that he had what he called a persistent sinus infection, and had offered to try, with Mary's help from a distance, to get rid of it for him.]

You felt the congestion yourself when you awoke—why ask when the answer will be apparent when he awakes? If he knows or doesn't know won't matter to you—or will it?

Frank: Matters to me if I'm inaccurately perceiving.

That is not a question at the moment.

– 4 –

I realize that I don't like the sleep tape because it doesn't let me change focus at will—and saying that helps me realize how far I've come in three months. Talking to Andrew and Len, especially, reminds me how far we've *all* come, on different paths. They each invented tricks to change frequencies. Andrew uses The Gentlemen Upstairs constantly to solve problems—college coursework particularly, but not exclusively. And he says he is working on winning the lottery by asking his future self to tell him the winning numbers—an ingenious idea. (But one that hasn't worked, at least so far.) Len has been getting in touch with emotions and problems he didn't know he had.

I write, "There's something about the energy here. It's like living in the future; I can't describe it better than that. Or as if someone from the future had designed it. And something from *our* future recognizes and responds to it. There is a calm sense of something different."

But all the first morning, Sunday, I drift through the tape exercises, to my disgust. I came with such high expectations, and nothing is happening! It is true, in one exercise I relate to several other inner personalities. But I suddenly realize that I haven't been asking my Higher Self for guidance. And I realize I forgot to use the anchoring technique. I go to lunch discouraged.

A tape introduces us to Monroe's method of healing, but Mary and I are already doing remote healing together, and the TMI method of visualization seems an unnecessary complication. I have no interest in it. By the time we gather in David Francis Hall after supper, I note that I am "considerably more chastened than I was yesterday—or even this morning." I go to 21 and write, "Gentlemen, the insight I got at dinner—that I depend too much on Mary for my purpose—is that accurate?"

Accurate in one sense. Certainly it prevents you needing to find your own inherent purpose if you can just go off to visit. But not accurate in that *your* own purpose—*our* own purpose—is ingrained in your being.

– 5 –

Case in point. The trainers have us pair up for what they call "Paired Intuitive Questioning." I pick a woman in her sixties. We are each to ask five questions, which the other will answer "intuitively." I suggest (figuring that this will reduce performance anxiety) that she and I alternate asking and answering, rather than consecutively doing five in a row, and this is what we do. We each write down five questions.

Her first question gets a direct answer from me, in the form of visuals. "You are describing the road to my house!" she says. Then, "You are describing my living room!" And the answers I give her make sense to her. It is startling enough to destroy her doubts; as for me, I didn't have any to start with. And her answers to me—given with great hesitation and even apologies—are right on the nail. (Her questions and my answers are her business.) My questions, and her answers, as I write them down at the time:

1. How will I find the group with whom to work?
   "Be patient. Be kind. Be pleasant. Smile. Be relaxed, at ease. Not pressured. Not trying to prove anything. Confident. Sure of your self, your knowledge and abilities. Calm surety."
   She also got an image of four soft white tubes filled with light, against a gold-yellow background. We don't get the image's significance, but when we put it to the group, it becomes obvious. "A light fixture," Len says. "The four elements," another says. Someone says that gold is the color of healing, and I realize that yellow is the color of teaching. Also, the four tubes are in parallel, not intersecting or conflicting.

2. What do I need to do to remove the remaining barriers to fully opening up?
   "Be good, in a spiritual sense, seeking the highest values. Not misusing. Truly seeking spiritual guidance, not winning the lottery. Seek truly that which is high and good. Not to compromise. Not to give in to temptation. Work hard at spirituality all day every day in some shape size or form, and to seek with real desire."

3. What is the most important thing I am failing to fully appreciate in my present situation?

"Your wife. Your home. Your livelihood. Your health (the fact that you are healthy). You're young and vigorous and able, intelligent, in an advantageous position, with a good future."

4. Describe my true life task from this point on.

"To be good. Spiritual. To develop spiritual capacities. To flow forth. To bloom. To develop—all spiritual sorts of things. To become more of what you are. To become a mystic. To be fruitful and multiply [not in the sense of offspring but] to be a blossoming to other people. To pass powers and abilities on to others. To bless those you come in contact with. And to give them grace. To develop so that the light that shines from you gives peace and blessing to all who come in contact with you. Peace and wholeness."

5. What is it that I am becoming?

"A saint."

She says no more than those two words, and I have no wish to talk about it; but when she says them, something in me nods assent; that had been my childhood ambition.

(A digression on saints: If sainthood is a matter of following other people's rules, I'm not a likely candidate. But if sainthood can be defined as the state of being in continuous communication with the divine within us; if it is living determined to harm no one intentionally; if it is developing our potential as best we can without thinking we on the Downstairs level deserve the credit—isn't sainthood an attainable aim for anyone of goodwill, pretty much regardless of belief? It should be obvious that I don't regard sainthood as having much to do with recognition by other people—let alone institutions—of one's inner state. As I always say, we can't judge other people's lives because we don't have the data. I smile, thinking of W. B. Yeats's father speaking before a hostile audience in Ireland.

"This island of saints," he said, and when they cheered, added, "of plaster saints." I think following other people's rules is for plaster saints. I would still like to be a saint; but not a plaster saint.)

Now, note that my partner in this exercise *believed*, before we began, that some people could communicate intuitively; she *believed*, theoretically, that she herself could. But when I told her that her initial answer was deeply meaningful to me—and when she heard me describing the physical appearance of her house—she was so astonished, it was funny. Big difference between belief and knowing. And hardest for her to believe was that she herself had been the conduit for valid information. It's a funny world; we are all so ready to believe that others are in touch, and so little ready to believe that we ourselves are.

I note also that at Guidelines, after getting no results from tapes, I got results from working with another living in-the-physical human being. Slow learners repeat classes.

– 6 –

As in Gateway, I am among the last to go to bed and am the first up Monday morning. It strikes me, sitting up in the early morning quiet, the *goodness* of the people there. No one comes to these programs seeking power or wealth or—particularly— gain for self at the expense of others. The process self-selects out those who think in such terms. Those who are left are not perfect—what good would the process be if only the perfect could profit from it?—but they are *good*. (And it looks like Mary and I may have fixed my roommate's sinus infection.)

Monday's first two exercises go unremarked. I run around outside, barefoot in the remains of the snow and ice, successfully relying on Focus 10 to protect me. At one point I am sitting on the wall at the corner of the building by the bell, and several guys are nearby. I dare them to try to hit me with a snowball. Inexplicably, they can't; I am deflecting the snowballs with my mind. The proof of this, oddly, comes when Andrew burns one in that I don't see till the last minute. That one gets me in the ribs. An interesting experience. I'm still looking to find the limits to what we can do with our minds, and not finding them.

The day's third exercise, to bring us into contact with what they call the Inner-Self Helper, or (in the inescapable jargon) ISH, makes clear to me that I am already in contact. I realize that my real task here (and from now on) is with people and not with the CHEC unit. Among other things, I get a channeled message stating clearly that my example is important to all around me, for better or worse, from now on.

$$-7-$$

Most of what went on that week does not belong here. Indeed, much of it is lost and gone forever, like Clementine, because by midweek I was getting too lazy, too contented, to make notes. But some islands in the stream of that experience seem worth noting before we look at my session in the black box.

- My roommate Joe was in a pottery class once, he told me, repeatedly trying and failing to throw a pot. It occurred to him to ask, "What would it feel like if I had done this tens of thousands of times?"—and threw it successfully for the first time. I wonder, what *wouldn't* that idea work for?

- I found out that the two tapes I clicked out on contain encoded signals that are supposed to lead to out-of-body travel. Apparently out I went, bringing back no notes from my travels.

- During the last tape before supper on Tuesday, I got a

terrific headache that I thought of as a channeler's headache—the result, one might say, of running too much energy through wiring that hadn't yet been upgraded. It was painful to the point of nausea, and I didn't know how I was going to get through the tape. The pain was still there at supper, but when I told trainer Bob McCulloch, he very simply counted me out again (that is, brought me fully back to C1) and manipulated a pressure point in the web of my right thumb. The pain was gone instantly! Pretty amazing. The following day, I was able to stop another man's headache in the same way. And although I didn't know it at the time, this was a milestone, marking the first time I was able to work in person, rather than at a distance, to help someone with a physical problem. In this as in so many things, I experienced things in the opposite order that most do. (I say little here about the development—or more accurately, the rediscovery—of my abilities to heal, not because I think the ability or the story unimportant, but because the other things I am discussing seem to me more fundamental, more universal. In any case, once you accept that we are the possessors of unsuspected powers, specifics are less important.)

• The same day, a different kind of healing. The woman with whom I had done the Paired Intuitive Questioning exercise said she was exhausted. I told her, "I will give you some energy," and had her hold her hand straight out, between my hands but not touching them. Then I somehow propelled energy over to her, not knowing how I did it—or how I *knew* how to do it—as a gift of love, not as a parlor trick.

- After supper, we were doing a tape consisting of Metamusic (music with Hemi-Sync tones in the background) without coded instructions or guidance. Nothing was happening, and finally I got enough sense to ask where everybody went, so to speak. The Gentlemen Upstairs pointed out to me that I hadn't been using my left brain, and I realized that somehow I had gotten seriously off track. I was looking for powers and abilities, when what I am to demonstrate is the reality and power of love. I wondered, "Is this a cop-out, an excuse for not finding what I went looking for?" They replied, "How can that be when in fact you *have* those powers? The [ability to see] auras, et cetera, is in your power now. But to have something that you use for the wrong reason or in the wrong way is worse than to have nothing at all." True enough— but in fact, as of five years later still I do not see auras consistently—which makes this statement not so much a promise as a pretended description of accomplished fact that does not square with reality.

– 8 –

Thursday morning three of us walk up Roberts Mountain Road from 6:30 to 7:30 A.M. Then comes exercise class and breakfast, and it's almost time for my lab session in the black box. I am nervous. "Gentlemen, any advice on how to use the experience?"

Keep your intensity high while yet being relaxed. If you can live at a higher vibratory rate while not living at tension's breaking point, you can do anything any reasonable person would want to do.

I ask, "Is there something I should ask that I haven't thought of?" They say, "Much, but nothing that will hinder." They tell me to be intense, yet relaxed.

So I go to the lab. Lab director Skip Atwater takes time with me to see where I am starting from. I tell him the things that have been happening to me; he says he can see why I am excited. He leads me into the isolation booth that I call the "black box," a sound- and vibration-insulated chamber. I climb the few steps up and then inside, and he helps me to climb carefully onto the waterbed. I get the earphones on, and he lowers a microphone to within inches of my head. He attaches three wires to the fingers of my right hand, then shuts the two doors (one inside the other), leaving me in darkness. After a moment he is talking to me through the headset, and it is much as though I were in a CHEC unit in the training center building.

I am very relaxed. After the initial period of preparation, when I am well in Focus 10, I ask what is the most appropriate thing for me to do in Focus 10.

All proceedings are recorded, and the following notes are from my copy of the cassette made then:

I immediately got a sense of a lot of bare trees, a wintertime forest. Woods. It felt connected to the John and Clara lifetime in the 1700s. I wondered, Why was I looking at forests? There came a sentence saying that I can't see the trees for the forest.

At first I took this to mean that they wanted me to look at something specific in the scene, in more detail, but nothing further came, and I followed a feeling that I should move to Focus 12, and then to 15. I asked if it was appropriate to try to heal leftover stuff between Clara and John at this point, if only from my end. I got that I should say to her that it was a long time ago, that I'm sorry and that it's time to give up all that, and to release it. I was told to hold the love and give up the pain and the loss and the frustration. I seriously doubt-

ed if she was consciously aware of my contacting her—of our contacting her, because I felt Mary's presence with me—and in fact I later learned that indeed she was not aware.

In Focus 21, I asked, "Gentlemen, what's on your minds this morning?" and the words came to me. Sometimes haltingly they came; sometimes a few at a time, sometimes fluently. I spoke them as they came, and I suppose this was my first conscious communication with The Gentlemen Upstairs. They said I had reached a point of departure; that I was going to see what the rest of my life looked like, "and what it looks like will be a lot like the previous except that the point of view will have totally changed and therefore the whole thing will totally change." They said that living out a conscious intention to give love and demonstrate love totally colors what you see and what you get. "It is true that you have everything you need and that all you need to do is concentrate on how to use it, why to use it, when to use it, rather than 'will I have it, will I get it, does it exist' and so forth."

Gently they reminded me that "there is such a thing as overreliance even on higher powers"—meaning overreliance on right-brain rather than partnership with the left-brain functioning. "We can guide, but you can act. Part of acting is thinking and analyzing and dissecting. Isn't all perception of patterns. Which is the initial message: You can't see the trees for the forest." They said, "You like trees, take your time with individual trees," meaning, spend less attention on what went on in the CHEC units and more on my fellow participants.

I asked for the correct name of David and his book, and asked why names are so hard.

"It is partly as Mary intuited, that he used more than one life—more than one name in his lifetime. He had a journalist's name, a pen name, that he used, which was David Peters, which sounded more English, because there was a certain residual prejudice against Welshmen, not a prejudice so much as an expectation of his readers that he didn't care to arouse. And neither did his editors. His name was closer to Powys, but the name on the book was David Peters. The name of the book: His title for it was always Waterborne Reflections. *It was like a travel memoir. Really it was disguised essays about people and how he saw people, but it was in the form of a travel narrative."*

I pressed them farther, but without success. After a few detours, they did say that "the feeling of the book is more important than the title and we want you to look more. If you had the title right now, that would be an easy confirmation, and if you could find the book, then you would say, 'Aha, it works.' On the other hand, you already know it works, and if you found the book too fast, perhaps there would be a certain amount of inflation, and perhaps that wouldn't be good for what's going on."

At which point I report a feeling as if I were spinning. Calmly (Skip is always calm) Skip says, "Welcome this energy in and ask what it is you're to be learning from this."

When I do, I get a knowing, after a pause, and say this:

"It's an access of more energy because I just opened something up. I just picked, I just—what happened? I

just—got with the program, somehow? I just, when they said that, I began to realize that's right, that I've been looking for the book because then it would be an objective outside proof of something that I already know. And what happened? I must have just released that because I realized that what I am is the proof of what I know. Thank you, good suggestion."

I remember that I want to ask about the focus levels left undescribed in the Monroe system. So I ask first about Focus 18, and as soon as I ask if I can go to 18, I get a headache right behind my eyes. Skip says, again calmly, "Welcome this energy in and ask what is the meaning of this." As soon as he does, the headache goes away, so I conclude it had been out to get my attention. I ask what they are trying to tell me.

I got a vision of a light blue light like a very pale blue neon light, with a solid on top and a solid plane underneath "and the light is in the middle a long way away." In fact, I had an impression that the blue was amid terrific distance and space. "It's really like it opens up into interstellar space," I said. [And in the desperate grammar that follows perhaps you can get a sense of what I felt as I attempted to express the words and, mostly, feelings, that flowed through me].

"It's like it's saying you've been living here for a long, long time. And that relates to the outer-space thing, sort of. You've been living here for a long time. Like, oh, it's like home, you know? And I'm getting the sense that they're talking about Level 18. Is that what you mean, gentlemen? Level 18 is a natural plateau for me, where I have been more than once in writing. That I will go to 18 not knowing really what it is or why it is, but that

when I write poetry or sometimes—the part of Messenger *that Mary thought was channeled was written from 18 and it is my one of my, it is been, it is my accustomed, my most something home. Oldest home. Which I hear as meaning that I was in 18 a lot as a kid, not knowing it. . . .*

"How can I find out what 18 specifically, what kind of abilities or more like what kind of point of view 18— [I laugh.] Ha, ha, ha, they're laughing *at me! Hah! The question was going to be, how can I find out what kind of a point of view it gives you, and of course that's the point of view that I had! Okay.*

[I laugh again.] "That's the point of view that's inclined to see the forest and not see the trees. [Pause] When I was a boy I was very aware of, what? What do you call it? I saw the patterns more than I could see the real things in front of me. I wondered about all kinds of things, because nobody saw it the same way. And, that's very interesting. Eighteen is the well of my creativity this particular lifetime. That's where I should be going. That's very satisfying.

"And they remind me of the times that I spent in the woods. The woods were my home, too. I'd actually forgotten there was a time before books. Well, Skip, you said [in our pre-briefing session] something might come in out of left field, and it certainly did. Very useful."

These interactions, and others unrecorded here, have used up almost all the time we had. But Skip suggests that I "ask if there isn't a special message for you just today." I go to Focus 21, and after a pause quote them to this effect:

"The message is the same message that you've been hearing more than once and have been hearing and we recognize that you've been hearing it: Love and persevere and continue and just keep on. With endurance comes success."

As Skip is counting me down, I suddenly get a great headache on the right side. When I ask them what is going on, I get a sense that the message is, "The experiment's not over yet!" I laugh and say, "Okay. I think that was in the nature of, 'pay attention.'" After which Skip counts me back to C1—normal consciousness—and eventually disentangles me from various wires.

I return to the debriefing room—they are just getting ready for the Thursday morning silent walk—feeling half in another world. And in a very real sense I never went back to the world I'd left that morning, for I never have left the newer world I entered. Have never again had the illusion of being alone. Never so far, anyway. Never ever, I hope.

– 9 –

At supper at one point, four of us sitting at a table have fallen into a comfortable silence. Bob McCulloch looks over at me with an indescribable expression on his face. I ask what's going on, and he says he's just enjoying my energy. In response to a further question, he says how much I have changed since Gateway. He's too tactful to spell it out, but I know that he's referring to how open I am now, and how closed-off I was then.

– 10 –

After supper we get a long talk by Bob Monroe, lasting past 9 P.M., then closing ceremonies, and it's time for quiet talk. At midnight, just when I am ready to go to bed, my roommate and I go for a walk in total darkness down a road we can't see. On our return, as we get near to the center, we can "feel" the positive vibrations of the hundreds of people who have come here to work on themselves. He and I sit up talking till 2 A.M.

After breakfast Friday I see Bob Monroe for just a moment, then drive Len to Charlottesville, stopping along the way to look at the old cabin (with the tolerant permission of the lady whose husband I had met a week earlier. She tells me that she has asked her husband for years to tear the structure down.) Len and I have lunch together—and I inadvertently eat meat again, just as I did after Gateway. I get him to the airport and take the long drive home.

– 11 –

I count myself fortunate to have attended two TMI programs while Bob Monroe was still alive, and I regret that I did not make notes of his talks to our Gateway or Guidelines groups. Some experiences make so immediate and deep an impact that one can't be bothered to make notes. In fact, taking notes never occurred to me. Because I *didn't* make notes, I can't summarize his talks, and can't even remember which things were said when. But I have two vivid memories, one from Gateway, one from Guidelines.

At Gateway, he was talking to us one night in the debrief room—the conference room off what was then the dining room. Probably in response to a question, he said that all of us were there at this time because we had *chosen* to be there. As he put it, we had chosen to be on stage rather than be in the audience when the once-in-many-lifetimes event took place. This, he said, was because we were deeply curious about the process. He said (and well do I remember it!) that whenever we read or talked about the upcoming disruption of ordinary life, "You *say*, 'How horrible,' but you *think*, 'How interesting!'" I got a fit of the giggles—something that doesn't happen to me just every day—and couldn't stop, because it so accurately described my own (perhaps cold-blooded) reaction to the subject. I had often thought, in some impatience at the Downstairs life I led, "Enough of this old stuff! Bring on the new world." And here was Bob Monroe describing my reaction exactly. I continued helplessly laughing, "Hee, hee, hee," for several seconds, until Bob craned his head around to see who had gotten the point so personally.

My second memory of Bob has him rather than me in my mental spotlight. It was the only time I saw him overcome by emotion. His reaction was quiet, for Bob was a man who kept his emotions under firm rein whenever possible. Nonetheless it was strong, and I remember the moment as clear as day after more than five years. Nor do I expect ever to forget it.

He was talking to our Guidelines group, again about the upcoming extensive disruption of life that is called, as shorthand, "the earth changes." I think he was pointing out that we would need all the mental resources we could muster if we were to successfully come through those times. Suddenly he stopped, overcome, and said something like this: "I talk about what is coming, the difficulties and the dangers, and to see you all calmly sitting there . . ." I knew what he meant. We were sitting there, not panicked, not fearing for our lives, not thinking about survival. Instead we were thinking about the new world we hoped we would have a chance to help build afterward.

It choked him up. Even at the time I thought, "Well, who has given us more to work with than you?" He got a sense, at that moment—or at least I hope he did—of how wide-ranging an effect his efforts were having, and would have unpredictably into the future.

NINE
(Non) Ordinary Life

After I did Guidelines in 1993, I saw Bob Monroe occasionally—usually in connection with Ed Carter—but never really had the long heart-to-heart with him that I wanted. Probably it never would have happened. Our lives weren't organized that way.

Certainly, I had other things to occupy my time. Shortly after I returned home from Guidelines, Mary arrived in Virginia. She took up residence on the Eastern Shore, moving in with Elena as a paying boarder. This was my bright idea. They were both psychics, weren't they? They could help each other, couldn't they? I had advanced it diffidently to each of them, and each of them had embraced it enthusiastically.

What I hadn't taken into account (because it never crossed my thick mind) was that Elena, associating me with the lost friend I resembled, must have convinced herself that she was in love with me. But I wasn't in love with Elena, I was in love with Mary (even though I was still married, and did not realize that I could free myself, and therefore had persuaded myself that nothing could come of it). It was almost a relief—but *only* almost—that the house on the Eastern Shore wasn't real close to my office in Norfolk, being seventy miles and a nine-dollar toll each way. Still, I figured it was closer than California, and although we couldn't have a romance, we still had work to do. At least, so TGU continually said.

I was oblivious to the cross-currents I had helped set up. Elena's attitude toward Mary quickly soured. She became increasingly bizarre and hurtful, finally one day throwing Mary's possessions onto a porch—damaging some of them in the process—and locking Mary out of the house. (Even months later, I didn't understand why this had happened, until finally my friends Upstairs explained it to me as I have explained it here.)

After *that* experience, Mary moved to Williamsburg—which was still out of comfortable driving distance. She tried again (as she had many years previously) to work at Colonial Williamsburg. All that year and into 1994, she continued to scramble to find or create a position that would employ her artistic, scholarly, and/or literary abilities. And she did, in fact, secure a position at CW as an interpreter, portraying (who else?) Martha Jefferson. But if she was subconsciously trying to structure her life to re-create something of that fondly remembered lifetime in colonial America, Upstairs had other plans. Repeatedly she would seem to be on the point of getting what she wanted. Repeatedly the prospect would recede, or prove illusory, until finally it became apparent to her that her work, this lifetime, was not in Virginia but in California, where she had been born. Besides, there was the draw of her children. Although her ex-husband had custody, she stayed in touch with them, and pined for them, and finally found herself unable to remain away from them.

– 2 –

But while she was here, we did some good work that could only have been done in person. In the spring and summer of 1993 we got together several times for a series of Paired Intuitive Questioning sessions. Working with two tape recorders (as insurance against electronic mishap, and to allow ourselves the convenience of each having a copy of the tapes) we went Upstairs together and went exploring. How better to look into past lives?

Now, one might think, if Mary is psychic, why does she need assistance? But working together proved very helpful to both of us. One would say something, or ask something, and the other would have a knowing, and would say something that in turn would spark the other to further knowings. The shared energy was greater, and the joint effort had the effect of aiding us to keep our minds focused on a given topic, not drifting as one might if working alone. To give just the flavor of the interaction, I include this small excerpt from the very first of our sessions, on May 22, 1993, about six weeks after Mary arrived from California. Right from the first, we zeroed in on David.

– 3 –

Frank: I wonder if you can find the most immediately important lifetime and why. Of mine.

Mary: David. The Welshman. For the reason of his searching. The tools that he used on his search, the things that he learned how to do, will teach you, right now—not merely in the manifestation of finding his book, but in how to follow and how to do what you're doing now. . . .

Frank: What was it he was searching for?

Mary: The way to connect things together, the people. The way to make seemingly disparate things show their true connection. And he did find it. . . . You have the tools again. You're using them now. He's always there, saying, "Remember this? This is how we did this." And this is where the brainstorms come from; always there, showing you.

Frank: You're telling me that David went a lot deeper and farther inward than anybody around him ever suspected. The external was just fooling around, while he was doing it. And he was fooling around with magic—In Paris?

With Yeats and all?

Mary: Yeah.

Frank: How could he?

Mary: He was a young man.

Frank: Yeah, he would have been. But Yeats was an older man!

Mary: Not at that time. Not at that time.

Frank: A little older. A few years.

Mary: Older than him.

Frank: Yes. In their twenties, or close, I think.

Mary: Yeah.

Frank: And he was there in Paris, I don't know how long, and he was fooling around. That was before he went to South Africa. If he went to South Africa. Do you get any sense of that? That he did or didn't? That was a long time ago and I'm not convinced that it was right.

Mary: Rhodesia.

Frank: Mm-hmm. Way inland. And he was—one time I got, working as a farm laborer, but I don't think that's right, I think he was working as a—an academic poor white, as somewhere between a journalist and a secretary.

Mary: Yes, I was just going to say, he was somebody's secretary.

Frank: Oh, *somebody's!* Not a traveling, but a—

Mary: In conjunction with somebody with a high position for a certain amount of time.

Frank: So the position just gradually tapered off? Ended. It isn't that he just—but he also got tired of staying in one place.

Mary: Yes.

Frank: So he wandered down—took ship again.

Mary: [Laughs.]

Frank: Reminds you of somebody you know?

Mary: [Laughs.]

Frank: And I suddenly think that he didn't go to China first off, I think he went to India. . . . But I don't know if it's the map or if it's real. Not India, maybe—Burma?

Mary: Burma.

Frank: What in the world was he doing in Burma? [Laughs.] I think he asked himself the same question, actually, and he left. I don't think he stayed there very long. What did he go to Burma for? Something about the plantations, I think. Was he wanting to see them?

Mary: There was something with somebody in England.

Frank: Was he writing up rubber plantations? Was he shipping back color pieces about it?

Mary: Yes.

Frank: And did not like something about it. Something about the labor aspect of it.

Mary: [Laughs.] Oh yes.

Frank: Coolies. Or some equivalent.

Mary: Yes. Good.

Frank: Couldn't stand it. Realized he was about to make himself very unpopular and decided to leave first.

Mary: Well, he would have been branded as a flaming socialist. [Laughs.] And that wouldn't have been very popular.

Frank: I think he might have just barely seen Singapore, and then gone.

Mary: Then he went north.

Frank: Siam?

Mary: No.

Frank: Annam?

Mary: No.

Frank: Up to China?

Mary: Just up, up.

Frank: Cambodia?

Mary: Calcutta

Frank: Oh, in India? He went back west again?

Mary: And then down and around, through Nepal and down the southern route and up into China.

Frank: Overland.

Mary: He tried to get into Tibet. It was the faster route.

Frank: But he was coming from British territory and they weren't wild about that.

Mary: No. So he had to take—it took a long time.

Frank: He had time.

Mary: Well, he could have gone back and taken a boat, but he wanted to see—

Frank: He liked mountains, I think. No he liked—Oh, you know who's bleeding through here: his predecessor [Smallwood, the roving transcendentalist], whatever his name is—

Mary: Mm-hmm.

Frank: because he liked being—

Mary: —in the wilderness.

Frank: Yeah. Well, that's not the right way to put it; to him, the wilderness was the middle of the city. [We laugh.] He liked being with God, although I don't think he ever would have used that word. I suspect he was probably— you know, the latest thing, kind of thing; God would be superstition to him, or that would be all he'd hear of it, so he wouldn't fool with it.

Mary: An atheist, in his own definition.

Frank: Yeah, which means that he, as somebody said, believed in no-God and worshiped him. And that bridge, I keep getting Canton, I don't know, but I never got anything else, no other cities. He was standing on this stone bridge in Canton. . . . Oh my lord! I just remembered, twenty years ago when I worked in the library they showed us a film about China and the opening picture of the film was a stone bridge across a river.

Mary: [Laughs.]

Frank: They never identified the city, but I bet that's what it was. Although at the time I thought it was Shanghai, I don't think it was.

Mary: Funny how these things work.

Frank: But what in the world was he doing in China? You know what? He wasn't just sightseeing, he was— That's why he wanted to go to Tibet, of course. He was looking the same way Gurdjieff did, he was looking for secrets.

Mary: Mm-hmm.

Frank: This implies that somebody was sending him?

Mary: Mm-hmm.

Frank: I mean, directing him?

Mary: Oh yeah.

Frank: The Order of the Golden Dawn?

Mary: Yep.

Frank: Would they have a record?

Mary: Yes, they will.

Frank: Would they have his name? Or would they have him coded?

Mary: No, they would have his name.

Frank: And yet, I've gotten that he was much more concerned with things like, painting and sculpture and human artifacts, rather than things like trees and wilderness and— you know, natural beauty; he'd done that route.

Mary: No. Along the way he picked up languages and managed to fit in with the people. It helped that he was not some blond Anglo-looking. . . .

Frank: He was probably sort of scrubby-looking like me.

Mary: Dark.

Frank: And not high. I mean, not tall. What you said about [the] Saint David's Day [parade] being five miles long and five feet high. And like [our mutual friend] Danny [Lliteras], in fact. And internally as well, because he did fit in; because he didn't look at himself as a superior European.

Mary: No.

Frank: He looked at himself as a searcher too. He didn't fit in with them—either!

I laughed, and the phone rang, interrupting us, as if to underline the point.

– 4 –

From that beginning, that day, we ranged far and wide for three sides of tape, about an hour and a half. We investigated David's life and those of several others—some connected to me, some to her. Long story.

Working together for many days—though those days were widely separated—we established much about her lives and mine; how they interacted and how they went their separate ways. What factors went into the making of the various personalities, and what effect those lives have had on the ones we are living now. It was a remarkable exercise, and I encourage you to try it yourself, if you have available a talented and sympathetic companion. If you don't have one on hand—ask Upstairs. When the student is ready, the teacher will appear; it's just that often the teacher appears in unlikely guises.

In Mary's and my case the love we felt for each other—past lives and present, if you care to put it that way—greatly facilitated, not to say fueled, the process, especially when added to the sexual frustration stemming from the fact that we were not lovers physically. In this too we were fortunate (or were steered by our friends Upstairs, more likely). Shared magical endeavors, I learned much later, are grounded—that is, either ended or prevented—by sexual union. The Gentlemen Upstairs had told us from the beginning that this time we had other fish to fry than romance. Not that the intense fascination inherent in having someone else to work with didn't cause plenty of strain! Particularly in my marriage. But I'd been waiting my whole life for something like this, hardly daring to believe that it could happen, and here it was. I didn't feel I could give it up, however unfortunate or uncomfortable the side effects, for of course nobody in range of either one of us believed we weren't carrying on a torrid love affair. Not so wrong an assessment, just a matter of definition.

Matters between Mary and me could not have continued indefinitely at such a level of intensity. No matter the amount of work we were accomplishing Upstairs, the strain Downstairs was considerable. Fortunately—I suppose fortunately—in August she met at Williamsburg someone else she had a past with, and we turned away from romance. This had the unfortunate side effect—I suppose unfortunate—of stopping all work between us for a while, as she turned her attention elsewhere. By then we had done nine taping sessions, however, and had accumulated a good deal of information on my and her other lives.

Again, this is not the place to detail this information, particularly as I have given so little time to attempt to prove any of the information as it applied to me. The net effect was not to provide us with information with which to prove anything to anybody, but to give us a great deal of information about ourselves, our psychological makeup, our motivations, hopes, and fears. That's a lot. Even if the stories were someday proved to be Upstairs or Downstairs fabrications, they would have been worthwhile in what they taught us. And in going through the process, I learned to have a greater confidence in what I knew Upstairs.

– 5 –

Before Mary returned to California she and I did participate in one other experiment that deserves notice. Early in 1994 I asked Skip Atwater if the institute could use the black box to detect telepathy. That is, could they wire up two people, have them attempt to communicate with each other, and measure whatever happened. Skip replied that my inquiry was quite timely, as the institute had just acquired new software that would allow them to wire up two people together in the black box, and was anxious to test it. He and Mary and I coordinated our schedules, and one day in February 1994 I drove her up to the institute and Skip and Dave Wallis wired us up and put us in the black box—the isolation chamber. If memory serves, Mary and I were the first two people to be tested there on this equipment.

The results were extremely suggestive. Mary and I went Upstairs to communicate, one to the other, and as we did, our brain waves were measured. Analyzing them later, they found no evidence of synchrony in our brain-wave patterns. It isn't like we got into resonance of some kind. (Mary, told this, said that's because when one was pitching, the other was catching. But whether a reciprocal pattern of some kind could be discovered, I don't know.)

What was of interest is that when Mary went "out" for something from Upstairs, her brain waves went up beyond the capacity of the instrumentation to follow. She went "out there" for information, then "came back" to deliver it. Two quite different wave forms. Mine, on the other hand, showed a very different pattern altogether. I didn't go "out" as far as Mary did, but I demonstrated what they said was a rare ability to be "here" and "there," Upstairs and Downstairs at the same time, in a sort of permanent split focus. This seemed to describe what we have experienced: She is more powerful, more "natural"; I straddle both worlds.

– 6 –

Another incident from this period was the strange affair of July 2, 1994. (Not the least strange feature is that when I came to write this up, I found that all my documentation was gone. I had had computer files, postings and printouts, and I know where they should be. All gone. Very strange.)

I had been having intense back pain. Excruciating pain. By then, whenever I began to experience apparently uncaused pain, I was suspicious.

I cannot now remember how it was that I first thought to contact Smallwood. Suffice it to say that on July 2, 1994, I did. He was in the battle of Gettysburg, I think. I think he got injured that day. (On a hunch, I had someone look up the members of the Second Minnesota, which incurred eighty-two percent casualties that day, but he was not listed.) My impression is that I seemed to him to be the by-product of delirium. Indeed, maybe it was only because of the pain from his wound—a clubbing on the spine with a rifle butt, or maybe with the barrel—that he was able to perceive my contact. Who knows? Anyway, I remember telling him that the war could be over in the next two days, but probably wouldn't be. I tried to get him to remember hearing the names Grant, Lee, and Appomattox, 1865. I haven't heard from him since. For all I know, it was fantasy, nothing more. But it did have a certain feeling of veracity. Just one more thing in the endless list of things to check into when time and ability permit.

– 7 –

Of course, in my life, as in yours, many more meaningful things happened than can ever be recounted, or even recalled. In 1994 I was occupied mostly with matters involving Hampton Roads, and that long story has little place here. Suffice it to say that we struggled along, repeatedly in trouble, again almost losing the company to debt but somehow surviving. Born to hang, I suppose. My domestic life—of which, you will notice, I say almost nothing here—continued to have its ups and downs. I was always aware that I wanted to be out of my marriage, but could see no way to leave. It seemed impossible emotionally (I had made a commitment, hadn't I?) and financially. So matters continued much as they always had, sometimes better, sometimes worse.

Ed Carter and I continued to talk on the phone, exchange faxed messages and—after a certain point that I can no longer remember—exchange e-mail. He got ever more interested in talking to The Gentlemen Upstairs. He also began to invest in the company, first in the short-term STP loans that he and I invented, then by underwriting a limited line of credit, then by buying preferred stock. Step by step he got more interested in the business and more involved in discussing our problems. By mid-1995 this would lead him to become an owner, under circumstances that enabled—forced—us to reconfigure the company in a more businesslike manner. Just about in time, too. Not only were we short of cash again; the *Conversations With God* phenomenon was about to hit, which would take us several steps up the ladder from being an unknown small company to being—whatever we would become.

And amid all these externals ran the unseen subsurface current. What else could I do to develop my psychic abilities? What else could I learn? Whom could I work with?

– 8 –

A constant thought was that somehow I could find a way to work with Bob Monroe. If only I could figure out what he needed and what I could do. I didn't want to be a trainer, I didn't think, and I knew I didn't want to be a TMI employee. But then, what could I do to help?

In the fall of 1994, thinking about the information on Focus 18 I had been given while in the black box during my Guidelines program, I asked TGU for information on the focus levels the institute never talks about: Focus levels 2, 4, 5, 6, 7, 8, 9, 13, 14, 16, 17, 18, 19, and 20. In late November 1994, Ed Carter and I had lunch with Bob up on Afton Mountain, and I sketched out what TGU had told me. Bob said it sounded right to him, but I looked forward to discussing it with him at greater length, after he had looked at the letter I gave him spelling it out. I thought maybe we could figure out how to test the information.

On February 24, 1995, I drove up to the institute to share the Friday morning breakfast with a graduating Gateway attendee, and afterward I sat with Bob Monroe in the lounge and asked him his reaction to my letter about the focus levels that TMI doesn't use. He sat there and smoked and said he didn't disagree with anything TGU had said about the various levels, but we didn't get to talk in depth because, of course, he was Bob Monroe and everybody who was around wanted some of his time and attention.

– 9 –

That was the last time I saw him. Three weeks later to the day, on Friday morning, March 17, 1995, he died an old man's quiet death in a hospital in Charlottesville, with his children at his side. He died of pneumonia half a year after his seventy-ninth birthday.

As it happened, I was in New York City that day. My friend Sandra Martin had gotten me an invitation to meet Colin Wilson at a party in his honor, and I had come up on the train, rereading *The Mind Parasites* (which will always be, for me, the book that started it all). A major item on my agenda was to try to persuade him to come see the Monroe Institute, but Sandra and I were greeted at our hosts' door with the news that Bob Monroe was gone.

The next morning I bought the Saturday *New York Times,* just to read Bob's obituary—which wasn't there. I thought, "You don't have any idea how important he was, or what he accomplished," and I remembered Emerson saying of Thoreau's death, "The country knows not yet, or in the least part, how great a son it has lost."

A week later, TMI held a memorial service, and I attended. When I returned from it I wrote up some impressions, thinking of those who knew and loved him who couldn't attend. I posted these impressions to the Voyagers mailing list, an Internet group centering on TMI-related stuff that was established in late 1994. I predict that there will come a day when even these notes will have a minor historical importance, strictly because they represent a firsthand account, however inadequate, of what will come to be seen as a historic milestone. In another hundred years, I think, scarcely an educated person on earth will not at least have heard Bob Monroe's name.

– 10 –

March 26, 1995

Dear Friends, here are some notes on the Friday, March 24, 1995, memorial service for Bob, for those friends who couldn't make it in the body.

We drove up to the training center. The unusual began immediately: people directing parking on the lawn. Folding chairs, set up outside the sliding doors of David Francis Hall, faced westward toward that lovely view of the far mountains. Facing the chairs was a microphone and a little platform, and two enormous sound speakers. At a table off to the side were Mark [Certo] and two others, to control the special effects. The day was bright, sunny, with a wind that gusted stiff enough to make us warm on the south side, cold on the north side.

We milled around for a little bit, hugging old friends, looking around to see who could make it. Bob McCulloch was the first person I met, Bob who had been one of my trainers in both Gateway and Guidelines. And there was Karen Malik, a trainer from Guidelines. She and I had last seen each other three weeks before, which was also the last time either of us saw Bob. And so many others were there: Dave Wallis and Skip Atwater, Helen Warring and well, you know, the staff. And there were what I call the extended family, too. Eleanor Friede, nearby residents and associates. Then we all sat down, listening to the Metamusic from the speakers, and waited for the family to file in.

In my experience, religious ceremonies often have at least patches of emotional deadness; places that don't resonate, words that are only empty words. This ceremony, conducted by the Rev. Shay Saint John, had none of this deadness. But then, how could it? The first thing to come over the speakers was Bob's voice, repeating the affirmation he wrote long ago. You may have heard the words once or twice: "I am more than my physical body. . . ."

Rev. Saint John spoke of Bob and then invited each of the family to speak. Bob's brother Emmet; his stepdaughters Penny and Scooter, and Scooter's husband, Joe McMoneagle; his stepson A.J.; his daughters Laurie and Marie. I am sorry I cannot give even a précis of what was said. I used to be a journalist once upon a time, but this day I was not in reporter mode; the words came washing in, affecting me to the core, then washed out, leaving little or nothing in short-term memory. I am left not with the specifics but with visual memories, and with the memory of the emotional impact. Scooter read a poem Nancy (Bob's wife) had written him, I remember that.

Then the family gathered in a circle, holding hands, holding the two white helium-filled balloons that had been whipping around in the wind the entire time. Rev. Saint John told us what would happen and invited us to stand up at the proper moment. Over the speakers came Bob's voice, reading the climactic point of the "Going Home" tapes, advising the dying person that he or she was going to find that he or she was everything he or she had ever learned, ever been. And at a certain point the family released the balloons, and that terrific wind whipped them off to the south. As we had been invited to do, we all stood and watched the balloons fly off, two white points against that deep blue sky, climbing and also covering the ground at an incredible rate, and then they were out of our visual range, and Bob's voice was giving his final advice, telling the departing soul, "Remember. Remember."

– 11 –

"Remember," he said. As though we who are his heirs could ever forget. As though our inner connection could ever cease. We all, each time we come back into this world, set ourselves tasks, some of whose aspects are internal and some external. The greatest tasks take the longest to show their full effects, and are therefore the most easily underrated, and those who accomplish them are underrated correspondingly. It takes a while for people to see what they had in their midst. Bob Monroe set himself a great task, which was basically the transformation of the world. He did the best he could, and his best was pretty good. The day will come when it will be more obvious how much he facilitated; how good his best was.

TEN

Connection Between Lives

Bob Monroe's death wasn't the end of the institute, and it certainly wasn't the end of his lifework. Every Gateway program extends his work to that many more people, as it transforms their lives by opening them to new abilities, new possibilities. Perhaps this applies even more to the graduate programs such as Guidelines and Lifeline.

By the time I came to do Lifeline in July 1995, I was a very different person from the closed-off, Downstairs-bounded individual who had walked into the center two and a half years before. I had gone into Gateway seeking some tangible proof of what I believed, and doubting that such proof was there to be had. In Guidelines, similarly, I had *hoped,* or rather (in light of my Gateway experience) I had *expected* to acquire specific "psychic" new abilities. And this had happened, in that my connection with The Gentlemen Upstairs became a steady, dependable, almost mundane resource. But there was nothing I hoped or expected from Lifeline. I couldn't see any advantage to traveling to Focus 27, and I wasn't particularly interested in retrieving lost souls. I did the program, in the last analysis, mostly because Ed Carter asked me to and made it possible. *Because* I had never intended to do the Lifeline program, I arrived seeking neither abilities nor confirmations nor specific experiences. I was open to whatever might happen. And this, as it happens, is pretty much the ideal way to approach any transformational program (not to say life itself): in a state of expectation, but without specific expectations.

Ed and I roomed together, discussed our experiences, even conducted a joint experiment or two, but of course my notes from that week concern mostly my own experiences rather than his. No point would be served in my attempting to go into every significant thing that happened in Lifeline, as I tried to do for Gateway. Instead, I will follow only certain threads. My purpose is less to give you a sense of the process than to show how certain themes developed themselves, what I learned, and what it means, by implication, to our discussion of what is real.

Sunday

Our first tape Sunday morning introduces the Dolphin Energy Club (DEC) method of healing. In Guidelines, I had resisted Monroe's DEC techniques as needlessly complicated, but I see now the worth of the techniques. The DEC tape will bring us to the mental frequencies used by healers, as a first form of helping others in the physical, before going on to those who are in the nonphysical.

We form images of our physical, mental, and emotional bodies, which TMI calls our Living Body Maps. I am thinking that I should remember to work on healing my teeth, when I receive a vision of a shape like a skull, starting just below my nipples and ending at about my navel. With the vision comes the distinct sense that this is a message for the group in general, not just for me.

I am reluctant to bring this vision and message to the group, for after all we are mostly still strangers, and I don't want to look like I am trying to bolster my own self-importance by imagining that I have a "special message to deliver" to the group. (I suspect that this kind of embarrassment prevents a lot of material of this kind from being delivered.)

Nonetheless, when we meet to debrief the tape I do describe what I saw, and I add that I get a sense that in general we need to put more mental energy into the area of our chest and upper abdomen. Then I say that I had a sense that the message was meant to be given to someone in the group, and I ask, in some embarrassment, if it is meaningful to anybody. I am relieved when a woman about my age named Joyce says that indeed it is. But it is meaningful because she is in remission from breast cancer. The rest of the message is right there, staring me in the face, but I don't see it until forced to, nearly two years later.

The next tape is a Free-Flow Focus 12 (expanded awareness of the physical and nonphysical) with periods for reporting on tape. As usual my consciousness flows to this and that, and I don't necessarily retain all or even much of it. Realizing that it is almost time to start recording brings me to a sharper focus, and I think, "Well, what do I have to report?" The words come. I get that I (and presumably we) should be observing and reporting and weighing the forces around me, in the way that Abraham Lincoln did, for instance. Weigh the strengths of various forces to show what's going on and what's happening.

Then the competing thought comes: Of course, if you do that you have to sacrifice time and attention on the external that might otherwise have been spent strictly on the internal. I go back to my mental floating, and at the second opportunity to record, I have a real sense that we are all surrounded by invisible influences from the thoughts and emotions (influences direct and indirect) of other people—and not just people—and that it's a matter of being open to it but also monitoring it and deciding what is mine, what is for me, what I want to create. This implies the questions, What materials do I want to use and which do I reject? What building plan? What ultimate shape?

I see that perhaps I haven't been doing that, but have been accepting all influences indiscriminately. This is a variant of the theme of weighing opposing forces; in this case, internal forces. Weigh what I want to become, and what influences I want to allow to shape what I become. I emerge with a sense of the need to pick and choose among alternatives—thoughts, influences, emotions—from *all* my environment, internal and external. In one of the visions that came to me I saw towers, with holes and windows in them. I understood that to be an analogy: We shape our own towers—the physical lives we lead, the mental and physical worlds we live in, with holes or windows from which to see the rest of the world—by what we choose to make part of ourselves, and what we reject.

And I realize that I get such influences, such guidance, chiefly by words rather than pictures. TGU come in through words—*if* they are asked; if I turn on the switch that allows them to come through.

After Sunday's long midday break, we do a Free-Flow 21 tape—a tape that brings us to Focus 21 and leaves us to our own devices. I drift, experiencing small visuals and pseudo-conversations. Drifting, almost daydreaming, I speculate about connections with people like Joyce, the woman who responded to my vision on the skull on my chest. TGU say Joyce and I have been friends and lovers before, but they add a sense of, "Who here hasn't been?" And the longer I live, and the more contact I have with others—true emotional contact, rather than arm's-length transactions—the truer this appears. We all have a past with each other, like it or not, know it or not, play it out consciously or not.

After supper we toured Focus 22 and 23, our first excursions past 21. In the course of doing this tape, I experienced something I dared not share with the group, and did *not* experience what we were expected to experience. This brings up two points:

First, our vulnerability to ridicule. In this tape I had experiences that I would later describe to the group at debriefing, but one

I did not tell there (though I will tell it here) for fear of appearing to suffer from delusions of grandeur, or exhibitionism. Later, when I came to type up my notes for my own sake, the fact that I, who have so little discretion in such matters, had not dared describe a meaningful encounter for fear of skepticism *in that group* makes me wonder what else gets experienced and not publicized. Our fears, our vulnerability to ridicule even when and where ridicule is not to be expected, leave us very closed off. In a society that welcomed and honored visions, many more visions would be reported, which of course would increase that society's sense that visions were commonplace and to be expected and honored.

Second, the intractability of my own experience. From the beginning of my Monroe experiences—back in 1990 when I was using the tapes at home—I was unable to see or experience anything that had been described to me in advance. Unlike my experience with Shirley MacLaine in 1987, when a directed-visualization exercise had elicited an internal image, Monroe tapes never produced this response. The tapes that gave me meaningful experience, and gave me growth, were those that brought me to a given focus level and left me to see what I could see. But the tapes that tried to tell me what I would experience left me uselessly straining to see what I expected to see. I could be directed to move from focus level to focus level—well aware that I moved only if *I* did the moving—but no amount of suggestion (what they call "front-loading" the experience) ever resulted in my seeing what I was told I was going to see. For instance, I never have experienced the park that Monroe described as the reception area in Focus 27. After a while this reassured me rather than frustrated me, for it indicated that if I was making it all up (a continual suspicion for all who do this kind of work), at least I wasn't making it up on demand!

Focus 23 is understood at TMI to be the "place" where souls go who are disoriented, or for some reason get stuck. Bob

Monroe well described it in his books, and it has been experienced by many people since. But I note—with the benefit of the hindsight gained through two Lifeline programs—that from the very beginning my visions of Focus 23 differ significantly not only from what I expected, but from what is more or less silently taken as a given.

I go, as directed by Bob's taped instructions, to Focus 23, expecting nothing in particular. After a bit I get a clear vision of a waiting-room sort of place, then another room off of it. Gradually I see that the place is packed with people, like railroad stations, like airport terminals. And there is a huge outdoor restaurant, where people can eat (or anyway, they think they do, perceive they do) while they wait.

A waiter passes in front of me with a tray of glasses. I take a glass, he not noticing, and drop it on the path behind him. Because no one notices, the glass never hits the path and shatters; instead, it is back on the tray. (Why this should be, I don't know—but the sequence and cause was clear at the time. It didn't occur to me to wonder why I was moved to try that experiment, or why it went just as I expected. Looking back, I can see that as usual I was being guided, and as usual I was assuming it was intelligent old me.)

The food looks different from ours, in the way foreign food would be different. I smear butter on a roll-like thing I break apart, and taste it. Tastes good, and not all that different. In other words, in this vision—this reality I am experiencing—I not only have vision and hearing but touch and taste. Yet there is something dreamlike and automatic about it, as when the dropped glass never hits the path, but returns unnoticed to the tray like a piece of film looping.

This is all very interesting, with its own persuasive reality, however different it is from what we have been led to expect. But then (as I did not later describe) all at once it is as if something pushes my face to the left, and pushes me out of the restaurant. (Again, at the time it did not occur to me that perhaps this hand was a helper, moving things along. At the time I noted the push, but didn't think about it.)

After a moment of floating, I ask to see someone I know. I am taken to Britain, then up to a northerly part of an island, and I know it is the west coast of Ireland up by Sligo, and I know that the person I see wandering alone by the sea and the mountains is Yeats—W. B. Yeats, the poet, my old friend in the life of the Welshman David. Willie Yeats, still there after all these years. And suddenly I am right there with him.

I establish contact, saying, "It's Owen." In that, I surprise myself, for all this time I have been thinking of the Welshman as David. A part of me asks myself (in the middle of the experience) if maybe my name really had been Owen; then I think that maybe it was Yeats's name for me because I was Welsh. Only when I began writing this book did I find in an old journal that in my one and only hypnotic regression in 1987, which I had thought a failure, I had called him "David Owen." Nothing my subconscious mind wouldn't know, of course, and if you will tell me what a subconscious mind is, I will be entirely persuaded that there's nothing in all this.

I say to Yeats, "I was younger than you when we lived, and I died earlier, and I came back after you were already dead—and now I return to find you still here! It's time for you to move on." I tell him, "Make your presence known, remember the physical, and then go, my old friend." We agree that he is to get a brief taste of the physical again and then go on, after making his presence known.

In the CHEC unit after the tape is over, I recite what I can remember of one of his poems, "To Be Carved on a Stone at Thoor Ballylee." Why that one, I don't know, but Mary much later points out that this poem was Yeats's statement of his personal identity, as opposed to his family, and maybe that's it.

So why don't I mention this in debriefing? I don't want to seem to stand out; don't want it to look like I am nurturing delusions of grandeur. And part of me suspects that this is exactly what I *am* doing.

I wonder what the others are not reporting.

After supper, we debrief at David Francis Hall, practice some healing energy, and have our choice of watching a movie or repeating the Focus 22–23 tape. I do neither. Instead, I get out my oil paints, which I have brought for some reason unknown to me. I am restless, silently waiting for any contact from Yeats. I paint a small picture of a fire in the night. After a while the movie ends and people drift in. One of those who watches me finish the painting is a tall, humorous man from Wyoming named Rich, and we are old friends meeting.

I stay up talking, but it is not late when I go to bed. And in the morning I awake only when I hear Bob's voice say he is going to count back to 1 from 27. Meaning that I recall nothing between going to sleep and awakening. Which is very unusual.

Monday

Many things happen Monday, including Ed using automatic writing to channel his old friend Bob Monroe! This is Ed's first contact with Bob after Bob's death, so far as I know. Ed has been feeling discouraged that he hasn't made better progress on the first few tapes, so he asks his old friend what he is doing wrong. "Slow down," Bob tells him, in effect. "Don't try to rush through the long slow count upward at the beginning of the tapes. It was put there for a reason. Slow down and you will go farther." In general, he says, go slower and you will notice more. Ed passes the message on to me, which leads to good results the next day.

During a tape on Monday morning, The Gentlemen Upstairs suggest to me that Paired Intuitive Questioning would broaden the Lifeline experience. They say, "Your idea—it's not necessarily *your* idea—about having several people talk to us together would be a very productive thing. Pick them carefully. Or rather, let them pick themselves."

So I take my tape recorder and sit in the lounge during the long break Monday to see what will happen. Ed asks rather impatiently how anybody would know, but TGU had said they would self-select, and they do. First Rich comes over; then, one at a time, five others including Ed and Joyce. We record nearly ninety minutes of tape, and everyone but Joyce gets to answer a question before we run out of time. The following transcript of the first few minutes, in which Rich and I are alone, should be of interest in connection with *your* access to guidance.

Frank: Monday July 17, 1995. The idea for this session was given to me this morning as a way of various members of the Lifeline class sharing experience and being given stuff that we wouldn't get otherwise. The only other information that I have is that the person who asks the question should then do the channeling on the next go-round. That way there would never be pressure of the questions on the person trying to channel. That's all that I know about it, and we're going to rely on people showing up who are called to be here.

Rich: What can I do to establish a strong link with my greater self?

Frank [Upstairs]: Well, you're in the right place at the right time. This experiment is an example to show you that the link is there all the time, and can be used in your daily life without any elaborate preparations. You know how to get to 21, which is one way to do it, or some people can do it from 10 or 12; just fool around and find it. Once you are persuaded of the reality of the process, you won't have to have anyone else involved in it unless you want to, or unless it's something so sensitive that you can't get your own emotional body out of the way. So you could write the questions in a journal or on a piece of paper and then ask yourself the questions. If it would help you to get out of the way, you could ask the questions on a tape recorder, and then wind it back, play the tape recording and stop it, with yourself in 21, and answer your own questions. The physical details of how to do it are not at all important, but the process—once you're confident of the process, that's all you need. . . .

That's not the only way, but it's a very simple way for somebody who's had the advanced training that you've already had.

[Downstairs]: And by the way, I do this with my eyes closed because I've done it with my eyes open, but all that visual information is distracting; that's the only reason why. . . . All right, are you ready to try it?

Rich: Um . . . [Pause.] Yeah.

Frank: [Pause.] If there's a new technique or a new approach that will help us all to accomplish the goals of this Lifeline program, will you please outline it for us, or give us some experiments to try.

Rich: Uh—I sort of get the strong feeling, what we're doing here right now. That in a larger group, where you can just start out and go from person to person around the whole room, that there's several things that would happen. Number one, there would be a building of energy and confidence in the group as they went around, and there would also be a drawing of focus and power from the group that would help each individual person to make the connection and make it strong and get the information through.

Frank: Is this something that TMI is liable to resist, or embrace, or be indifferent to?

Rich: I see TMI as being open to it. To a certain extent I think that this is happening already in the group discussions;

it's just that it's sort of a group discussion in a different form. There's right now where we've got basically two trainers that take care of the group and keep things moving along. This would be sort of like a perpetual circular synergy or whatever. And you know right now we've got— there's— somebody will put out their feelings or their questions or their experience with the tape and in almost every instance, in fact I think that probably in some instances there's something that some person in the group has to say, but they *don't* say it, that would help that person. And in many cases they say it and it does help. And I think that by getting this into maybe a slightly different structure, and starting off in sort of a round-robin format and just moving it around, I think that it would help a lot. And I do see TMI as being willing to at least try it.

Frank: All right, let's give you another shot.

[Tape off. We listen to what we had just recorded, and Rich starts to give his reaction to it. Tape on.]

Frank: Actually, let's get this on tape! Were you surprised?
Rich: Yeah, I was real surprised. There was a little bit of a— it's kind of funny, there was a little bit of a stumble at the beginning as far as my confidence, but then, it's real funny it just starts to flow out of you. You know, once you start to pull the thoughts in, or to open up to it, it just really starts to flow in on you. I'm actually quite amazed.
Frank: I think the embarrassment factor is the biggest single damn thing that stops people.
Rich: Yeah. Definitely so.
Frank: And that tells me why we started with two [people].
Rich: Yeah.
Frank: And this has gone on with me now since Guidelines.

Guidelines started the process, and I learned why channelers talk sometimes in staccato ways, because you don't know how the sentence is going to end!

Rich: Yeah. That's right.

Frank: Stuff starts and you're just going with it and find out if it makes any sense, but if it doesn't, so what?

Rich: Right. In fact, there was a— it's funny, when you mention this, because there was a book that I read on channeling, about how to make connections with your guides and, you know, to open up to that, and one of the things that they suggested was to read questions into a tape recorder and then listen to the question, and again it mentioned the same thing you did, don't feel embarrassed or anything, just put the question out, you know. And they suggested maybe starting with a tape alone because of the fact that there's nobody else sitting around, to be embarrassed, and if you felt comfortable with it, have other people ask the questions.

Frank: But TMI is a protected environment, so I think we're a little more open to that kind of stuff. . . . But I find even with my partner or with Ed I have a question that I want to ask my guys Upstairs, and I ask them to ask it for me, because it seems easier than changing gears. And I don't think it's necessary. . . .

Rich: I think that may be one of the problems I have in asking my own questions, that sometimes I get in my own way.

Frank: Interesting . . . let's listen to this again.

[Tape off/on.]

Rich: Okay. What I'm seeing now, in listening to this back again, was that the group, especially— it kind of seems like the circular analogy can be expanded a little bit. Number one, I think the group should be in a circle. I see that as being important. The other thing that I see is that the group actually acts as a satellite dish, or a collector. And that as each person is getting ready to— is asked a question, that the group acts basically as a large receiver and almost an amplifier to allow that person to pick it up easier.

Frank: You mean the existence of the group helps everybody to focus easier?

Rich: Yes.

Frank: Which means it helps each person to get information easier.

Rich: Right. Yeah, and another thing that just occurred to me is—and I've read it in many, many books in many, many different places—is that the energy that one person has, or one being has, is like x; when two beings focus their energy into one endeavor, it's like x to the two. And as the group continues to grow, it just keeps growing exponentially.

Frank: Let me add to your analogy about the collector dish. When you were saying that I got a— it's not a *visual* image, it doesn't make sense visually, but— I got a clear image that all the members are around the various points of the circumference and that without somebody's contribution you'll miss something. In other words, somebody over there can get whatever hits that part of the dish—

Rich: That's right.

Frank: And if they don't contribute, it's lost to everybody.

Rich: That very well could be. You know, and it could be with the point of our growth right now, that what happens is that maybe we aren't quite strong enough in most respects to be able to get that collector dish large enough by ourselves, or to keep it steady enough, maybe, to take all the information in. And what we're getting is good information, it's just that we're maybe not getting the entire picture.

Frank: As individuals?

Rich: Right. In other words, there's a larger focus with a larger group, so there's more to draw on.

Frank: Again, fewer pieces left out.

Rich: Right.

In *Ultimate Journey*, Monroe quotes the INSPEC—the nonphysical being he encountered out-of-body—as saying that all we need do is ask for their help. He asks if they mean meditating? Saying prayers? They reply that words and rituals are meaningless; the thought, the emotion, is the signal they respond to.

It is as I keep saying. The guidance is available to one and all.

For me the most important thing that happens, certainly the most striking, takes place in the dining room after supper, when I begin to talk about Katrina to Joyce, the woman who had said that my skull vision was meaningful to her. As we talk, I realize what a lovely person she is, very soft and caring, yet with the strength of the trained psychotherapist she is.

When I first mention Katrina to Joyce, the name and the situation startle her, because *she* remembers a life in which she had killed her daughter, whose name was Katherine, in order to save her from the Nazis. The guilt and pain from that act lasted into another lifetime. My Katrina was not her Katherine, of course, as mine had been killed by the Nazis, and hers, mercifully, by her own mother. And anyway, Katrina's mother had died before the war.

When I tell the story, I am concentrating on the facts and focusing on Katrina's fate at Auschwitz, but when Joyce hears me refer to Katrina's parents as "the father" and "the wife," she says, "'The wife.' Do you mean your mother?"

Instantly I am filled with a devastating sense of loss!

Which confirms that I'm dealing with something real, here. But in the next instant, the emotion is cut off, against my wishes, by my internal control unit and a lifetime of denial of emotion. This, despite the changes in me since Gateway. (There are always more levels, it seems.) And at least for the moment, there's nothing I can do about it.

By the time we are ready to go to bed, Rich and Joyce and I have formed a strong bond. (In retrospect, it is clear that three of us had business together.) Joyce was one of the first Lifeline participants I noticed, reminding me in her looks, voice, and gentle manner of several women I have liked over the years. And both he and she separately told me that when they met on Saturday there was instantly a sense of recognition; dear friends meeting again. He and I, beyond our other interaction, share a sense of concern for her, a sort of protectiveness about her.

This night, Joyce mentions that she has been charged with so much extra energy that she has been unable to sleep. She has been taking midnight showers—"hydrotherapy," she calls it— trying to get rid of some of it. Instinctively I know that Richard and I can help. Standing with our hands near her head (touching auras, in other words), in a few minutes we take away the excess. She is surprised we can do it and that the energy exchange is so strong. I tell Rich, jokingly, that we're now in vampire mode.

Tuesday

Tuesday, July 18, is a beautiful morning, "misty and fog and spider webs and flowers and fir trees and the quarter moon and bird sounds and otherwise silence," as I put it in my journal. I wander around barefoot long before others are up. The world changes irretrievably after the sun is well up. As in every other TMI program, I am reminded what a garden this world is, how beautiful it is.

At breakfast, there are five of us around a table—Joyce, Rich, and I, and two others—including a curiously childlike woman I will call "Ingrid," who talks of her inability to deal with Focus 25. She says that when she sees the churches of Europe, she thinks only that they used to burn people. I tell her that when *I* see them, I think of how nobles pulled rock to help build them; how they were a collective expression of spirituality. In other words, that her reaction was not a natural inevitable reaction, but a highly personal one. I tell her that if she wants to find out, she can go to Focus 25 right then and there, and the others of us around the table will support her.

The suggestion startles some, who are not yet accustomed to bringing this stuff into everyday life, but the five of us, sitting at the breakfast table, hold hands in a circle, and four of us accompany Ingrid as she goes to Focus 25. I remind her as she does so that she is not alone now and wasn't alone then, though she thought she was. Within minutes she comes back, surprised, with an image of herself backed against the wall, with the bishop leading the community against her. I hope she will pursue it later, but that's all we can do at the time. Then, as Joyce is feeling a little drained, we all give her energy, replacing what Richard and I had drained off, perhaps.

The day's first tape is free-flow 25—bringing us up to Focus 25, one of the belief-system territories—and leaving us to our own devices.

"Belief-system territories" is Monroe's term for areas in which people of the same beliefs, which in practice means souls of similar vibration, flock together. (Those of us who are in bodies associate with others, in bodies, of all vibrational levels. This helps make physical-matter-reality—3D Theater—a unique teaching tool. Without the body, we can associate only with those of like vibration.) Think of the plethora of beliefs that people have adopted over the millennia, and you will have a sense of the immensity of belief-system territories.

I get a scene of the inside of The Monroe Institute, or someplace like it, and I get that I am in a possible future in which the institute is the center of a kind of a religious belief system. I hear somebody say, "Well, there was no joy in the center," and feel that this refers both to our morning's experience of the Church in the Middle Ages and other times (no joy at the center of the Church as an institution) and "no joy in the center," meaning that people then—whenever that was—have lost the joy of discovery and freedom, having no idea how little we here and now know, or how much fun we have exploring.

Then there is something about shamans in the past, and I get that I was a shaman in the dry country in Mexico or southern United States somewhere. (Nothing else on this, then or later in the program. Indeed, this little nugget would sit unnoticed in my journal until, as noted previously, I unearthed it in the writing of this book, only weeks after I had been told the same thing by a psychic who knew nothing of me, and certainly nothing of a vision I myself had forgotten.)

This tape brings me much more that I don't bring back, but I am not distressed about what I can't recall, because I know it is still there and still will be—a vast territory to explore, and plenty of time to explore it. I get the sense of the territory, and the sense that you can get a little bit of a travelogue at a time. But I see a vast number of people deplaning; coming downstairs from a plane (and only as I write this do I see the pun, although even then I knew it was a symbol of people coming off and it's like a way-station.)

Before the thirteenth tape of the program, "second run to 27," I comment in my journal, "We'll see if this gets any better results." Well! When we meet to debrief, I ask first, "Was it real?" Between novelty and content—it's almost too much.

I decide to go to Focus 27 in a train, with the focus numbers flashing by, the way station-stops do. (This, because visualizing is important in beginning the mental process, and the content of the visualization seems to matter little. At some point the process takes over, and we are along for the ride; until that point, it helps to "imagine it" along. I suspect that many inadvertently prevent themselves from entering the process because, not wanting to "pretend," they refuse to—or don't think to—prime the pump, and thus prevent the process from getting under way.)

The train brings me to the Thirtieth Street station in Philadelphia, which I know well in this life. I go outside and start to get a cab, then realize I have no idea where I want to go. The taxi driver points me toward a phone book nearby. It has so many pages (thousands) that it spills down onto the cement. From within the vision, I decide there must be a better way to do this. I find a computer terminal, and enter names and dates one after another. Each of my grandparents, my brother, Dave Schlachter. After each name, I get, "Not known."

I enter my father's name: "Frank DeMarco, 1915–1985." I get "E15," which puts me in mind of a poem I had written for a friend who got killed in Vietnam (a poem about the dead, in short), the title of which I misremember as "E15, Line 21," rather than "E33, Line 29."

I ask the taxi driver, "Does E15 mean anything to you?" He says it's in South Jersey (where I grew up). I get in and he starts driving me. Along the road I ask him some question like, "How many years since you died?" whose phrasing alerts him to the fact that I'm not dead.

I tell him this is a test-drive of a new kind of program, which seems to satisfy him.

He pulls up; we're at the farm where my father grew up, but the house (which I always thought of as Grandmom's house) looks new, with the barn and tractor shed restored. "I'll be damned," I say.

I ask the cabby, "How do I pay?" and he tells me, "Bring another one. You're already one up so this brings you back to zero." I know somehow he's talking about the help we provided Ingrid around the breakfast table.

And in front of the tractor shed there's Dad, younger than I am now (in his mid-forties, say), without all the extra weight he always carried, looking good. He is working on a tractor, wrench in hand. We each say a casual, "How you doing?" as was our way.

In the packing house there is the old soda machine, as had been there when I was a boy. I get an orange soda for him, grape for me. (Oddly, in my vision I see the brand name of the sodas as being Nehi. It takes some work, later, to remember that what we drank as kids was a brand called "Ale and Quail." If the name "Nehi" contains some meaningful play on words—other than its own inherent play on the expression "knee high"—I don't see it.)

I ask Dad, "Where are Grandmom and Grandpop?"

Shrug. "Not here. Nobody else here yet."

"Uncle Charles?" (Dad's favorite brother-in-law.)

"Charlie's here. He's a banker in Philly." I can't get over that. Bankers here? What would they do? He conveys an amused idea of them going to lunches and feeling important and enjoying each other's company. I remember the joke we told about Dad probably showing up when Uncle Charles died and saying, "We're going to the races, Charlie. Where have you been?" He says he heard us make the joke, and used it himself when Uncle Charles came over.

I ask about Bub, my cousin who died in 1978.
"He went back before I got here."
(Then something very private, which affects other living people.)

All this is very clear, as clear as my Focus 15 experience in Gateway thirty months earlier. Then Bob Monroe's voice calls me back. I tell Dad I'll be back when I can.

I turn on the light in the CHEC unit and make notes as fast as I can during the few minutes it takes for Bob to count us down to C1. I can't get over the feeling of the *reality* of it, but it's all so strange!

I read the conversation to the group, prefacing it with a question: "Was it real?"

Yet, it *felt* real. Every *bit* of it felt real. Interesting.

Tape 14 gives us a specific mission: We are to set up a place of our own design in Focus 27 and implant a marker to help us find that "place," that frequency, whenever we want to later, including—obviously, though it isn't stressed—when we die.

Creating the scene isn't hard. I'm up on a hill. To the north is a great vista of two forested hills across a river. To the northeast, a river flows from near or beneath the house to a vast lake like Switzerland's Lake Zurich, and these two vistas are very clear. To the southwest, part of the house overlooks an immense drop at the bottom of which is a city and behind which are mountains. Reminds me of Chattanooga, Tennessee.

But as I try to begin designing the house itself, it's very strange: I feel like it already exists and I'm just discovering it, not creating it. I try to create a room in which to paint, but what comes clearest is a log-cabin-like living room, fireplace, bookshelves, all wood and comfort and late 1800s, something like my idea of the Dakota house that Teddy Roosevelt built and lived in in the late 1800s. And I swear, it has its own reality. I see that living room from one precise perspective, as clearly as looking at a magazine illustration. I start to design a room for baths, and a bedroom, but I'm not nearly as interested in them as in that living room. I am tempted to have no roof, but decide I might want storms and cold and snow-storms, so settle for a large glass panel in the roof.

I invite Dad to look at the house, and his reaction cracks me up, it's so typical. He says, "It's pretty, but why did you make it so far from town?" I say, "Dad, there's no distance here!" and get a sense of him being embarrassed at being caught being "practical" out of habit.

I run out of time; can't finish. But I figure, I'll be back.

Meanwhile in C1, something is going on behind the scenes. By suppertime I am filled with an overwhelming sorrow that is just over my mental horizon. I'm trying to figure out how to get at it, and I have no ideas at all. Getting at my emotions has never been my strong point. Supper I eat alone, at one of the tables for two that adjoin the windows. Just as the meal is over, Joyce leaves her table, gets a cup of coffee, and comes to my table.

"Do you mind if I join you?"

"I was praying that you would."

She asks to hear the rest of Katrina's story and tells me more of hers. It is clear to both of us that I need healing, as she does. But, she says, she has never found it easy to ask for it. It is always easier to be the caregiver than the one receiving.

After supper we meet at David Francis Hall, and the first thing on the agenda is doing another healing circle. As part of that exercise, we are encouraged to ask beforehand for healing for anyone we know who needs it. I ask for healing for myself. (Joyce says later that she was going to ask for it for me if I didn't, and says I took better care of myself than she did of herself.) Sitting in a circle in the comfortable chairs at David Francis Hall, we listen to a healing tape played over speakers. At the same time, they show a wonderful film of dolphins playing, jumping, diving, doing somersaults, et cetera. Then we take a break, get pillows and blankets to be comfortable, get our share of popcorn, and return to David Francis Hall to see a movie, a fluffy Hollywood thing called *Defending Your Life,* which gives a view of the afterlife that at least provides relaxation and laughter, if not any particular amount of enlightenment. But lurking in the background, for me, are internal demons.

We emerge after the movie to a phenomenally clear starry night. Summer in the mountains at its finest. Awesomely clear. Many of us stand or sit gaping at the Milky Way and that tremendous profusion of stars. I go prowling around away from the lights of the building, looking for greater darkness—which phrase now strikes me as applicable to more than the search for a good place to view the stars.

All night, I try to *will* my inner demons into coming where they can be dealt with. All night, I wrestle with a long, slow-motion nightmare, partly involving me trying to kill somebody and having no luck with it. The feelings, I know, are connected with Katrina.

Wednesday

Tape 15 starts with dolphin energy, then fades into our first attempted retrieval. I "take the train" to 27 and I get several visuals; the net effect is a sense that I am a part of an entire community of lives. What's more, though I seem to myself to live in the present, I am not the most important part of the community that is me. As in any community, each individual is naturally his or her own center of interest; but viewed objectively, none is *actually* central, none is "the most important." As with the external community, so with the community within the individual. For the first time, I see that when we speak of "past lives" we distort perspective by putting ourselves in the center. Objectively—from the point of view of the whole being—one life is not the "past life" of another; they are more like a community of lives linked by an animating spirit. (But of course in practice I find myself saying "past lives" like anyone else. We don't yet have a vocabulary that would easily express the community concept.)

I don't have any doubt that this first retrieval run is for Katrina. Guided by Bob Monroe's voice superimposed on the Hemi-Sync signals on the tape, I move from normal consciousness "up" to Focus 27, and then "down" to Focus 23 and call for Katrina. As I head down to Focus 23, I am very conscious of the help of several others.

I find her without difficulty. She is there because she never realized that she was dead. Whatever the Nazi bastards did to her (and I haven't found out, nor do I necessarily want or need to know), she spent the last few days of her life psychologically dissociated. I call her to me. I look for Mama, but don't find her. But then, Mama died years before Katrina, of course, which might make a difference.

I take Katrina with me up to 27, telling her that if she doesn't fall asleep or get distracted, we'll find her brother Marcus. I know where he is: He is with Mary! As we ascend (to put it that way) I am calling Mary to have Marcus there. I get to 27 with her. Marcus is there, and Katrina is gone from my side in a heartbeat! No way am I or anybody going to successfully compete with the beloved elder brother!

Love.

I tell her to visit me sometime.

I have never felt stronger love than I do for that child.

Tears from the moment I find Katrina. Large quantities of tears, quiet tears overflowing my eyes and running down the sides of my head. And then I know, *this* is why we look for past lives, to make ourselves whole. This time, at least, I have no doubts about the reality of what's going on. I lie there feeling the tears flow, and the emotional reality is far too intense for me to bother to try to question it. I decide that this is what I'll do next. I will concentrate on survivors and bring them up. It comes to me that if we bring forth the trapped "past incarnations" of those who are in the body now, we will lighten the consciousness of living beings without them necessarily knowing one thing about it. "We'll lighten the whole world," is the way it comes to me.

When we do a second retrieval tape, I go back to the camp where I'd found Katrina.

I wear a German uniform to get the attention of the women prisoners: I form them up in rows and lines, and then I tell them. I show them!

I snap my fingers and the guards are gone. I do it again, and the towers are gone, and then the barbed wire, and then my German uniform. I know somehow that I look to them like an angel. I tell them that I am not an angel, just a person. Then I have them hold hands in a gigantic circle, these skeletal wraiths, and I tell them it is important they not fall asleep or I can't bring them to the place I want to bring them. I tell them to concentrate on sending love to the two people each of them was holding on to. (I never did succeed in telling anyone this detail without choking up.) And so I bring them up to 27. I still think of this one as the retrieval where I couldn't do anything wrong. Everything I tried, worked.

Again, anyone currently in body who is connected to

*these personalities: must they not be suddenly "lighter"
for no reason they can put their fingers on? Must they
not feel freer?*

*After I retrieve the women, I go down and find the
old man, Katrina's father. I look for him first in 24, then
in 25, and in 26, and I find him finally in a section com-
prising socialist Jewish atheist scientists. (Which
teaches me that one secret to retrievals is, the more
closely focused, the easier to find somebody.) I have to
argue with him. "You stubborn old man," I say finally,
"you've got lousy research facilities and I can take you
to a place where there's better research facilities and no
Nazis." He says something about staying true to his
convictions—meaning solidarity with the workers and
the oppressed, I think—and finally I tell him I love him,
but he is a stubborn old man and he has sacrificed his
children and his wife and his life to his theories and
that's enough. Then he comes with me and he meets
Katrina and Marcus.*

*Later, among the Polish Catholic section of Focus
25, I find the mother—I find Mama. I persuade her that
there are some people who would be happy to see her. I
tell her she doesn't need love, she has so much, but she
could certainly give some. I am able to bring her up to
27, finally, after persuading her that in fact she hasn't
seen judgment day, so that maybe things were different
than they always said in church. And she comes up with
me and the family is reunited.*

It is fabulous.

I am about to go down to 23 again, but then I say no, I feel
like I'd better just rest, and as it happens I've scarcely gotten
back into my cabin when Bob's voice says it is time to go back,
and we start on back.

"Wow," I say on tape, "what a wonderful day!"

We debrief in two groups, so I learn only later that Ingrid successfully dealt with the situation in the Middle Ages. And I tell Joyce that I had rescued Katrina.

Our briefing after lunch tells us that the next tape contains no instructions but is designed to help us bring various parts of ourselves into consciousness. Integration, in other words. The tape produces no particular images, and I expend no particular effort. At the time I think I am daydreaming. Later I realize in fact I *was* integrating things. I mention only two things here:

1. I take a fast train ride to Focus 27 to look in on the family to be sure they're doing okay. I remember, now, leaving Marcus and Katrina—originally—and telling them to get some meat on their bones, and telling her to learn to read from Marcus.

2. I remember, from Gateway, a vision of being sad and alone and going down the ramp that developed—going in my bare feet—to a table where I was joined by people popping in, a long table with endless room, and people appearing and filling it. I think: What parties we are going to have in Focus 27, just of my other lives! Let alone guests! Think of interacting with John, and Owen, and Katrina, et cetera!

After a short break and no debriefing comes tape 18, a free-flow 27 tape designed for us to explore who we are and what our purpose is.

At the end, I feel called to go rescue the men of Treblinka. But while I couldn't do anything wrong when I went to retrieve the women, with the men not much that I try works very well. I have a hard time getting their attention, or getting them to believe that anything could disappear, or that they are dead. I can't make them form a circle and hold hands, but have to settle for forming them in ranks, each holding the shoulders of the man in front. When I try to bring them up to 27, I can feel individuals peeling off in all directions, drawn to various belief-system territories. I don't know if I bring back even half of the number I started with, and it seems to me that maybe not all those still in the camp even started. I do the best I can, but I am not very satisfied with the results.

I barely get to 27 before Bob's voice calls us back.
A while later we do another free-flow 27 retrieval tape.

I come across one John of Penmorthy, an arrogant SOB still lying where he was killed on a battlefield in 1424 (or so I am told). I say, "What country are you from?" and he says, "Perth." I am very arrogant with him in return, else he would not pay me any attention at all. At one point I trick him into jumping up to show me that there was *so a battlefield around us—at which time he realizes that being dead is a little more complicated than he had thought. I bring him to 27 and tell him he can maybe find the person dearest to him who had been in the world. He calls for "Mary" and she thanks me for bringing him. I tell her to come visit me—and bring him too.*

Then I fool around some at my house in 27. Visit Katrina's family and persuade her hardhead father to get them a better house, with a solid floor, more windows, larger. It hasn't occurred to him that it is possible, I suppose. Tell the kids I am proud of them; tell Mama a child loves his mother, her mother. Tell her to keep the lessons, give up the pain. It's still in her face. Tell the old man to be easier on his Orthodox son; that the son's biblical beliefs aren't any wronger than his own "scientific" beliefs. Back to my place for a little bit, then down again.

And I have my first experience of what Mary (out of her theatrical background) calls the Green Room. (In theater, the Green Room is the place where actors hang out between scenes. The equivalent in Focus 27 is where our Higher Selves—our Upstairs components, I'd say now—hang out and interact before and during our interaction on this level. I'd sometimes thought that was a literary conceit of hers, but now I see that it is a description of reality that she perceives "naturally" and I had only just learned to. I don't know how better to describe it than as the place where the actors consult before going on stage in 3D Theater.)

Thursday

Thursday morning, a lovely walk before sunrise, pacing through the dew-soaked grass under a last-quarter moon. Then we come to our last morning exercise class, and breakfast, and our morning briefing. We are told (what I should have anticipated) that we will have a morning of silence, doing three tapes in a row without debriefing, and then lunch—also in silence if we choose.

The tape begins as a DEC tape, then moves into rescue and retrieval. I already see that these experiences, like dreams, often feature abrupt transitions and seemingly meaningless episodes with no obvious context. As I did my initial exploring, I thought it important to remember as much as possible—which meant extensive journaling—on the theory that maybe some things would make more sense later. Here's a sense of it:

I get up to 27 smoothly. My living room. That love-ly view, or rather three views. I go down to the river and get a canoe. It's a big river, a long way, so I borrow from something Ed Carter had told me he did, and I make it thought-powered. It is fast, smooth, silent.

I come to a house upriver on left side. Shack-y, sort of. A family there to get to know. I'll be back.

Back to my house. It's too dark in living room for daytime; I need new room. I see fully the unsatisfactory nature of my unplanned house.

To see Dad, back at same moment I'd left. We're talk-ing, when violently, suddenly, I am pulled to another place; I am hearing some woman's voice talking about something erudite and educated. Joyce? Just before Bob tells us to start our retrieval run. Then, no follow-up, ever.

I go down to 23. Is anyone here part of me? (They'd know by the feel of the energy.) None.

I had determined to find a Russian prison camp next time, don't know why. And it is only in the writing of this book that I realized how little the Downstairs "I" directs my life, and how often and extensively "I" am *placed into* scenarios—in C1 quite as much as at other focus levels; in ordinary life, quite as much as in TMI programs. I begin to think of us as human torpe-does—not in the sense of implements of destruction, but in the sense of devices that are continually receiving and executing minute course-correction impulses.

I go scouting. All over Russia, Siberia, then drift west, looking for the one that feels right. Siberian gold mine above Arctic Circle? No. Urban prisons in Moscow or Leningrad as in Solzhenitsyn? No. Where?

I wind up in Poland, near the Czech border. I ask for any Polish, Russian, or Czech prisoners, and collect a ragged bunch of them. I try snapping my fingers to show them it is illusion; it doesn't work. I can't get them to form circle either. I feel quite unprepared, with time (on the tape) running out. Finally I tell them, the war is over, the Russians are gone. I can take you to a better place. I have them line up with their hands on the shoulders of the man in front. I bring them out, feeling myself lose some of them at every step, as we pass through belief systems. Some of them get to 27 anyway; and no matter where the others wind up, it has to be better than the camp. When we get to 27, I tell them to call for loved ones. I ask what nationality they are, and am told Russian, Czech, and Pole, as that is what I asked for. I resolve to be more ready, more careful, next time.

Bob calls us back. As usual, I pull out my journal immediately, while he is still counting us back from Focus 27 to C1, and write as much as I can remember, while I can still remember it. While I was retrieving, Bob had said get details for verification if possible; but I think, the hell with that, I'm not interested in verification, somebody else can do that.

After the tape, in our morning of planned meditative silence, there is time and space for journaling. (In this book I am necessarily leaving out most of the things that happened, trying to stay on the main threads. In this, I hope not to emulate Adlai Stevenson's definition of an editor as "someone who separates the wheat from the chaff and prints the chaff.") I make note of a few things, chief among them this: The world of 27 has objective existence in the same way as our world of C1 does. That's something of a surprise, as there's always the temptation to regard it as a creation of imagination *here and now* rather than, perhaps, imaginations of other places, other times. That

house with the poor people, on the river, came to my consciousness; I did not create it any more than I did that living
room, which I did not create, but discovered.

At some point—an important moment, though it went
unrecorded—I had made a deal with my left brain: You record
what goes on and we'll discuss it later. This works. It prevents
the left brain from inadvertently ending an experience by trying
to interpret prematurely, and it saves me from returning with
nothing recorded. Simple technique, very useful. So after Tape
22, free-flow 27, I ask left brain, "What went on this time? You
did a hell of a lot of recording. Did you get it all?"

His report: "Went up smoothly and rapidly to 27. In fact,
by the time Bob says you're in 27, I have already been down to
23 and found John Cotten of the John-and-Clara lifetime. (At
some point earlier I had gotten or guessed his surname, I forget
now how). John knows me as a voice he'd heard in his head,
during his life. It takes some persuading to convince him he was
dead. Finally I have him reach behind and realize the arrow was
there."

"That must have broke [sic] my back!"

"You'd better believe it did. And you bled to death. But
dying isn't what people think it is," etc. [Getting sick of making
the same explanation all the time.] I bring him up, he holding
my hands with his. He trusts me from past contact.

In 27, John and I talk about all this. As I mentioned earlier, it doesn't seem accurate to say he is one of my past lives, or
I his future life, because this gets things out of perspective. And
it isn't only a matter of which life is more important. It's a question of the nature of time. What we call past lives can't be simply "past." Not only do we have abundant testimony to the
relative nature of time (as seen from outside 3D Theater), but
time after time I saw "past" lives continuing, whether in one of
the Belief-System territories or within our psyches. To say he is
one of my *past* lives, or I his *future* life, implies that one present

is more real than the other. Yet from our own point of view, we are each always in the present!

Sometime, somebody is going to figure out the connection between lives. Maybe John and I, or Katrina and I, are merely aspects of a larger being who share emotional characteristics and therefore, being vibrationally close, share access to each other's memories. I have no idea whether that idea even makes sense, let alone if it is anywhere close to the truth. I know only that our idea about past lives is skewed somehow. If I continue to speak in those terms, it is only for lack of a better mental "bucket" to put it into.

But that John and I are connected, I have no doubt. I ask him to give me full access to his memories and tell him I'll give him access to my memories. I believe he agrees, but the memories never arrive. On the other hand, I have yet to do the work that might bring them in. As always, there are interruptions undescribed here.

I take John, in Focus 27, to a shack I found by the river earlier in the program. He takes it to be his cabin. Maybe it is, though of course he was in the mountains of Virginia and this is on a river. But that way of thinking won't go far in Focus 27!

I tell him about the complications between Emily and me that might make it hard for me to find Clara, his wife (whom I had looked for, but had been unable to find. It will be another two years before I find her.) He and I will do some working together, I see. I invite him to come over for supper sometime. I go back to my cabin to rest, and soon Bob says it's time to leave.

The encounter gives me some interesting things to ponder. If I can get John's memories, verification will be possible—but it means a hell of a lot more than that. It means increased integration. It means the various parts of myself (and of so many of us) can be put together to form—what? Something unprecedented? Or something often described and misinterpreted and forgotten? Retrieving past parts of ourselves that are stuck, as Katrina was, is significant enough in its possible effect on the world. But to be able to integrate those memories actively . . .

I think: John could be here with me now, enjoying a silent lunch as part of me. And eventually I could enjoy his life as well, which may have entirely as much immediacy and "life" as mine always has. After all, no part of our long lives is ever "here and now" except for one moment. Yet each of these moments in turn is experienced (at best) as "here and now." That is a paradox stemming surely from incomplete perspective.

Then (I ask myself), what happens as each of us becomes more closely in touch with our other facets (if they may be justly considered as such) and in turn interact with others who are also in closer touch? I haven't an answer, for I haven't yet had the experience.

I maintain silence through lunch, and as always I find it tremendously centering. (Why don't we do it every so often, as a part of our routine?) After our break, we do a "tapeless tape" exercise. That is, we are instructed to return by ourselves to the new focus levels, so that we will absorb the fact that we are not dependent on tape signals to get there.

> *To 27 by myself, rapidly by train. The house is still there—what I've constructed of it. The landscape is there, though one of the views is a little blurred now. I find a new place upriver beyond John's cabin. Tidal marsh, sort of. Wetlands.*
>
> *I find Yeats in Focus 26 with others of the Order of the Golden Dawn (I specified British, Irish, English, et cetera) but I do not find David (who Willie calls Owen) with them. I take at least some of them up to Focus 27*

*and tell them they are free. Ask Yeats to wait for me, to
get me verifications. He says he will.*

I run out of time, as the tape kicks in and I have to run to
Focus 10 for the color breathing and integration tape. There
was a time when Focus 26 and Focus 27 got sort of confused
with each other. I expect this happens when the tuning wan-
ders. (And, strictly as a scarcely noticed aside, I find a couple of
young girls acting as ghosts somewhere. Mischievous and
bored. Maybe early teenagers. Took them to 27 and released
them, told them they were free, suggested they find boyfriends
or whatever. Hardly noticed the incident until later.)

A nice TMI tradition is a birthday cake for any participants
with birthdays that month. At supper they bring out a chocolate
cake for Joyce's birthday and mine, and we are both touched.

Thursday night goes by in a lot of random motion on my
part, ending finally with an unforgettable long night walk with
another of the participants, barefoot, all the way up the road to
the llama farm and back, beneath an eerie layer of mist and fog.
I think of it as my walk "at the bottom of the sea." Finally, at 1
A.M., to bed.

Friday

Great sadness. It is hard seeing people go, these people I
mostly didn't know before and mostly won't see again. For a
while I sit around with Rich and Joyce and Ed, but then centrifugal force sends us our separate ways. (It is very true—as the
aftermath to Gateway had taught me—that to part is to die a little. I made good friends at Lifeline. Except for Rich and Ed, I
haven't seen any of them since.)

I have Hampton Roads business to attend to in
Charlottesville—very difficult to deal with, my mind being in

another place and my mind and body both being very tired from the intense concentration of the previous six days. Interestingly, as I am getting onto Route 6, a few miles from the institute, just as I start really feeling my deep sadness at leaving my friends, my car begins to overheat, taking and holding a significant part of my attention for the rest of the day, first into Charlottesville, then all the way home to Hampton Roads.

Friday night I return to Focus 27 to do some tomato transplanting with my father—and I find myself reliving something that really happened, so many years ago, that had significance but is too private to share.

Saturday

Saturday morning and afternoon are taken up by chores and the little things that make life—and make life difficult! It is not until 3:15 P.M. that I get a chance to lie down and return to Focus 27. I have my left brain (LB) use the technique I call "LL-R" (Lifeline remember), recording sound and vision for later recall, so I am able to reconstruct it in my journal afterward, like this:

Up to 27 by train. I decide a lookout point is needed for my house. Not just a piece of ground, enough to walk around, but a high pinnacle overlooking the junction of the two rivers before tree-covered hills. It occurs to me to re-create some of the rooms in Shangri-La as I had envisioned them in my novel. Some I know quite well already. And the walk I'd described, along the barren, stony hills, that leads to the dead-end promontory—I decide to construct that somewhere as a retreat.

Then, to a retrieval. I had thought I would pull back the dead from American prisons, maybe because I had recently been reading Jack London's novel *The Star Rover*. Instead, I found myself pulled to Andersonville, among the

Union prisoners.

Some were asking me who I was (thinking I too was a prisoner). I said I was born in New Jersey, and was now from Virginia. Realized that, in context, this sounded funny! They asked my name, and I started to say Josiah Smallwood; then wondered if he was there; prospected for him. Was he maybe captured at Gettysburg? But he wasn't there and I don't think he ever was.

I could see their suspicion that I was a ["sowbelly"? "sawbelly?"]—which meant either a Reb pretending to be a Yank, or a Yank who'd gone over. I suppose this was the equivalent to "galvanized Yankees"—captured Confederates who were released from POW status if they would take the oath of allegiance and agree to go to the frontier to fight Indians.

I went to the commandant, who was *not* the real person that they hanged after the war. That one was gone, along with a lot of the others (most, I suppose), both blue and gray.

In charge was a major from North Carolina named Major B—— [It was clear then, not later. A name like "Bruckner," or "Buckner," though it wasn't either of those two.] I talked to him after internal guards challenged me. Yanks that got too close could be cut down or shot, I gather. But I came on anyway.

At some point somebody tried to kill me with a vertical saber cut and was dumbfounded to slice right through me without effect. Can't remember where in the order of things that happened, though.

Eventually talked to Major B. and to the ranking prisoner, Captain Williams of Rhode Island. We three shook and held hands right to right, left to left, and left to right after I persuaded them that the war was over, and I took them up (running out of energy), telling the men they could follow at will by concentrating on either B. or Williams, who would meet them.

Sunday

I have a sense to go to 27, then I know somebody wants me elsewhere—it isn't to go hang out at my house, as I'd first thought. I descend to 26, 25, 24, and am not at all surprised to come to 23.

Back at Andersonville. I formed up the men. Now they said it had been Captain Miller. [Left brain says, oh sure, first Captain Williams as in Roger Williams of Rhode Island, now Miller as in Roger Miller! But we agreed that LB would record again, on condition that RB would consent to examine it all later.]

Anyway, persuaded blues and grays it was time to close up the place. Told Union men to strike the tents. Got lost in change of phasing for a bit. Refocused, persuaded the Johnnies to come, marched out of there formed up. Told them not to be surprised if men disappeared around them; those who didn't stay awake, I told them, would wind up somewhere else, but I didn't know where.

Somehow seeing the officers disappear with me earlier conditioned them to believe, this time. I don't think there's anybody left there now. I asked how many Rebs there were and was told 350, the remnants of seven companies. Again that seemed unlikely to me, but who knows?

Why couldn't I recall the name of the Confederate officer? It was clear enough originally, then lost, now the men themselves were exchanging blank looks. If I—or something within me—made up a name, why not be able to recall it later? And if I *didn't* make it up, if it was factual, why wouldn't I be able to recall it later? It doesn't make sense.

A busy week followed, as we began preparing to pick up the company and move it from Norfolk to Charlottesville. I had set us a deadline of August 24, and found it hard to stay unfrazzled in the face of various problems this created.

On Wednesday, July 26, I went to 27 at lunch hour, lying on the couch in my office, and among other things engaged, with Mary, in a TGU-to-TGU chat. I went after some energy, and got it, and other things happened that later I could not recall. "Better hurry!" said a little voice inside. "You aren't going to have a whole lot of spare time soon." As I well knew. I find it significant, at this distance, that in going to 27 at lunchtime at work, I had begun to integrate Upstairs and Downstairs reality in a way even more direct than before.

You will have noted that after Lifeline, the Focus 27 experiences blended into everyday life—as they should, if they are to enrich our lives. On Friday standing in line in a bank lobby, I had a little chat with TGU. I suggested that we talk by computer in my room in Focus 27, but then first came the suggestion that we talk by phone, so to speak, then—face-to-face! So, I decide, I will set up a conference room at my cabin in 27. Why not? On Saturday I talk to Rich, and that night, or rather at 3:40 A.M. Sunday, July 30, 1995, I take another trip to Focus 27. From my journal record, expanded for clarity:

> Last night, several hours ago, I created a room with tele-porters à la *Star Trek,* and sent myself forward to December 1995, so it would be cold and I could have a fire in my living room and still be comfortable. This because it was hot (our house didn't have air conditioning) and I wanted relief.
>
> That worked. I remembered TGU's offer to meet, so I invited Evangeline to come through, which she did. And then came others of The Gentlemen Upstairs.
>
> Then came Francis—basically, Saint Francis. Then Anne, basically a sensuous, lusty woman. Finally—finally for the evening, because I was getting tired—a soldier, who appeared in various uniforms, various centuries and styles.

Each of them represents or embodies an aspect of my character, I know well. Evangeline asked, did I want to see her naked, which crystallized (made me aware of) the fact that her essence was *not* a sexual presence but a woman of wisdom, she choosing an aspect perhaps in her forties. This was not the old woman I had once sculpted, but a high-cheeked, strong-featured woman in midlife.

Anne on the other hand *is* very much a sexual being. She went into the bedroom to wait for me, in fact, taking off her clothes there, while I sat in some embarrassment in the living room with Evangeline and Francis, who smiled at my discomfort, knowing me well and being well beyond pretense.

Francis is the aesthete, the one with no use for material things—luxuries and indulgences of any kind. Playful, though, not serious and gloomy. *Puer Aeternus,* to some degree.

Other things happened. I started to design a conference room, but preferred talking in the living room before a fire. I built the fire though I didn't have to; I could have just had a fire there—and other times I will. But it's like Dad working on a tractor; sometimes you just want to do the thing yourself. Speaking of Dad, isn't it interesting that my image of him is changing—readjusting—after all these years, all of a sudden, in response to meeting him in 27? Another argument for the reality of the process, if another were needed.

This book is about my exploration of what's real, rather than being about business or about the business of living ordinary life. But perhaps it is worth stressing periodically that in the middle of all this exploration came what to the outside world looks like ordinary life. I was responsible in this period for all the innumerable details of moving our company from

Norfolk to Charlottesville, a move that required finding a new office and new warehouse, moving the existing files, furniture, and office furnishings, and hiring new people for nearly all staff positions, as only two of our Norfolk employees decided to accompany us. The physical drain of so much planning was considerable, to say nothing of the actual physical activity involved in packing, driving the rented truck, and assembling the warehouse.

Yet the two worlds needn't be—shouldn't be—considered separate. I asked TGU what I should ask people, in interviewing potential employees, and used their advice. And going to Focus 27 was a good respite from thinking about so much physical activity. I notice in my journals a recurring theme throughout this period: I missed my new friends from Lifeline, and wanted to talk to them. They weren't always available. Focus 27, though, was.

On Saturday, August 5, I spent a couple of hours there. From the outside, it would have looked like I was taking a nap, but actually I was visiting. (It occurred to me, afterward, that probably I have done this before, not knowing.) Having returned, I asked my left brain what had gone on, and it brought back quite a bit.

I'd gone back to Dad's house. He wasn't around, so I looked through Grandmom's house. I realized that he had it probably more or less as he likes to remember it. He apparently sleeps in the big bedroom, and has the old, old big stove back in the kitchen, the stove that I remember from my boyhood that would burn wood as well as whatever else it used—gas? There is a refrigerator, but nothing much in it but some milk and a bottle of cold water. I suspect he isn't as interested in cooking as in just enjoying the eating. I meant to check to see if the barn has animals in it, but forgot to look. Odd, how vivid the back stairs of the house are, more than any other part of the house, perhaps. But then, that would be the part I'd remember best.

At some point I went down to the river and took one of the boats out, to think about Hampton Roads' problems and prospects. I took a look in at the train station in Focus 23 again, but didn't have the staying power to continue there. I did get a strong visualization of a creek or river, without context. There was more, but most of it is lost and what's left is not necessarily for here. For one thing, much of it is in fragmentary images whose context or explanation never arrived.

On Sunday I visualized a staff meeting at Hampton Roads, and made a note to myself that this was a good practice, to be continued and expanded. But I forgot about it in the press of events. Before that, I had a meeting with my two Gateway and Guidelines buddies, and with Ed Carter. It occurred to me that it is not the plan for all of us who are connected Upstairs to clump together Downstairs, but to leaven the loaf. And speaking of Downstairs, I began this day to reread Monroe's *Ultimate Journey,* and it struck me again that I had been privileged to know one of the great men of our time.

On Monday, August 8, I talked to Mary and realized that a very real closure between us had occurred with my retrieval of Katrina. The link between us that was so strong was between Katrina and her beloved elder brother Marcus, not between the two lovers in Scotland, and certainly not any of the other rather tangential ones we have unearthed. All that time, little Katrina was alive within me, crying for Marcus. Now she is free, and the link, the unconscious connection, is gone. I can see in this conversation that it has been replaced by a more comfortable, more normal distance that has in it no indifference, only independence.

Does this not have ramifications for all of us? If we are linked internally (Upstairs) in unsuspected ways, *must* it not affect our behavior? May these links not go some distance to explain so many inexplicable subconscious compulsions that move us?

Later I went back to Focus 27, and promptly felt drawn to the train/plane station/restaurant where I'd gone in my first

Focus 23 experience. I realized I could increase the intensity of my experience by narrowing the *width* of my awareness, as if by narrowing focus. This from having just read part of *Ultimate Journey* and suddenly being struck by how much more vivid than mine Monroe's experiences were. *This realization came while I was in Focus 27*, so far as I can recall. Later I would recall that in Guidelines I had stumbled upon what I call the "Megahertz scale," the intensity meter. By turning it up, I'd intended to be able to intensify my experiences. Now it appears as yet another workable tool. It seems to me that if I can control the intensity of focus, probably I, or anybody, could repeat all the experiences Bob reports in *Ultimate Journey*. Of course, within the context of my life, rather than his, but the point remains: Controlling the intensity of the experience may be the key.

Another striking thing happened. I was thinking about something—pondering it—when I suddenly realized I wasn't in my living room on the couch at all, though I had thought I was; and that in any case my living room couch did not face a fireplace. I realized I was in a visualized place, something made of my remembered (transmogrified) house here and my cabin there.

Another example of evidence that my internal activity may be merging, enabling me to experience more than one focus level at once. From within Focus 27, I brought awareness from Focus 1 (or wherever I live these days). Thinking I was in Focus 1, I realized my surroundings could only be Focus 27. A sort of intrusion of one kind of consciousness overlapping another. Very interesting. Of course, I've been noticing this right along, as my consciousness has drifted. A stray noise—sometimes a thought—will snap me out of one state, requiring me to count or intend myself back.

I think, LB (left brain) does such a good job of storage and retrieval! When I think of my *years* of wasting effort, trying to do without him—sabotaging his efforts (by telling him to get lost and stop bothering me) and then suffering his sabotage in return (in the form of crippling doubts about a process from which he was excluded) it is to laugh, or cry, or a little of each.

And I am beginning to understand things in a different way. In 1990, I well remember, when I was practicing at home, attempting to have an OBE using TMI tapes, I began envisioning myself in a control booth looking through a wall of glass at an unconscious body that I was monitoring and guiding. This image returns to me with a haunting familiarity. It is an image out of Focus 27. But the consciously designed image came in 1990. Formed of what raw materials? And to whose design? At the time, I thought it was one of my (Downstairs) bright ideas. I am beginning to see that, in fact, as usual the bright idea came from elsewhere. If I weren't a Leo, I'd be in danger of learning humility.

On Saturday, August 12, I made several trips to 27, the most important of which involved finding Yeats. He talked, and he promised to give me a poem via automatic writing. Sitting in my cabin by a fire, I asked him, this intense middle-aged man of penetrating eyes and prominent cheekbones, if I could succeed in transcribing it. You can get it, he said, but whether you can understand it is another matter.

I sat down at my journal and was nearly stifled by performance anxiety. I got so far as a title, then a first line—then I was quarreling with the next lines, trying to make something coherent and losing it, then the phone rang. I tried again, and got this:

Sentinel
There are those think the day a long weariness,
Life a long never-releasing swampland clinging.
Can they never in their ceaseless counting and reckoning
Look up to the bird on the wing, or the hour?

Cease telling your beads of worry and amassing.

Your prayers are in every breath you take,
will it or not. The grave's no prison
to match that spun by blind men building.

We who know pass you this directive;
Live your limitations as a blessing bestowed;
Build your castles but omit the bars;
Pass through the glowing.

After the poem came to me, I said:

"Maybe it's Yeats, though it certainly doesn't sound like him. And I can't make sense of that title and this content.

"Nor does it sound like great poetry to me—or even competent rhyme. Would Yeats write something unfinished and crude?

"Ask him, maybe. Can I do that here and in 27? Let's see. Mr. Yeats—"

"Different rules apply in new circumstances. What you value may seem child's play or child's distraction to us, sense and sound detracting from other attributes. Study the poem and see if it has anything to say to you and you may decide it's not so bad after all."

I asked if that was the "indisputable sign" of his presence that I had been promised.

"No. This is the sign: David Poynter. Little Portraits: Waterborne Reflections 1887–1913, printed 1921 in London. Murragh printed it. Limited edition of five hundred. Available in a few places, not so highly valued. Look in belles lettres. Good-bye and my thanks to you."

TGU, asked about it, said, "Yes, what you have experienced

has been solid, has been—as you put it—real. Even the thing with Yeats—David."

"Wise guys," I said. I reflected that at least I knew what to look for, but that whether it did or did not prove accurate, it wouldn't prove a thing about Yeats. "Why is it that the thing that had the most evidential value for me was his farewell: '. . . and my thanks to you'?"

You know the reason for that. It was a human touch, a thanks from a man who had been rescued by an old friend from wasting time on illusion. More or less. And you went looking for him among the Order of the Golden Dawn, you think; in fact, you will recall you went looking for *David* among the Order of the Golden Dawn, and found him [Yeats]. A different story, no?

And in fact I had forgotten that this is what I'd done.

I didn't see how the poem could really have been from Yeats. It wasn't at all his style, and didn't seem to me very good poetry; scarcely poetry at all, though perhaps I am no judge. Yet when I posted it to the Voyagers Mailing List, along with the story of how and why it came, one of those on the VML said that reading it solved a psychological problem she'd long had. I can't figure that out, though I'm glad it happened.

True encounter? Fantasy? Still undetermined. Such is the nature of the unconscious life I live (or perhaps I should say, such is the nature of the compartmentalization of my life) that I had forgotten that Yeats—if it was Yeats—had given me that name of the man and the name of the book. I never followed up on either, though one would think it would be easy enough. On the other hand, what would follow-up prove to anyone but myself? For me to say that I had found verification would still leave you, the reader, wondering if I was telling the truth, or at least wondering if other insights might explain it away. I am content to report what I find—to act as a sort of pointer—and leave it to others of a more scientific bent to do controlled experimentation and verification.

In any case, these experiences (and others unmentioned here) persuaded me that we extend far beyond the present-life self we commonly recognize. Not only are we intimately connected Upstairs; we are connected to other personalities leading other lives, now, in the past, and presumably in the future. Whether or not we reincarnate in the way commonly believed, I don't know. But in one way or another, we live more than one life; of that I have no more doubt. And it seems clear enough that those various lives affect each other. As a matter of fact, I am beginning to think that it would be simplest merely to say, as a scientific statement of the way things are, that "we are all one"—just as religions and other metaphysical systems have always said.

ELEVEN

Connection Between Individuals

My life, like yours, is mostly orchestrated behind the scenes, though the orchestration is not always evident. Looking back, I see that I did the Lifeline program (which I had no conscious intention of doing before Ed invited me to join him) just about in time to help me deal with the death of several people who were important to me. And those deaths taught me something about the way we as individuals are all connected beneath the surface of things.

If I had not done Lifeline in July 1995, I might have had to wait a long time before another opportunity arose. Literally on the day Lifeline ended, Ed Carter (newly a shareholder in HRPC) and Bob Friedman and I were enmeshed in the details involved in moving the company from Norfolk to Charlottesville. All fall I worked hard, first at moving the company, then commuting between Charlottesville and the Hampton Roads area (where my family remained until the following spring). In December Ed and I rented an apartment together, which gave me a place to stay weeknights and him a place when he came to visit HRPC and TMI every so often for a week or ten days at a time. An unexpected bonus to this mutually convenient arrangement was that it gave us a convenient place and time to have sessions with The Gentlemen Upstairs.

– 2 –

In the first week of January 1996 I got a message slip saying that Jack Dunbar had called me. Jack? I called him back and said, "Jack, is Suni okay?" He said, "Frank, Suni's dead!" After all those years, her cancer had come back a few weeks before, and she had gone rapidly. I hadn't even known she was ill, and it was typical of Suni that she wouldn't have told me. Suni only wanted to look at the bright side, not the dark.

I hung up the phone and cast back, looking for the last time I had talked to her and finding that I couldn't remember. I remembered the years right after the Shirley MacLaine seminar, when we used to have foodless lunches together, talking about everything under the sun. I could make her laugh, I remembered. Then somehow we each got busy with other things and the phone calls got less frequent, and then the company moved to Charlottesville, and now all of a sudden there weren't going to be any more phone calls, let alone foodless lunches. Life is a strange thing. We come into each other's lives, and become crucially important to each other, and then, mission accomplished (or mission abandoned), we leave again. I knew her a little less than nine years, yet she was vitally important to my life. Many others I have known for fifty years have made little impact. Life is more than mathematics.

– 3 –

A little more than a week after I learned that Suni had died, Joyce called (having gotten my new phone number from Rich, thank God) and told me that her mother had died of cancer over the holidays, and now her own cancer was back, in her ribs and liver. She told me she was going to fight hard, including coming out of the closet as a psychic. She was going to work on her book and work on healing herself. She was going to use vitamins, naturopathic medicine—and chemotherapy, though, she said, not the strong stuff she had been using before. I hated the idea of her using chemo, but she said she wanted to try everything that might help.

I suggested that she contact the Dolphin Energy Club to get on their list of people requesting distant healing energy, and that she get Mark Certo at TMI to make her a Focus 11 tape for the script she was preparing for herself. (I think of Focus 11 as the place where one programs one's subconscious mind. For a fee, TMI will make tapes underlaying one's self-help programming with Hemi-Sync tones designed to get the message to the right place.)

Of all those I'd done Lifeline with—other than Ed Carter, of course—I kept in closest touch with Rich, via telephone or e-mail. I got very fond of his dry and absurd sense of humor. "I was up to my place in 27 last night," he told me flatly one day. "I think I've got termites." Every so often one or the other of us would call, and we would swap jokes and generally fill each other in on the latest absurdities in our lives. At the time, we were working together via the Internet on the institute's Voyager Mailing List, trying to spread more light and less heat. Sometimes we'd discuss what went on there.

And of course we discussed Joyce, particularly after we learned that her cancer had recurred. In a long Sunday chat one day he said he had a sense of Joyce's liver cancer being connected to a stab wound in a prior life, which I realize must sound like lunacy to many. But we—and not we alone, by a long margin—have repeatedly been involved in situations that seem to involve just that. A few days later, I told him that TGU told me that she can't be in tune with both her inner and outer circumstances, as they don't line up. She would need to deal with a certain situation left over from the past. We wondered if we dared tell her.

In the course of conversation, I realized that she had been hesitant to reach out to us partly out of a sense of unworthiness to be loved. (God, what a sad world!) Part of that feeling could easily come from a life in a concentration camp, combined with the necessity of killing her daughter to save her from the Nazis.

Think of the ramification of that! We are what past experiences have made us. Easy enough to see in the context of one body, one lifetime. But our lives are far more extensive and more complicated than that. The experiences of these other lives carry through into ours, mentally, emotionally, spiritually. Therefore also physically.

I had experienced my Katrina as a child, crying within, because she had died bewildered and alone. And I periodically have suffered crippling back pain related to injury in at least two lifetimes, not counting this one. Similarly, my friend Bruce Moen had nearly died in this lifetime of sarcoidosis (as told in his book *Voyages Into the Unknown*) because of an unresolved wound "long ago." When he dealt with that root cause, "elsewhen" so to speak, he recovered from his illness. Rich had a sense that a root cause of Joyce's cancer was much like that.

– 4 –

In March Joyce went to Spain to see Alex Urbito, the psychic surgeon, who worked on her all week. When she returned to the States, her voice was strong and vigorous again. She said Urbito had told her it might take three weeks for the healing to manifest. He gave her the phone number of a man he said he had healed. That man told her he had a previously scheduled scan only a few days after his healing, and the doctors found no trace of cancer.

Joyce said that her husband was with her as Urbito worked with her—seemingly putting his fist *into* her stomach. Could see only the backs of his hands, though. Saw him put two clumps of something into an ashtray. He worked on her prior to working with the public, because, he said, she was his wife's special case. I said in my journal, "God, I hope!" But I asked myself, "Is Joyce doing okay?—or dying?"

In May she sounded very good. Scans showed that at least one liver tumor was shrinking. She had some bad days but now was better. She sounded optimistic, even happy. (But she was continuing on chemo!) Was working on her manuscript when I called. She told me she now realized love is all around her.

But on the twelfth of December she called to ask for prayers. She had gotten another bad report, and was scared again. I told her she *will* beat this, and will beat the underlying issue, which was that she has been repressing negativity rather than allowing herself to be less than perfect. In January I asked my friends on the Voyager Mailing List for support for Joyce.

Michael, a cyber-friend (i.e., a friend I haven't met), replied:

I will be happy to add my energies to the effort. . . . If a time is picked nights are best for me, but I can get by anytime. Sorry to hear about your friend. I lost my mom to six years of suffering with cancer two years and eight days ago. The emotions are still strong and easily brought back. . . . Whatever I can do for you, Rich, or Joyce, just let me know. Take care.

Richard said, by e-mail:

Thanks for sending out the request for healing for Joyce. We didn't get a chance to talk for very long last night. I think this has hit her a little harder than she wants to let out right now. Especially coming right after the death of her mother from cancer.

I am doing DEC for her each night and will also participate in any group healing. I am also sending her energy whenever I think of her during the day (which was more than I could count today). . . . I just wish we were all closer physically now.

Christel, another cyber-friend from the Voyager list, answered:

> Thanks for asking us—and you don't have to explain just how wonderful the person is, you know—a simple request from you is enough. <s> I've started sending her love already.
>
> Of course your description helped me tune in on her. I'll also try connecting with you and Rich to sort of link myself to your sending her energy and so hopefully help intensifying the energy you send, you knowing the target better.
>
> If you all decide to join in at a certain time, I'll do that, too. Only it's my experience that it works just as well above time. But anything you decide will be fine with me. . . .
>
> Sending love and light and healing energy is a wonderful thing to do also for the person who is allowed to do it. I'll keep sending her love for as long as it takes.

This loving reaction from friends shows how life—life in general, even life among strangers—*ought* to be, and still *can* be. I can't help wondering, Why isn't it?

On Thursday, January thirtieth, 1997, I called Joyce and was shocked at how weak she was. Her mother-in-law had to hold the phone for her so we could say a few words. I offered spoken prayer for her after I hung up. And sobbed.

The next night I was at my friend Dave Wallis's house on the New Land, the land around The Monroe Institute. Dave was an ex-Lockheed engineer who had worked on a volunteer basis to put together most of Monroe's laboratory, back in the early days of the institute. His open heart, his constant willingness to help at any time, and his great mechanical abilities made him a fixture on the New Land. He had put together a few people that he called the "Dream Group," meeting every other week or so to

perform various (nonpharmaceutical) experiments in con-
sciousness-expansion. At my request, we directed a group
prayer for Joyce, my first spoken prayer, sent with great emotion. Bruce Moen said he had seen a "cable" come from the
direction I think Texas is in, and saw a powerful beam coming
from me, arcing out in that direction.

Did it do any good? I was afraid to ask her, for fear that she
had felt nothing, or felt worse. What I hoped was that she would
feel so inexplicably healed that she would call me. Of course, I
knew that the healing a person needs isn't necessarily the healing we expect. On the other hand, we want results, and want
some indication we aren't fooling ourselves.

On February second I asked The Gentlemen Upstairs if
they had comment.

We are *so* happy, and happy for you (which is happy for us,
as you understand). Love *is* all there is; it's just that curiosity, work,
play, et cetera are *aspects* of love—or aren't. If they are, they come
with (and from) joy. Otherwise they are dead, or at best neutral. A
marking of time.

Your work for Joyce bore fruit *within you,* as all work for others does. Continue to love, continue to learn to love. Grow in *that*
direction, and cease to shrink from hurts and rebuffs now long
gone in your life. Remember—but remember only as spice of your
current knowing.

You are alive again, more alive than you have been for many
a long and short lifetime. Rejoice! All is well for you and those you
love. Only expand your circle. Cast your net widely. Cast it widely, and more widely. Think of Eleanor Roosevelt.

And thinking about Joyce, who *didn't* have a reaction to
Friday night, I got so angry all of a sudden. *Human life is not
supposed to be this way!* It doesn't have to be this way. But how
do we change it?

Joyce died February thirteenth. I had known, after what turned out to be my last conversation with her, that I should call Dr. Walter Weston, a minister who for many years had been doing healings by means of what he calls "therapeutic prayer." I knew I should ask him to pray with me for her. I didn't quite dare, I guess. I wondered: Might the power of that spoken prayer have produced a miracle? Did my reticence cost her her life?

Absurd thought, I suppose. She was at the center of her life, I only at the periphery. But I'm not all that sure that this way of thinking really makes as much sense as it seems to. If we are all connected, we are all connected, and each part affects every other part. Mentally, emotionally, physically.

– 5 –

From the day I learned that Joyce had died, I found myself getting upset whenever I thought about her. It was a little bit inexplicable to me. My beliefs about death and the afterlife aren't such as to make me think death a tragedy, so why the emotion? I didn't know, but at least I had learned not to deny what I couldn't explain.

In May I went to the meeting of the Dream Group at Dave Wallis's house, and went looking for her at various focus levels as we did a tape, but I couldn't find her anywhere. And not often, but every once in a while in the next few weeks, Joyce would come up in my thoughts or I would tell someone what she had done for me at Lifeline, and I would again realize how upset I continued to be. I wondered: Was it just because my efforts at healing—and those of so many others—hadn't brought her back to health? I didn't think so. But then, what was going on? I would not find out until July, when I would visit my friend Louis in Florida.

– 6 –

Ed Carter, unlike Joyce, left 3D Theater easily and (I believe) painlessly, in December 1996, on his own schedule.

Schedule?

Back in December 1994, at a time when his physical ailments had brought him to a point at which he might have left, he felt he faced a choice. He decided, he told Bob Friedman and me, to "renew his contract" for two years, with an option to renew at the end of that time. He told me repeatedly that he enjoyed being here, but that if it ever came to the point that he couldn't enjoy himself because of physical—or worse, mental—disability, he would want to, choose to, leave. By "choose" I don't mean suicide; I mean that he was confident that Upstairs and Downstairs would disconnect.

Sounds highly unlikely, doesn't it? Think of all the people you know, trapped in their bodies and longing for release, or longing to live and incurably ill, or victims of accident that fetches them off. Highly unlikely. Yet I cannot think of Ed's death without recalling the nature and timing of his last consultation with The Gentlemen Upstairs.

– 7 –

Ed made more use of TGU than anyone but myself, perhaps because he knew I was always delighted to "go Upstairs" and talk to them. During one of his visits to Charlottesville in early 1996, I was living with a wracking, painful cough that had gone on for two weeks, not getting better or worse, but not going away either. I couldn't figure out what it was or *why* it was. It wasn't asthma, and it wasn't a cold. I had gotten used to it, and saw no reason to let it stop me from doing anything I wanted to do, so one night I offered to talk to TGU for Ed, regardless of the coughing. I lay down on the couch in the living room, and Ed asked questions and worked the tape recorder, and we filled a side of tape with their answers.

At the end of one side of tape, as I got up to go to the bathroom, Ed asked if there was anything I wanted him to ask them on my behalf. (In those days I found it easier if others posed the questions for me, so that I didn't have to alternate between reception and transmission, so to speak.) I said, half-sarcastically (the sarcasm aimed at them, and at life in general, rather than at Ed), "Ask them how come the entire time I'm talking to them, I'm not coughing, and as soon as I get up I'm coughing again." Before I got to the bathroom door I knew the answer, but when we started taping again Ed asked the question and I got a fuller description of their version of what was going on.

(As usual, I find myself relaying information that I am not competent to judge. It was only after I started talking to TGU for others that I understood why Edgar Cayce feared the information he received, and said that if ever even one person was injured because of it, he would never do it again. It is a great responsibility, passing on information that may or may not be right. But what else can we do, but pass it on and see if it proves out? *Caveat lector.*)

TGU told us that our physical health is actually a relationship between our various bodies—physical, emotional, mental, astral—and our innumerable mental states, and that our health may be affected by changing *either end* of the body-mind polarity. Changes to the bodies tend to persist but are harder to bring about. Changes in mental state are evanescent but are, therefore, quite easy to bring about. (As in 1987, when my watching the Shirley MacLaine TV special changed my mental state—and instantly cured my intolerable back pain while I wasn't noticing.) They said this explains why people with multiple-personality disorder may have one personality who is diabetic and another who is not. In each case, the *body* is the same, obviously; but the *mind-body equation,* so to speak, is not. Changing the mental state has changed what is; it's a different mind-body mix, and the result is a different state of health.

Thus, when I was "where" I go mentally when I talk to TGU, the specific mind-body combination that had resulted in my coughing was in abeyance because one end of the polarity had moved. In returning to normal consciousness, I moved back where I had been, and the coughing resumed.

Sure enough, as soon as I ended the session, I started coughing again. But this time, I reached for the state I had been in when talking to them, a calmer, more expanded state. I brought the coughing to a stop. It began again the next day, but I again stopped it, and it did not recur. After that, Ed and I took their explanation as a given.

– 8 –

That was sometime in February, probably, of 1996. At the end of November he sent me by e-mail a question to ask them:

> Both my earth brain and my eternal mind accept as a fact that C1 existence requires three spatial dimensions plus the dimension of time. While my brain does not comprehend it, my mind can accept as reality the assertion that I also exist in the totality of all mind states, however many that may be.
>
> The question: When I die and discard the earth body I chose to occupy during my C1 life, do I then only exist as "the collection of mind states," or do I also exist as some kind of C1 image, and if so how does this work?
>
> Note: I am painfully aware that I do not have the words to express what I am trying to convey, but I expect you know what it is.

I took Ed's question to be motivated primarily by intellectual curiosity. TGU's response, delivered via the computer keyboard, came on Thursday, November 28, 1996, beginning at 6:02 P.M. I was aware even at the time that it was more like an interim statement than a full reply.

> Can you exist only as "the collection of mind states?" Could you? We'd like to see it, if you wouldn't mind demonstrating.

The concept lacks any organizing principle. You, Ed Carter, exist as a unit that is body, soul, and mind, or however you care to phrase it. Take away the body and what have you? Mind and soul together, with nothing holding them as a unit? (To the degree that you in a body are a unit anyway; less so or rather differently than you think.)

What do you think your body is? A convenience to keep you anchored in a certain place/time? Well, that's not so far off, in a simple view, but it is far from the total. It's also and even primarily an expression of the soul and mind that created it and are somewhat modified by it and its experiences.

On Wednesday evening, December 4, 1996, Ed called me from his home in New Hampshire and we had had one of our long phone conversations, in the course of which he made a point of paying me a couple of compliments that had the air of having been long thought and never previously said. In retrospect, the call was a farewell.

I went to bed and awoke a few hours later, at about 4 A.M. I sat down at my computer, and at Ed's request (and also out of my own curiosity) asked TGU to expand on their prior reply. For my own sake I also asked, "What was going on last week when I asked on his behalf and got this constrained answer?"

What was going on was stage fright, as you well know, and you well know, as well, whose stage fright it was. [Mine, in other words.] It's just another stage in development. Knowing that Ed knew something and knowing that you had read things, and *not* knowing if we knew the "right" answer, you choked, somewhat, and what came through was the limit of your audacity. Not that you need be ashamed of choking, given that the reaction stemmed from concern lest you pass on false information, but there is a certain amount of ego involvement here as well. Like all who bring in information from what you call "the other side," you want to have good information come in; you want to be known to bring in good information, and you don't want to get caught, to see us get caught, flat wrong. And of course there is doubt still. Do The Gentlemen Upstairs know what they're talking about? Do they even exist? Are you making it all up as you go along? But doubt is its own punishment. (Not that a "wrong" attitude warrants punishment, even by way of correction, but you know what we mean.)

So having answered your more important (to you) question first, on to an explanation of our previous answer. Reread it, then reread the question.

Now, remember that in trying to bring across information, you were painfully aware of having read something on the subject in one of the manuscripts you are incessantly reading. And you were determined not to let that information "contaminate" ours. Result, deadlock, because you were attempting to do two incompatible things: 1) bring in information by, as usual, being receptive without judgment, and 2) judge the information as it came in. You see the result, or lack of result. Now, note, this is not our way of "punishing" you. It is not the water's way of "punishing" the hose when the hose gets kinked up and the water can't flow through it. Neither is it the hose's "fault"; these things happen. We are only deepening your understanding of the process.

Of course you continue to have a body when you leave; your subtle body is the "organizing principle" we are hinting at. It is from the patterns underlying the subtle body that the physical body is constructed; this is why scars and other distinguishing marks are carried forth from one lifetime to another; it is also why weaknesses created in one lifetime (wounds, for instance) manifest in a succeeding lifetime; the pattern has been altered.

Now what should be of interest to you is this. You live, as we have said more than once, not consecutively as seen in earth time, but consecutively—to the limited extent that such a concept is meaningful here (that is, outside 3D theater)—in terms of soul growth, of soul experience. An individual soul may experience earth life in 1700 before it experiences it in 1325, then go to 1950, then 2000 BC. You understand? To speak of a soul's chronology is somewhat misleading, in that in an important way it all happens (as you would perceive it) "at the same time," or "at once"; or, let us say, that is as good a description as saying things happen one thing "at a time," for how can things happen "one at a time" when here there is no time? Of course, there is no "here" either, but you see the difficulties of communication between the two "playing fields," ours and yours, particularly when "ours and yours" are of course shared, and are only perceived in this analogy as separate.

Note too that when you change something "in the past" as you did on July 4 a couple of years ago, concentrating on your past in Gettysburg, you change not only that past but your present, as you healed your back at that time by healing "another's"; it is not a mere stylistic convenience to say "you are all one." But if an event changes now, the body that resulted in the past from—

Let us try again, as it is easy to get this twisted up.

You exist in 1996, but you previously existed in 1749, say. Now let's say (though in your specific case this is not true, but let us say) that in your soul's progression the 1996 lifetime came first; hence from the soul's point of view, the physical experiences in 1749 follow the physical experiences of 1996. And since the body is the expression of what happened to it previously—DON'T LET LOGIC GET IN THE WAY OF THIS, JUST TAKE IT DOWN—since the body is the expression of what happened to it previously, your changing yourself in the present changes what happens to bodies in the soul's future, which can be in the chronological past; hence potentially changing the past; which impacts on where you are in the physical present. A circular process, you see, and far less constrained and "determined" than you (plural) usually think.

Now (Frank), reread and absorb and we'll deal with objections.

God! All right, if that's the way it is, then someone in my soul's past, inhabiting a future body, can change my "inheritance" now? And creates a new body each time it changes its own reality?

Not bad. That's probably as close as you can get right now to getting our meaning. It begins to capture the evanescent quality, the now-you-see-it,-now-you-don't quality, of life that your logic-choppers never get. This is why there are infinite alternate realities, by the way: every choice sets up new conditions in the soul-future and in the body-future, and these are curiously interlinked with the body-past and soul-past, so that each new decision is a carom shot that sends repercussions bounding wildly in all directions. Which by the way is the fun of our continual creation; and by "our" we of course do not mean TGU alone, but you and other dimensions as well. Think of life as a great game on a self-creating pinball machine. Fun! It ain't all solemn purpose; experiencing is fun. Otherwise why do it?

Well, you've given us some stuff to think about. I'll send this out to some friends and see what it generates. Thanks.

As always, no charge. Just think of what some of your "past incarnations" just added to their subconscious memories tonight.

I had the computer mark the date and time as usual, and so I know that this consultation ended at 4:54 A.M. I sent it off to Ed as an e-mail message, which means he had all day Thursday to read it, though nobody can positively state that he did. Sometime that night, he left us. Was there a connection? I know only that the two things happened closely together in time. *Something* in the universe linked them.

– 9 –

By this time, Ed's daughter Ginna Colburn had come to work for us as chief administrative officer. For the first few months, before she moved to Virginia, she commuted from West Virginia, staying at her father's apartment during the week and returning home for long weekends. I called her there from work on that Friday, and Ginna told me that she had just been told that her father had been found dead by his computer, having died apparently swiftly and presumably painlessly.

Calling the staff into the conference room and telling them was the saddest duty I had ever had there. We all held Ed in great affection. After a while Bob Friedman and I went into one of our offices and turned on the tape recorder and I went Upstairs, to see what The Gentlemen Upstairs had to say about it. Here are excerpts from my transcript:

Bob: Do you have any comments about the reason Ed chose this particular time to leave us?

Although what you call his Downstairs level sort of forgot, itself, he'd been telling you for more than two years he was going to leave this month. He later was hedging his bets, but this was the plan. He was surprised to go, actually. We will give you the assurance that he's not disappointed, however. He has finished— There would never be an empty agenda, because he was always one to put more into the mix, but he finished all the things that were the most urgent, and he more than accomplished what he came here to do. [Pause.] You will find that he didn't leave you without final messages, some of which were already delivered.

Bob: Do you know where he is now?

He's where he always was, but—disconnected from this body, let's put it that way. If you mean, is he aware and conscious at this point—unlike the people who need time to recuperate, you know?—yes he is. Very quickly and easily and we can talk to him if you wish.

Bob: I'm not sure we wish, except to wish him godspeed, and that if he has any messages for us, to tell us, at this point.

We smile, passing on his smile, because he's saying something that amounts to, "Don't worry, I'll have messages for you." [A laugh.] To-do lists. . . .

Bob: Anything else you wish to say?

We remind you that Ed Carter went downstairs in a Heartline program after a particular tape and looked around and said everyone in the room was an angel. And we tell you that he saw true. You understand? . . . You're all surrounded by angels. Which means, of course, that you're all angels. Not meaning you're not human, but meaning that humans are more than you think you are. And we say you with an asterisk, because it's more like "we," but you make the distinctions.

Bob: I don't know if Frank has any questions or not.

Frank: Well I don't have questions, but I have a feeling there's something waiting to be said. Or waiting for us to precipitate it, I think. Gentlemen, you want to give us whatever's—or, why are we doing this—I mean, do you have an agenda here?

When you find your heart opened, cherish the feeling. Cherish the ability to have an opened heart. That's Ed's last gift.

As part of a message to Ed's family, they added:

Ed very late in his life learned that love is the only thing in life that counts. He *believed* it a long time, but he *learned* it and *knew* it toward the end, and that's what he became.

That is very true, and everybody who knew him was aware of it. And I suggest to you, reader, that this book will have been worthwhile for you if you absorb nothing more than the idea—the truth—that love is the only thing in life that counts. By now the statement is a cliché—but statements become clichés because they are endlessly repeated, and sometimes they are endlessly repeated because they are true.

– 10 –

A few months later, in July 1997, my old friend Louis asked me to visit him in Florida. The coordinated timing of his life and mine was interesting, as always. Not only were our mental and emotional outlooks still the same; our lives were eerily similar internally, even though they couldn't have been much more different externally. I was a father and married; he was single. I was a businessman and writer; he was a schoolteacher. I had moved from field to field while he had stuck to one thing since he graduated college. Yet as I got off the plane in Florida we faced similar crossroads, or rather, to put it more accurately, we similarly seemed to be facing looming dead-end signs. Neither one of us could see how we were going to be able to go on living the lives we led.

Lou's story is his to tell, should he ever choose to. And my story is as little communicable as ever. Suffice it to say that neither of us could see a way forward. It was odd, how different our problems were, and how similar. I don't mean to be cryptic, but that's as much as I'm going to say about it. The point of saying even this much is to indicate what should be obvious anyway; that acquiring new mental abilities does not bring you to perfection, or enlightenment (whatever that is), or even, necessarily, contentment. Life is still boot camp, and like boot camp it is educational, but it is rough, and hard to get through.

Like boot camp too, it's a great place to make deep friendships, whose value is more than gold.

Our week was perfect. Not an unkind word, not an awkward moment, not a clash of temperaments or wills. I value friendship, and I have been blessed with having many friends, from one year to the next, but this was the only perfect week I have ever known or expect to know.

Externally, not much happened. We went to the nearby Gulf beach, we listened to music, we went out to eat or he cooked for us, and we talked and read and made bad jokes and sat in companionable silence, and talked some more.

And talked. And talked. Even in this, we were perfect, neither of us chattering when the other wanted silence, neither refusing talk when the time was right.

We talked about the impossibility of living this Downstairs life. The incredible cruelty that people can display toward one another, and the kindness. The senselessness of ambition, and yet the aimlessness that accompanies lack of ambition. The difficulty of living a blameless life and yet the blamelessness of one and all, when seen in a certain perspective—for truly, the strange truth is that people are doing their best.

I was down there only a few days—taking a flight one Tuesday and the return flight the following Tuesday—but the brief week turned his life around, and mine. How? Not the talk, exactly, and not the quiet, unhurried activities that filled our days. Not the music from the stereo or the books from the library and bookstore, or the oil paints that I lugged along from Virginia that resulted in one nice painting.

What was the magic element? Empathy, I suppose—for truly we could each understand the other, and the other's dilemmas, however different they would have appeared to the outside world. I think the old saying has it that sorrows shared are sorrows halved. True words. We each spoke the pain and confusion and guilt and anger that filled our lives, and in speaking them to a sympathetic ear, found ourselves healed.

– 11 –

And a very interesting thing happened. Among the many things we talked about was Joyce, and how she helped me, and how she died, and how bad I felt about her dying, and how for some reason I could not reconcile myself to the fact. Months after the fact, I still found myself at the point of tears when I thought of her, which produced in me not merely surprise but impatience. Louis and I talked of many other things, but I noticed that over several days, he came back to referring to her. And he repeatedly said, "Been there, done that," an expression I had never heard him use before or since, an expression I associate *exclusively* with Joyce, who used it a lot at Lifeline.

One day after lunch, as we each sat half drowsing in the midday heat, I suddenly realized that maybe something (someone?) was using him to tell me that I should go looking for her. Sitting in a chair in his living room, I closed my eyes and went Upstairs, and this time I found her, quickly and easily, lost and wandering in some focus level very much *not* 27.

I didn't get it. The ability to make our way to 27 when we die is one of the prime objectives of the Lifeline program. That's why we put markers at that level, and construct "houses" there, so that we will have something familiar to aim for when we shed our physical bodies. Why hadn't she been able to do it?

As soon as I put the question, the answer came. She had died confused, lost in the physical pain and the brain-dulling effects of the painkillers.

Okay, enough of that. I surrounded her with love, and moved with her to Focus 27, and showed her my cabin there. Then others came for her and she went off with them. What is interesting and inexplicable is that she was met by others *from her life as Katherine's mother,* not from this life. I thought that was very strange, even inexplicable, even while I was still in the experience. I tried to make sense of it; couldn't. I even criticized myself for getting confused and fantasizing. Still, there it was, and my self-reproach didn't change it. Nor do I understand it yet.

– 12 –

When I came "back" a few minutes later, I got up quietly (Louis having fallen asleep in his chair across the room), went to bed, and slept deeply for a very few minutes. Expedition and recuperation together didn't take above half an hour. After I returned, and since, I have not felt the awful pain that even the thought of this lost love had been provoking. And Louis stopped mentioning her. Also, I have never again heard him use the expression, "Been there, done that."

Where she had been, I don't know. But I do know she is there no longer, and is okay. Hedge and waffle as I would, I concluded nonetheless that I did succeed. As with Katrina, I felt different. Changed.

Immediately after I got her safe in that midday retrieval—within hours—other things happened (that are no part of this story) that left both Louis and me seeing more calmly and clearly a possible path ahead, at a time when all roads had seemed closed. I wondered, later, could it be that she was again helping me, as at Lifeline? But maybe this was not Joyce's initiative, but that of the same invisible helpers who prompted me to go Upstairs that day and help her.

It is tempting to think that in bringing Joyce to safety we have brought her story to its logical conclusion, but given the way we all interact on this plane and others, I wonder if any of these stories ever do reach a logical conclusion. Every set of events forges or strengthens or complicates or weakens or resolves emotional links between souls.

Surely this is what is meant by karma? The endless play of interaction? If her soul and mine meet again in another life, presumably we will not recognize each other Downstairs. Neither she nor I, of course, will be the same person that we were in this life. Not only will our physical identities be different—with all that that implies in terms of different genetic inheritance—but our souls themselves will be different because of whatever has happened to us by the time we meet again. And the story line of that new lifetime may enmesh us in God knows what relationship Downstairs, complicating or rather overlaying our relationship Upstairs. But will there not be then—at least at the beginning, as there were this time—seemingly uncaused strong bonds of gratitude and affection between us?

I am very aware, writing this, that what I have just written is a lie, in that it takes time-space for granted, as if "future" lives are in a future that doesn't yet exist, and "past lives" are in a past that is over. Yet to speak otherwise—even to think otherwise— would require that someone invent a new subset of our language, as mathematicians and physicists do.

Actually, I think this language already exists in several places, in unsuspected places. Monroe has a piece of it. Hindu and Buddhist scriptures have a piece, as does modern physics. Swedenborg offers clues, and so do the mystics of all religions, if we can find the key to what they experienced and are attempting to express. Christian theology is a major source of understanding, if reexamined shorn of the anti-reincarnation bias that was imposed as a political decision seventeen centuries ago. I take it as self-evident that nothing that has occupied the minds of serious scholars over a long period of time should be dismissed, without examination, as nonsense. To examine and explain the profound insights of past generations, and other belief systems, in light of what we know today, would be a massive job, but a productive one. And obviously I agree with Monroe: the key to translation is personal experience.

TWELVE

Connection Across Time

A few weeks after I returned from Florida, without much prior thought I did the Lifeline program again. I had been expecting a visit from an out-of-state cousin. I learned, on a Thursday in late August, that he and his family would be unable to come. I called the institute to see if there was a slot open, and on Saturday there I was, not quite knowing why.

I knew the trainers, Ann Martin (who had been a trainer in my Gateway Voyage in December 1992) and Dave Mulvey (Lifeline trainer in July 1995), and liked them both. Other than them, I knew none of the participants, not that prior acquaintanceship usually mattered.

I went remembering Joyce, of course, and Richard and Ed, and a couple of other friends from two years earlier. Haunted by ghosts, I was, in that sense. During the Focus 10 reset tape on Saturday evening, I looked for Ed Carter. Nothing. Joyce, nothing. Looked for my Uncle Lew, who had died only weeks before. Nothing. Then Bob's voice called us back to C1. Nothing for the whole tape. But it's all right; this is only preliminary.

Sunday

Sunday I am up at 5 A.M., journaling, walking outside before dawn. Something moves me to raise my arms in salute to the coming day, and it feels very natural and right, very connected. During Sunday morning's first tape in Focus 10, I experience a vision of the universe being composed of something spinning. But what is it that's spinning? I lose it as soon as the vision completes, though I try to keep it. Very strange. (I will learn what is going on before too long.) After a while I click back into consciousness, realizing that I have missed much of the rest of the tape. Maybe—it occurs to me with a smile—maybe *this* is why I sleep so little at Monroe. I sleep during the tapes! Actually, though, I think I have "clicked out," in Monroe jargon: I have had an experience, but haven't downloaded the memory of it, leaving me with nothing.

Before the Focus 12 reset tape, I ask The Gentlemen Upstairs for ideas on what purpose I should bring to the tape.

You can always stand to improve your connection with others in your life, with the situations in your life. Why not try to think through your concerns, concentrating not on what "feels right" but on what "makes sense"—given that what makes sense in Focus 12 may be different from what makes sense in C1.

This is what I do. Sure enough, what makes sense from 12 is different from what makes sense in C1. The reset 12 tape works better than it ever has before, because I *think*, I don't just drift around and wait for something to happen. Proving there's always more to learn about even the things we've come to take for granted. In the middle of the tape, I have a sudden knowing that Bob Monroe's voice is going to invite us to record, and immediately thereafter he does so. Among other things, I record this:

I had forgotten the thing I did at sunrise this morning. . . .
I want to be more connected with the earth and with
everything than I am. I want to be a healer and to be

whole and be in my power. I'm very much aware of that as I am here, the longing to come into my own. I am aware that it is right around the corner.

After the tape I wander around outside, speaking to no one. The feeling that soon there is deep stuff coming has returned.

During the long break I talk to a woman whom I will call "Lucy." She and I feel connected to each other, for reasons I won't go into here. Suffice it to say that rather than romantic attraction, we seem tied by bonds of mutual emotional support. Later, in a break between tapes, I tell her she may be the reason (beyond my personal reasons) I so suddenly decided to come to Lifeline. I had called Louis and told him I was inclined to do Lifeline again, and didn't know why. He had said, instantly, someone needed me to be there. She says she may know why. She had been told a male figure at Monroe would give her a piece of crucial information.

I don't expect much going into the "Introduction to 22 and 23" tape, but it proves highly interesting. In 23, I get a clear picture of a church, and of a little house, and before either of those, of a grand arched outdoor cafe or garden, very pleasant, just as I had at my first Lifeline. And I realize that there are infinite numbers of places to choose from, lots of thought-created structures. There was much time to have created them, and they stay, once built. It's more like the place Bob Monroe's friend built (as mentioned in *Journeys Out of the Body*) than it is our idea of 23.

Even for the souls in 23, I hear, there is a nighttime sky. I see vast, endless cities and trees, a world bigger than ours, more populous. I get an image of a bridge over a vast, deep, chasm. One half of the chasm's wall collapses, crumbles, millions of elements crumbling. A sign of the coming catastrophes. They depopulate the earth and thus vastly increase the population of 23. Not a crumbling civilization, a crumbling of the physical structures, tumbling millions into 23 and other places.

Existence in 23, I realize, is quite as real and as definite as ours to us in C1. It is vague to us only because we can't see it clearly from outside—as they do not see clearly any but their own creations/perceptions. One thing that is coming clear (I write after the tape) is how little of what I know can be conveyed to individuals in speech, as opposed to writing. I decide that maybe I will have to write a book after all—and, interestingly, at some point during a briefing, a woman announces to the room in general that she has been told (Upstairs) that someone there is going to write a book, and should share the royalties with The Monroe Institute. I learn later that she first went to Lucy and told her the voice named me specifically as that person.

Monday

Monday I get up at 5 A.M. and walk around in the dark. At about seven, armed with coffee, I sit at the table in the center room near the conference room, at the bottom of the stairs, and write:

> Ritual, it struck me this morning, is anything we do routinely and habitually but in a state of awareness, with intent to connect. Connect with the earth, or with animals or other people, or even with the self we are at other times. Thus, we impoverished white tribes could return ritual to our lives quietly, inconspicuously, even in things like commuting to and from work. But the seed consciousness needs to be there.

Lying in my CHEC unit writing as I wait for our first tape of the day, I find that I am reluctant to start, for some reason. Something guides me to "stay right in Virginia." I try to work TMI into it, but can't. (One argument against the suspicion that we are making all this up is that sometimes—often—one can't move a vision or experience any way but the way it wants to go.) I say, well, is there anybody here I can help?

I remember Clara. And find her. She is still on her deathbed, still dying of the allergic reaction to the stings from what they called "bees," which I think were yellow jackets.

In real life—life in physical-matter reality—she had lingered several days, in agony as her throat swelled up inside, preventing her from eating, drinking, almost from breathing. And after she died, apparently her mind—her soul, call it what you will—never got free of that scene. Without her physical body to drag her through time, she remained stuck in the same place, in an endless moment that went on and on.

No wonder the atmosphere of that cabin affected people negatively! No wonder Emily had hated being there. All that time (if you want to look at it that way) Clara was lying there in an unending agony. Like the boy Patrick of Monroe's famous Patrick tape, she had been caught in an endless scenario that never progressed, for the dead have no time. For whatever reason, too, the helpers on the other side had been unable to help her free herself. Now that I think of it, the situation closely resembles what happened with Joyce. Joyce had died disoriented by pain and the effects of chemical painkillers. Whether Clara too had painkillers interfering with her mental clarity, I don't know. In any case, she had fewer resources than Joyce to deal with the situation.

No matter. In both instances, our invisible friends needed help from someone who was still in the physical. In both cases, they chose me, presumably because of the strength of the emotional links.

I am clothed as John, of course. I put a sort of woven mat made of reeds around her throat, telling her that I have found an Indian medicine that would cure her. I tell her that the swelling will soon go down. After a bit I tell her that I think she could take some water. Meanwhile I am lying to her about how fast the medicine works, et cetera.

Before long, I get her to sit up, and I tell her that she needs to get outside again, and see the kids. (Kids? Presumably John and she had kids, but, as so often in retrievals, I find myself saying things without any idea where the prompting is coming from.) I help her walk to the door of the cabin, using the distraction that this causes to move us to Focus 27.

To my surprise, the cabin in Focus 27 is—the cabin I had found there waiting for me, back in my first Lifeline program two years before. Somebody created it there for me, maybe for just this purpose. For all I know, maybe I created it sometime in what is still the future for me as I write this.

As we stand at the doorway of the cabin, her parents come for her. Her father wears a big, broad-brimmed hat. Her mother is in gray.

"But—my parents are dead."

"Clara," I say, "you died of that sting. Your parents will take you from here—" And I say good-bye to her, and come back to this world.

This description may sound calm and in control, but in fact as soon as the actual retrieval was over, I was wrenched with great sobs, sobs of sorrow and relief, as when I retrieved Katrina two years before. And after the tape ended, while Bob's voice was counting us back down, I wrote in tremendously powerful, heavy pen strokes, "Oh God! Oh God," and then wrote down a fast, sketchy description so that I might remember as much detail as I could. These experiences can be of searing intensity, yet fade quickly from memory unless swiftly anchored.

I asked myself—and do yet—if maybe Emily feels the difference? I know *I* do.

This experience was a healing of another, *and* a retrieval, *and* a working out of a relationship problem, even if only Upstairs. (I doubt that Emily and I will ever be reconciled Downstairs, much as I regret it.) It was closure going back to Gateway. I trusted Guidance and it did not let me down. Rather than push, push, push, I was open yet alert. The concentration on staying in Virginia paid dividends! Now I see that it is no wonder that I was unable to find her during my 1995 Lifeline. It had never occurred to me that she might be still stuck in her terminal scenario from that life.

The more I think about it, the stranger it all is, this life of unsuspected connections that we lead; and the wider the ramifications extend. I learned after I retrieved Katrina what a difference in this life here the welfare of our other lives makes, regardless whether or not we even suspect that those other lives exist. Once I retrieved Katrina, I *in this life* felt the difference; it was, as I have said, as if a part of me that was a lost, crying child was suddenly all right. And if my perceptions are accurate, the personality that was Clara of the 1700s had been stuck in her deathbed scenario all through Lidian Emerson's lifetime in the 1800s, and Emily's in the second half of the 1900s up to 1997, not to mention any other lives that may be connected to her/them in other times. In retrieving her, presumably I have lightened all those lives by just that much.

Think what that says of our ability to help or harm our fellows! Hurting anyone hurts all the lives to which they are intimately connected, as healing them heals the other lives. The greater the hurt or healing, the greater the effect. Seen in that light, how great the damage done by a Hitler or a Stalin or a Mao! But the damage we each do in our blundering around, until we learn to step more carefully, is great enough.

I do not share my experience of retrieving Clara during our debriefing after the tape, merely because it would have taken too long to put in all the requisite explanations. But when I tell Lucy about healing Clara, suddenly she sees that what she had seen as a bird's nest in the sunshine (a vision in the tape experience that had puzzled her) could also be interpreted as reed matting like I had used on Clara, put into the sunlight so she would notice it. We seem to have shared aspects of the tape experience.

In fact, two experiences. For, in the tape following the one in which I retrieved Clara, I see some interesting line drawings of people's heads, and when I come back I sketch them (incompetently) in my journal. Lucy and I debrief that tape one-on-one, and she tells me about seeing people's heads, quite distinctly. I am glad to be able to show her the sketches, so she doesn't have to take my word that I had really seen much the same thing.

Tuesday

Tuesday at 6 A.M., after my morning ritual, I write:

The world outside at night is different each hour, and different every night. Today it is intense fog, and only a sliver of moon—well past third quarter—riding in the sky. The trees I walk among are not ghostly presences, but solid presences amid a ghostly atmosphere.

I do love this earth, this miracle.

Tuesday's first tape brings us to Focus 25.

At Focus 25, a sense of an endless building—cathedral? monastery? priory? Something quite other? Stone, unending. Waited for it to end, told self to wait and see what it meant, rather than jump to conclusions. Aerial shot, rising. Vast lands, trees, houses, centers of various kinds.

Went to one particular house (didn't know why, but trusted guidance); went in very close to the wall, didn't know why at first, later realized it is a pun: what I am seeing is only a sliver of what exists. Saw a room, with a man sitting in it. The bottom fell out of half the room, leaving him sitting next to nothingness. But I didn't follow the man; I followed below the floor to a stone pillar on which the house had been constructed. Then a sense of catacombs, and people living like burrowing animals—and the number of them there had been. A sense, in other words, of extent in time and space and number, for those who lived in catacombs are represented in belief systems too.

Then more sense of extent, and a knowing that these territories aren't so much for illusion, or comfort, as a foothold for people. Again, millions who won't be on earth—but earth at C1 isn't the only game in town. That's the message. Treat these places seriously, they are work places.

Lucy and I agree that I will look for her symbol in 21 and try to accompany her, to help her get to 27. A tape brings us to Focus 27 for the first time. On the way up, at Focus 10 or thereabouts, I am all intent on trying to help and I get a grotesque face with a clown-like gesture. I laugh and say, "I get it, no drama." I remember carrying Lucy, briefly, between level 10 and 15 maybe, saying I want to do that: support. I doubt she got the *image*, but I was hoping she got the *feeling*, the protection. I click out after a while, trying to keep her okay. I don't wake up till Bob's voice is bringing us to Focus 25 on the way down. As we pass 23, I sit up in my CHEC unit and start writing. When Lucy and I compare notes, she tells me she felt she *had to* go from 23 right to one! I hadn't thought that my popping out into C1 might pop her out too, but I'm just as glad it happened, as it shows that we seem to be sharing our experience. Very gratifying.

For the first tape after lunch, we meet in 21 by agreement, and I see us in the sunny corner of a house, having breakfast together. Once we get to 27, I hold up my physical hand in my CHEC unit to remind me, and to stay conscious, and mostly to be a symbol of my staying connected to her without trying to tether her in any way.

Then I go to my cabin. It is changed! Now there's a big porch with very modern windows, very comfortable. The whole thing is modern now inside. Mission accomplished, I'd say, so far as Clara is concerned.

When I meet Lucy again at the time we are to begin to return to 21, I tell her (down through several layers), "Remember that you are loved. Remember that you are loved. Remember that you are loved." And not till I came to write this book did I recall that this is the same message I gave Clara, five years earlier. And Joyce. Why is it so hard for people to believe that they are worthy of being loved? At 21 I leave Lucy (waiting till 21, this time!), so that I can write in my journal, knowing that she'll be fine.

During the next tape, in which we are to build a place for ourselves in Focus 27, Lucy and I agree to meet at 21 again, go to 27 together, and wing it from there. At 27 I invite her to see my place. It has changed again. It now is open to the view of the river—windows gone. I play around a lot, realizing that I have no place for writing, no place for nutrition, no place for elimination (bathroom) or cleansing (bathtub). Granted, logic said two years ago that it wasn't necessary. But I see now that it represents unfulfilled necessities. Elimination of used-up nutrition, for instance.

I place a table and a desk for me to write and to store manuscripts. And need a place to paint and to play the fiddle, which I can fill in later. *And,* I realize mostly, I need someone to *share* it with; never before a perceived necessity. At least as a temporary or guest situation.

Wednesday

On Wednesday I get up at five, as if to an alarm clock, because the day before at lunch one of the young women had said she had never walked before dawn and would like to join me. But she is not around, and so I do the same morning ritual that I have done Sunday, Monday, and Tuesday morning. I return to see if she is up, but she is not, so I go out again, this time walking straight down nearby Rainbow Ridge Road, never dreaming that in less than a year I would be living there.

Coming back, I am moved to run, and listening to some instinct, I do so in a strange flat-footed run that in a quick sequence reminds me first of Don Juan teaching Castaneda and then of an Indian runner in the Andes. (Funny, I never thought of those runners as having personal lives.) My gift in getting up to walk with someone if she really intended to walk is that I got up and did it, culminating in a run and a realization. And so to journaling, and exercise class, and breakfast, and our first retrieval tape.

The DEC portion of the tape has us visualize our physical, emotional, and mental body maps. As we do, I get images, all of which deal with nutrition, which I finally figure out. While dealing with the physical body map: I see myself starting to eat a meal, and pouring hot sauce on mine. (Which I translate as meaning, I can have it the way I like it.) Emotional body map: I am walking out of a building against the tide of a few people coming the other way. (Heading toward the outside, and mountains, and freedom.) Mental map: I am in a cafeteria. (It is up to me to choose my own nourishment. I have the right and responsibility to choose what I eat.) And this third vision refers all the way back to the cafeteria vision I had had in Gateway five years earlier, just before I watched my transcendentalist friend Smallwood visit Emerson.

Then I escort Lucy from 21 to 27. At 27, I go to my house, then upriver very briefly, and downriver. This time I don't turn back, but go on and on, into an indefinite and undefined future, into a picture where you couldn't tell the river from the surroundings because of distance. A *good* feeling.

Then I am in 23, at the podium of a lecture hall. I say, I know there is a person here that I love; please contact me. But nothing happens (yet).

The retrieval itself proves difficult, if ultimately enlightening.

I see a young woman essentially naked on a wet grassy hillside. She has been raped and strangled. I have to figure out how to approach the problem. I know tenderness won't work, at least not initially. I get a blanket and cover her body up to the neck—that is, I treat her as a living person, not a corpse. I try to get her to sit up, to tell her help is here, but she won't respond. She has retreated as far from the situation as she can, and intends to remain "safe" by not responding to anything, least of all to kindness.

I think—now what? I get a red and blue police light going, as if on a crime scene, and Bob's voice on the tape interrupts; time to report. I give a few clipped sentences, ending with, "I gotta go"; I am filled with urgency. Back to the scene. I set up a good cop/bad cop routine. I know somehow that she won't respond to tenderness, couldn't relate to it. So I'm a cop.

Other cop says, "Leave her, Louie, she's just a spic."

I say, "Shut up, Charlie, I'm Spanish too."

He says, "She's just a whore."

I say, "No, she's a good person."

"Well, get her off the lawn, or I'll throw her in the morgue with the other meat."

I get down near her head and encourage her to sit up so I can get her to help. I try and try and try. Takes a long time before she responds. I tell her she is wrapped up in a blanket, and I'll get her to the hospital so she can be treated. Somehow I wind up carrying her in my arms in a fireman's carry, and get us to 27 that way. When we get there, there is an ambulance and a stretcher and I tell her they'll take care of her, I have to go fill in a crime report—and there's Bob's voice, right on cue, saying to report.

This is the hardest retrieval I have yet done, because of the delicacy of approach needed and the difficulty I have in figuring out an approach that might work. However, as it turns out, "I" am not the one doing the figuring out. And during debriefing I see that each of us had been given a retrieval situation tailored to what we could handle. It is interesting to watch people change as the experience changes them. One man who had been extremely doubtful of his ability to do it reports offhandedly that he had brought several people to 27. He gives no details, saying, "And that's about it." I laugh and say, "Another day in the office, right?" Another man, who was extremely skeptical, had found a woman standing on a hill, staring down at a harbor. He had walked up to her and said (perfectly in character), "Excuse me, but do you know that you're dead?" We laugh as he tells us this, but in fact that was exactly the approach needed. "Yes, I had about decided as much," she told him calmly. He suggested that she go aboard the ship in the harbor, and this too accorded with what she had been thinking.

In my case, I had been through Lifeline before. I knew the basics. So they had given me something harder than I had done before. And as an extra, they had thrown in a bonus in the form of the interruption from Bob's voice. That interruption showed me that the flashing police light wasn't *my* invention, because I had no idea what I was going to do with it. When I came back, I knew, without doubt.

It reminds me, now, of what Monroe said in one of his books, about how he kept getting into situations and then flawlessly out of them. Like him then, I thought maybe I was good, but I knew I wasn't *that* good. It was the first time that I saw, front and center, how much we are guided by invisible promptings that seem to us to come from ourselves.

A lot of what I was beginning to suspect came clear on the next retrieval tape.

I couldn't figure out what was going on. I was in 23, back at the same auditorium I had seen earlier. Who was I supposed to retrieve? I started to go into the audience, thinking it might be a younger aspect of someone I knew. Then I thought—maybe more than one at once. And this was a thought-bridge that proved to be the key, for it moved my expectations. Then I knew that somehow I was to bring the whole crowd.

The difficult part, actually, was accepting that somehow a crowd of people to be retrieved had been assembled. Once I decided to take that as given, I winged it and it was fun, in a sort of self-mocking way. I decided (or rather, I strongly suspect, I was prompted) that they had been assembled to experience an OBE workshop! I told them to put on the earphones by their seats! Then I did my best Bob Monroe imitation, telling them, "Anything you may feel—dizziness, a sense of motion, flying, or nothing at all—is perfectly normal." In the process I concentrated their attention on an expected experience. It was easy to bring the whole auditorium with me to 27, room and all.

But then I stayed there and asked guidance for an explanation, because I couldn't figure out who these people could be. Aspects of myself? Past lives? If so, how could they have known about OBE stuff? And how could they have been assembled?

Finally I got it, and it tied in to what I had gotten some days earlier. In 23 not everyone is disoriented and isolated. Many, perhaps most, are just stuck because they don't know they should be moving on and won't listen when told so. So they live in these communities such as I saw, those vast areas. It was a small thing to get a small percentage of them together for an OBE lecture and workshop!

Of course, the whole scenario into which I walked, playing my role ad lib, reinforced my growing sense that in these sessions we are being guided through scripts prepared for us in advance, little though we may sometimes realize it. We are walk-ins in these worlds, not choosing the drama or the personnel or the situations, only doing our best, with guidance; stumbling through. I'm developing a different perspective on all this.

It may be that we don't yet understand very well the purpose of the belief-system territories. In the tape Sunday night, I had recorded that "even for the souls in 23, there is a nighttime sky." I saw vast endless cities and trees, and got a clear impression of a world bigger than ours, more populous. And there was that definite sense I had of an infinite number of places to choose from within 23: lots of thought-created structures like houses, churches, cafes, built over a long time. Once built, they stay. Existence in 23, I gathered, is as real and as definite to them as ours here is to us. It is only vague to us because we from outside can't see it clearly, just as they do not see clearly any but their own creations/perceptions.

The tape on Tuesday had showed me Focus 25 as a seemingly endless building, then a vast land with trees, houses, and centers of various kinds. Beneath the houses were foundations down to endless catacombs. It gave me, in other words, a sense of how far the belief-system territories extend in time and space and number. And I knew that these territories aren't so much for illusion, or comfort, as they are a *foothold* for people. Again, there are millions who won't be on earth. These places are *work* spaces.

On Wednesday I had been told that in 23, not everyone is disoriented and isolated. Many, perhaps the vast majority, live apparently normal lives, in communities such as I had seen—those vast areas. This was reinforced by another example from another member of the Lifeline group. She went to see her recently dead daughter, who said the equivalent of, "Mom, come with me, I've got something to show you," and took her to 23. There she saw a grown man, with family, and realized that this was the baby boy she had miscarried at six months, thirty years ago. Somehow, in 23, that life is being lived out as it had not had a chance to be, here in C1. There's *a lot* we don't understand yet! It may be that in a few years we will look back with smiles on our present understandings of how things are. These experiences, which were clearly orchestrated somewhere, persuaded me that we don't yet have the final word on the true nature and purpose of the various focus levels.

Bob Monroe used to say, "You go find out and come back and tell me, and we'll both know." It seems to me that's our task now—to keep going out and finding out, and coming back and telling. For all we have learned so far, we are still only at the beginning.

Thursday

Thursday. Last day of the program. I get up at six and do some journaling. I take my little morning walk/ritual, though it's abbreviated, because since I'm wearing long pants, I can't go through the tall grass. But I get in the salute to—whatever is where I'm saluting; it is not in the direction of sunrise, but rather north of that, maybe northeast.

As always, Thursday will be a silent morning—three tapes, no debriefing, then lunch. I look forward to this; I like it each time I do a program.

In the next tape, I see faces, some defined, some less so. Indian faces: South American Indians, some of them. I get a visual of a man and a woman, South American Indians, on the deck of TMI, where Lucy and I had stood just before the tape. I got that. He was broad and tall for a man, but not by our standards. They were smaller people.

I see a South American Indian climbing down wooden steps that change into a ladder, steeply angled so it can be climbed like stairs, only the rungs aren't the flat surfaces we use. He keeps changing back and forth, and so does the ladder, and I take that to be a metaphor for him and me. Another phase of being. This is where we loved. I had had an idea—that night on the road—that he was a runner, a courier along those high lofty roads amid the mist-filled peaks. And I realize that the weather we have been having this week—misty and ethereal each morning—has helped me bring back these memories. Think of the implications of that. The weather was there for all of us; did it mean something different to each? However, I was the only one who went prowling outdoors each morning before dawn. Perhaps it was a matter of each paying attention to the specific clues that internal guidance pointed out.

In the next free-flow 27 tape, I go back to 27 to see about the woman I had rescued from the hillside. I go to the hospital as a cop taking a report. She is hard-eyed, weary, wary of cops. I take off my uniform coat and even my shirt, and tell her I'm not a cop. I start asking questions. She is twenty-two. I ask, "The man who murdered you—did he mean to kill you, so he raped you too, or did he rape you and then murder you so you couldn't talk?" She says he intended to kill her, as she knew too much about something he was involved with, drugs, probably.

I ask, does she know his name? Impatient shrug. "He said Johnny, but since when did people give their right names?" She has a savage satisfaction: he won't do it again. She had kicked him hard in the testicles, and even though it was her bare foot, she knew she'd hurt him. Says that's one reason he killed her quickly instead of slowly as he'd planned. She knows she's dead; she's just a little blank about what comes next.

And I sense I was brought back there to let me know, back-handedly, that lives go on. There's something wrong with our concepts of reincarnation.

Friday

Lifeline ends, and the participants go their separate ways. I take Lucy to the airport. Saying good-bye to her (though Downstairs I hadn't known she existed, a week earlier) is painful. But pain is the price we pay for having feelings, for being alive emotionally. And if people's personal experience at Monroe programs teaches any one thing, it is that this one life in physical-matter reality is important, but it is hardly the only life we live. We are much more than our physical bodies.

Case in point. On the way to the airport, I stop to show Lucy the old cabin. Interestingly, the junk that had filled and surrounded it is gone. The owner (after owning it for fifty years) suddenly (coincidentally?) decided to clean it up. And for the first time, it emanates no forbidding or oppressive atmosphere. Clara has been retrieved, and now, finally, the cabin is clear, after more than two hundred years.

Afterward

Originally I ended this narrative just before Labor Day 1997, at the close of my second Lifeline experience. I ended it there not only because the end of the program was a convenient moment of closure, but because I began writing this less than ten weeks later. Plenty has happened since then. My life has gone through major upheavals. Still, every account has to end somewhere. Life contains many small endings, but no one big final ending, happy or otherwise, not even death.

Although I haven't talked about it here, much of my second Lifeline program consisted of my searching for guidance as to where my life could and should go. I got that guidance—very definite guidance—not only from visions during tape experiences (and there were many) but from things people said around me, and memories or daydreams that popped up spontaneously whenever I happened to be in a receptive mood. In this, I see no departure from what I have learned these past dozen years: the guidance is always available. It's a matter of us asking for it, and listening to it.

The day after I returned from Lifeline, I went out and rented a little cottage and there I spent an increasing amount of time happily alone. There I wrote the first drafts of this book, going back through ten years of journals, annotating and remembering. There, as the months passed, I realized (observing the difference in me) that I needed to get out of my marriage—just as several visions at TMI said. This process was hard, if only because it involved hurting people I had no wish to hurt. Yet I was confident that, in following the guidance I had asked for and had gotten, I was not falling prey to Psychic's Disease. I had looked long and carefully, using logic as well as intuition, and checking my perceptions and feelings by asking trusted others. I hadn't exactly leaped before looking.

But in the end a leap is still a leap, and is either made or not. You can't make half a leap. And you can't both leap and stay where you are. Long before I heard of The Monroe Institute, or Hampton Roads Publishing Company, long before I met TGU or even The Boss, I knew that a part of me hated my life and was anxious to radically change its pattern, regardless of how hard that would be. For a very long time—years—I shrank from doing it, or maybe I was less shrinking than subconsciously waiting for the time to be right. When the time was right internally, it became possible externally. I take that as a sign that all will be right, and for all concerned. I have learned that much: All life is one, and we Downstairs are connected Upstairs whether we love each other, or hurt each other, or go our separate ways.

I can be slow to apply what I learn, but I have learned to live *one* life; that is, to bring each aspect of my life to bear on all other aspects. What I have learned about our life applies to *all* parts of life. If we are all connected Upstairs, then we are connected even when we don't happen to be thinking about metaphysics. We're connected when one of us owes money to another, or gives it, or steals it. Life is many things, yet it is also all one thing, all interconnected. If your way of seeing life has to be disconnected when you switch from "doing philosophy" to commuting to work, or dealing with co-workers, or meeting a payroll—then you need to do some work connecting your mental compartments—your mental buckets, I call them—so that they talk to one another. We shouldn't have to continually ignore inconvenient data, or put them into separate boxes that don't communicate with the rest of our mental world or with each other. Life is confusing enough, without hampering ourselves with incorrect certainties.

I have hung this narrative on my own life, but that doesn't mean my experiences are only my own business. They are first-hand experiences, but they illustrate many phenomena that our ordinary way of seeing things forces us to put aside as puzzling or impossible. They shed light on who and what we are.

And that has been the theme of this whole book. The world contains real forces and abilities that haven't yet been explained, and cannot be explained away, but can be experienced. When we find ourselves habitually putting aside entire classes of phenomena that nonetheless continue to be reported over the years—over centuries—we ought to take that as a sign that our worldview is inadequate. We can remedy that inadequacy—but only by knowledge, which is always based in personal experience.

THIRTEEN
Interim Report

So what does this whole book amount to? It doesn't amount to *proof* of anything, that's for sure. For all you know, I'm deliberately deceiving you, or am deceiving myself. My data may be wrong, my reasoning may be wrong, my "knowings" may be wrong, my conclusions may be wrong. As always, you're pretty much on your own, and you're pretty much going to believe whatever you allow yourself to believe. The only other choice is to find an authority to follow, trying not to remember that belief in authority is itself a belief, not a known.

I wrote this, not to persuade you of anything, but to present a clear statement of first-hand experience that might suggest to you that your life is more magical than you may have thought. I have seen, first-hand, that there's a lot for us to learn about many things that have been reported for centuries and denied only in the past few hundred years. These phenomena, if taken seriously, cast serious doubt on the materialist fantasy that has passed for science and common sense in our day. Among those inconvenient reports: ghosts, out-of-body experiences, spirit possession, witchcraft, telepathy, afterlife experiences, the power of prayer, the ability to heal by touch or and at a distance—and plenty more.

Do such things happen? Is the commonly accepted view of the world significantly different from real life? There's only one way to *know*. You have to investigate. You can't just take another person's word for it, except as an interim report. I know that stepping off the beaten path can be somewhat scary. But the land beyond the beaten path is not a featureless wilderness. I hope that my few muddy (not, I hope, muddled) footprints in the grass have given you whatever excuse you need to go find out for yourself. Herewith, a summary of my own interim report.

– 2 –

My own experiences (including reading and thinking, trying to make sense of these experiences) convince me of ten interrelated points:

1. *We are immortal spirits temporarily inhabiting bodies.* Although by habit we identify with our bodies, this is a mistake, or a partial mistake. We are *somewhat* material, *somewhat* mortal, *somewhat* human. The identity we call ourselves—Downstairs, as I call it—is linked to the earth in many ways, some known, some not. Our bodies are of the earth. Our genetic memories, our physical ancestry, our everyday interests, are all firmly rooted in the earth. To our physical bodies—the human part of us—earth is home. It is rightly said that we are spiritual beings having a human experience; that human experience is an experience of living "*in the earth*," that is, in 3D Theater—physical-matter reality. Therefore it isn't "spiritual" to hate our bodies or our lives, however much our moments of deepest homesickness may tempt us to.

But we are more than our physical bodies. We are spirits, *forming* and *maintaining* and *living in* physical bodies, and neither this beautiful earth nor any other physical place, here or in the next galaxy, can be home to a spirit. We come from Elsewhere (or perhaps I should say Else-non-where); we're just visiting here. Therefore, neither is it "scientific" or "realistic" to think that the body, or even human existence as body/mind/spirit, is all there is. Too much experience flatly contradicts this. Therefore,

2. *This life is not our only life.* As immortal or relatively immortal spirits, we lived before we were born this time, and will live after we die this time. Before and after this one physical-matter-reality life, we exist. It seems likely that we're somewhere (physical or otherwise), doing something (whether imaginable to us now or not). And in fact explorers before and since Monroe have found just this.

3. *We "individuals" are all connected one to another.* The lives we lead seem to be separated between Me and Not-Me, with the dividing line seeming to be our physical bodies, but even science now knows that the division is illusory. We touch each other and are touched both in and out of body. Our scents, our auras, our thoughts, all touch at a distance. We often know each other's thoughts, and "spontaneously and fortuitously" intervene in each other's lives when needed. We engage in dance-like, perfectly executed interactions in ways that do not originate Downstairs and cannot be understood strictly in Downstairs terms. I think this is because . . .

4. *We as individuals are fragments of a larger being that cares about us and can be trusted.* What Monroe called the "INSPEC," what religions call "God," what New Agers sometimes call "The Universe"—something vastly greater than us is yet an intimate part of us, as we are an intimate part of it. It is our connection to the larger whole that makes our lives possible, and gives our lives meaning. We are as fingers of an immense hand—which analogy demonstrates why the intentions of the larger being can be trusted. Does a finger distrust the hand it is part of? And if the finger comes to grief for whatever reason, does it suspect that the misfortune came

from the hand's malice? Obviously not. Where there is identity, there is identity of interest.

5. *Nonetheless, this larger being sees things differently.* Down here, immersed in 3D Theater, we can't help identifying with the here-and-now. Indeed, that's what we're here to do! But naturally anything that had its being in a framework outside of time and space would see things differently. What is desperately real to us would be a dream to it, and what is important to it might be nonexistent to our consciousness. We almost always forget the larger reality when we enter this one. Mythology had it that we forgot as we crossed the River Styx. Monroe says the noise of unfocused human mental and emotional activity is too great for us to function if we were to stay at the level of awareness natural to us outside 3D Theater (that is, in the nonphysical realm he called "Locale II"). Other mythologies and cosmologies explain it in other ways. Different ways of saying the same thing. We forget. But the larger being remembers, and it is there to remind us.

6. *The larger being is a source of foresight and wisdom.* The larger being cannot live our life for us. This would deprive us—and thus itself—of choice, and of growth, which is the result of choice. But it sees outside of time, and it knows our purpose for this lifetime, as we cannot, and it has insights that can help us stay "on the beam" and live this life to the fullest. Think how wise we would be if we could remember the experiences and conclusions of thousands of other lives *from the inside.* Think what wise counselors we could then be to one who was within such a life, with its sensory and other constraints. Access to wider knowledge, combined with intimate insight and identity of interest, makes the larger being a trustworthy source of unlimited wisdom, relative to even the wisest and best of us fragments.

7. *The larger being contacts us,* sometimes sending dreams, sometimes visions, sometimes hunches or "knowings" or precognitive flashes. It works through intuition, regularly, and sometimes automatic writing, spontaneous recall, coincidence, you name it. Anytime you hear or see something that resonates, your larger being may be taking advantage of an opportunity to get something across. Monroe said noncorporeal beings communicate exclusively by nonvocal communication rather than by words. Isn't this precisely what dreams do? Dreams usually set up pictures, scenarios, symbols, leaving us to decode them as best we can. Sometimes, it is true, we get words; sometimes words, even sentences, of great power. But primarily dreams send symbols, which we can learn to read. (Let me say in passing that all means of divination, including tarot decks, the I Ching, and those not yet devised, seem to me to work by helping the larger being to communicate with us, if only by concentrating our attention on symbols.) And this is not a one-way street.

8. *We can contact the larger being.* Some call it prayer; some, meditation; some, asking for guidance. The names vary according to time, culture, and tradition, but the means of access are well known. Regardless of context, the underlying reality is that we as fragmentary individuals have access to a trustworthy source of relatively boundless knowledge and wisdom, ours for the asking. We need only to learn how to communicate, and to practice doing it.

9. *Thus our lives need not be disconnected and solitary.* We are always in intimate connection with the larger, wiser being we sometimes call "our" Higher Self; because we are *part of* this Higher Self, as fingers are a part of a hand. (Is a hand a finger's Higher Self?) Without this intimate connection, we could not live, any more than a finger could live apart from

its hand, or the hand away from its arm, et cetera. Therefore it is impossible for us to be alone in this sense.

10. *Nonetheless, we may often lose communication.* The intimate connection cannot be severed, but communication may be, and often is, distorted, neglected, or forgotten. Many never even learn of the possibility of such intimate communication, having been taught otherwise. Obviously if you don't believe it exists, you don't try to communicate with it, and don't listen when it communicates with you. And even those who know about the larger spirit sometimes forget, mostly in those times when "the world is too much with us." At such times, be it a period of forgetfulness or a lifetime, everything you might have learned from that source is closed to you, not as punishment but as a consequence of your own forgetfulness or disbelief. But regardless of belief, we *can* contact the larger being, using many tools internal and external. Thus our lives *don't have to be* disconnected and solitary. Thus we need not live our lives alone, even if all contemporary society says otherwise.

It seems to me that thinking in terms of our connection to a larger being clears up a lot of mysteries. It opens up unsuspected possibilities for us as individuals as well as collectively as a species. It means more, suggests more, than the words "God" or "Higher Self." If the concept still poses perplexities, and if it still leaves vastly more unexplained than explained, so what? That leaves all the more work—and fun—for us and those who follow us. But it does give us a point of departure.

– 3 –

The experiences I have shared with you in this narrative cease to be inexplicable when viewed in this context. They become what is only to be expected. They become (dare we say it?) ordinary. And the things religions have tried so hard to tell us, these many generations and centuries, make sense in an entirely new way.

We are immortal spirits temporarily inhabiting bodies, and so this life is not our only life. We "individuals" are all connected one to another, if only as fragments of a larger being. This larger being cares about us and can be trusted. It is a source of foresight and wisdom, but nonetheless, it sees things differently. The larger being contacts us, and we can contact it, and so our lives need not be disconnected and solitary. Nonetheless, we may often lose communication.

Immortal spirits, temporarily inhabiting bodies? My contacts with living beings who no longer live on this earth—including some whom I did not know when they were alive here—would be enough to convince me, if I needed convincing, that it is demonstrably untrue that "one life is all you get." The only way that saying is true is in the limited sense that a given personality in a given historical time is somehow significantly different and distinct from other personalities and lifetimes that are embodied by the same soul. Thus, one might reasonably argue that a given life is not really a "past life" of another, but "another life" of some common-denominator soul. Or, one might make the counterargument that all beings are at bottom part of one great being. It's only a conflict of viewpoint. I can't see how it ever could be resolved, and I don't see that it would be important to do so.

As to this life not being our only life, here are a few of the lives I have found to date: Bertram, a Norman monk of the Middle Ages; John Cotten, the eighteenth-century Virginia farmer who married Clara; Joseph (or Josiah) Smallwood, the Vermont nature mystic; David Owen Poynter, the Welsh journalist and seeker of hidden knowledge; Katrina, the Polish Jewish girl; Clio, the Roman diviner in fire; Senji-san, the Japanese monk; and unnamed others, including at least one (if the evidence may be believed) on another planet. I don't expect it to convince anyone else, but it goes a long way toward convincing me.

As evidence of our connection one to another, I might cite every instance of so-called telepathy mentioned in this book, and more to the point, perhaps, all the mutual assistance so freely offered and received. Think of the interaction between Mary and me, for instance, or Suni and Ed and Dave and so many others named and unnamed. We tend to take love and friendship for granted, considering them to be part of ordinary life. So they are. But the very prevalence in our lives of love and friendship may blind us, sometimes, to how very strange and interesting they are as symptoms (not merely symbols) of our deep interconnectedness.

That we are fragments of a larger being that cares about us and can be trusted has always been an axiom of religion. My experiences, inner and outer, convince me that this is a straightforward description of the way things are. And although Monroe calls that being INSPEC and others call it God, Monroe made it quite clear in his book *Far Journeys* that INSPEC (on INSPEC's own say-so) was not God. Yet he also said that he could see how people in the past, catching just a momentary nonphysical glimpse of INSPEC, might decide they had seen the deity. Just so, Carl Jung once described what he called the racial unconscious in terms that he explicitly said resembled the traditional conception of God, including, among other attributes, (relative) omniscience and omnipresence.

Certainly, a larger being connected to all of us, and existing outside time-space, would be a source of foresight and wisdom. Certainly, it would see things differently from those of us enmeshed in 3D Theater. Yet it would be willing and able to contact us, and would encourage such contact. I have given many examples in this book of the simple process of establishing and deepening connection with the larger being. What else was it, when I learned to talk to (listen to) The Boss, or The Gentlemen Upstairs? When, before that, I connected with my Higher Self in the image of a unicorn? The information I have gotten has proved reliable on matters mundane and practical, no less than philosophical and abstract. And when I listen to hunches, it is the same thing.

But you must be willing to connect. What is leading an exclusively Downstairs life, if not loss of communication with Upstairs? This is the long, hard, solitary Downstairs road, with a vengeance, and it is no fun.

This new overview is all right there within the context of my experiences. I promised in advance to speak of what I know of my own knowledge. The same knowledge, by way of different experiences, is available to you. It is merely a matter of going after it.

– 4 –

Every religion I know of testifies that we are spirits in bodies, and that we are an integral part of an eternal being that guides us and cares for us, and is essential to our moment-to-moment existence. "In Him we live and move and have our being." Religions have greatly discredited themselves by their quarreling over the way they see things. Nonetheless, I think it would be a great error, almost a laughable one, to ignore the existence of so many thousands of years of religious testimony, testimony that coincides.

Experience unites; opinion divides. Those who give testimony to personal experience of what they call God describe what has happened to them as best they can. Of course, their testimony is going to differ as to detail and emphasis. But the reports are similar. It is when we get into opinion about what that experience means that we meet intolerance, the construction of logical prisons, and the laying down of rules and the beginnings of religious wars. Little minds attempt to interpret great experience, and the inevitable result is distortion, and quarreling over the nature and attributes of God, and the nature of humans, the nature of reality, the nature (and existence or nonexistence) of heaven and hell, and of the afterlife in general.

Different religions emerge, shaped *by* different types of people, *for* different types of people. They place their emphasis so drastically differently that they seem to be describing differences *in essence* when in fact they are describing difference *in nuance*, or *in interpretation*. What they cannot spread and often do not share is the *experience* of the very real existence of the larger being of which we are a part.

One of the greatest Christian mystics and seers in history, Emanuel Swedenborg was also the most famous European scientist of his day. For more than twenty-seven years, beginning in his fifties, Swedenborg conversed with spiritual beings he called "angels" and was granted visions of heaven and hell. He interpreted his experience entirely in a Christian context, but they sound remarkably like what Lifeline participants experience. Shared experience does not imply shared interpretation. Yet the experience is real.

– 5 –

We are in one of those historic moments when a civilization's old way of seeing things is breaking into fragments, and a new way is not yet born. It is exciting, challenging, liberating— and also disorienting, frightening. No matter. This world we are moving into was not called forth by us and it won't be banished by us. All we can do is meet it well or badly. And the only way to meet it well is to live our greatest truth and see where that brings us. Neither materialism nor fundamentalism contains enough truth to be worth the distortion they include. Neither offers us firm ground upon which to found our new lives. Only experience, followed by reflection, does that.

So it becomes a matter of personal exploration. My Upstairs link provides me with whatever assistance I happen to want, along with quite a bit that I need but don't have sense enough to ask for. Do you have reason to think your Upstairs is any less interested in helping you? Is yours any less practical than mine? Why not ask your own questions?

Of course, any process of interpretation includes distortion. As an example, I suspect that often people experience the larger being as an external spirit, because it seems to them to be something outside themselves. In a sense, it *is* outside themselves: it extends far beyond the bounds of their own personality. In another sense, it is *not at all* outside themselves: it is an integral (and often unsuspected) internal part of the larger being that they are. Each viewpoint is *sort of* correct; neither is exactly correct. The distortion caused by viewpoints can be recognized and allowed for, but not prevented.

The same thing goes for this overview. It is (at best) sort of correct, from a certain point of view. As far as I can see, "sort of correct, from a certain point of view" is about as good as we can do while still being in physical-matter reality. Even at best, anybody else's ideas and experiences are no more than an interim report.

Afterword

Pointing at the Moon

April 29, 1998

Gentlemen, are we really finished?

Really finished in terms of new material and new divisions of material. What needs to be added—Suni, for one—can be added to existing material as you edit it.

Somehow I don't get a sense of completion.

This is for you to find as you reread your material, carefully annotating.

Anything here to be put into the book?

This book was not written to be admired, or enjoyed or used as scripture. It is not a work of art, or of beauty, or of truth, so much as it is a finger pointing at the moon. The reader who—

Wait, I get it, and maybe I should have thought before. Would you write the Afterword?

With the greatest of pleasure.

This book was not written to be admired, or enjoyed or used as scripture. It is not a work of art, or of beauty, or of truth, so much as it is a finger pointing at the moon. The reader who comes to the end of the book and puts it down—with whatever feelings—and follows these clues no farther does himself or herself a disservice.

For, those who read this book—as any book—were called to read it. Your Upstairs, as Frank calls it, did not bring you to this book by chance. Nothing in your life is by chance.

It is true that often you cannot see a mark of meaning in the little events that make a life; nonetheless, this does not mean that all is chance, or that *anything* is chance. We taught this to Frank by one means and another over many years before he leaped to the conclusion we had been holding before him.

This book is a teacher that appeared. If you were not ready, you would not be here reading it. But not every student heeds every teacher, and not every time. It is up to you. It is always up to you. But the setting up of scenarios is up to us (so to speak), and the scenario you are in brought you to this book, however unlikely it would have been by chance.

Well then, why? What's in it for you?

We well realize, from dealing with Frank "over many years" of change, that you in your position find it difficult to understand us in our position. It tempts you to think that those who are not encased in bodies are all-knowing, all-powerful, all-anything. Conversely, it tempts you to think that we do not, because we cannot, exist. It is hard for you to envisage us as we are.

Impossible, probably, because you cannot even envisage yourselves as *you* are. This is said not with contempt, at all; nor with sympathy, which would be undeserved; nor with despair, which would be unwarranted. Frenchmen speak French; Russians speak Russian. Some scholars speak Latin, some read Sanskrit, some read the times and the eternities. What we're saying is, different environments reflect themselves in different modes of being, which reflect in different externals such as language.

To put it more plainly, we on our home turf are different from you on your home turf, more because the turf is different than because of any inherent differences between ourselves and you. If you will think through the implications of this very true statement, you should find them very encouraging.

Afterword

What Frank calls The Gentlemen Upstairs—what Monroe called INSPEC and Swedenborg called heavens of like souls—what are they, what are *we*, but (shall we say) ex-humans, or rather, ex-individuals, many of them ex-humans, now cooperating together in a way that preserves individuality within a larger structure.

Frank despairs of that last paragraph, so we will rephrase it to suit his perceptions. We will put it this way: you are already part of a larger being. It is in the larger being that you exist, for if you were cut off from it you could not live one second. And this is what your theologies have been telling you; only they could not give the reasons in a way that could be heard by you. This was no accident, for it is time for new conceptions, in order to make possible new ways of being.

Every age has its own characteristic way of seeing things, of reacting to what it sees, of becoming. The Middle Ages had possibilities closed to you at the new millennium. Similarly, ways that are open to you are closed to it, and for good reason. To allow anything to manifest, contradictory manifestations must be suppressed. You see? The life force that is moved into vortexes to produce a rose must, in so doing, suppress everything that is *not* rose. Can a rose be a rose while also manifesting daffodil, or turtle, or elm tree? Yes, it is true that on the highest scale, everything is one; it is also true that that distinction is meaningless in nature, in what Frank calls 3D Theater.

Emerson said, "All the thoughts of a turtle are turtle." We had Frank copy that down months, actually years, ago; he copied it down in the computer and it has sat there till now with him having no idea how or why or if it would be used. Yet, trusting, he put it there, and now it appears in a connection he could not have suspected beforehand. Can you see that in your life it is the same, always? What appears for no reason, and appears meaningless and shapeless will appear in due course in its proper relation, and suddenly all your fears and perplexities will reveal themselves to have been waste of time, waste of breath.

To manifest what is, one suppresses what is not. A rose by its nature is only rose, and not anything that is not-rose. And what you *are*—all of it—is essential to the making of you. Where you think you can pick and choose, shape and reshape, accept parts of yourself and reject others, you mistake yourself, and yet at the same time it is no mistake.

It is a mistake in that you are larger than your own idea of yourself. It is no mistake in that you are here to choose, and choose, and choose again, to make yourself what you wish to be. The wishing, and all the background for that wishing, come from what you are—which is the sum of what you have been, combined with what you can be, divided by what you cannot be and do not wish to be.

It is only an analogy.

May 22, 1999

I received the above from TGU in one fluid motion, stopping as abruptly as it had started, or rather as abruptly as I had realized that they wanted to write it. But it seemed merely to stop, rather than coming to an end. As I didn't know what else to do, I left it, waiting to see if anything new would come. More than a year passed, during which I, thinking the book completed, tried to market it. Then I began to rework it, and finally in May 1999, I began to see daylight. On this Saturday, even though I have not (as I write this section) completed my revisions, I am moved to give over to them again, to see if they have more to say. Gentlemen?

As Mary would say, "You hear very well." It is worth pointing out to the reader that during the course of writing this book, life continued, and your life changed notably. In some ways, you realized the freedom you had never allowed yourself. In some ways, you have yet to allow yourself this realization.

Afterword

Reader, during the past few weeks, we have been drumming into Frank's mind (though he usually thinks he is doing the thinking) that the gift he has to offer to the world, insofar as it is contained in writing, is the unique viewpoint that sees the affairs of "this" world and "the other" world as equally important, equally real. Most choose one or the other. The result of making so false a choice, we suggest, is a crippling unreality. This is the false choice, the wrong turning, if you will, that has crippled your culture. How can one find the most productive road if half the possible choices are unsuspected, if half the landscape is unsuspected?

We end as we began. There are not *two* worlds, but *one* world, not *two* realities, but *one* reality containing an infinitude of seeming realities. Not a dream world and a real world, but a world that is a real dream. That is, reality is a dream; the dream is the reality. Same thing, said seemingly differently because of the difference in starting point and emphasis.

You—we, everyone, everything—are part of *one* indissoluble reality. Thus everything impinges on, colors, everything else. Nothing can exist in isolation, because there is no isolation to exist in! All is one; separations are illusion. Not that it is a magic trick, or a delusion, but that the appearance of separation masks and blurs an underlying connection. Just as space is not separate, just as time is not separate, but each is considered to be made of separate parcels so that they may be apprehended; so reality in the widest possible sense is not separate, but all one thing.

Live in that knowledge. Know that you overlook any one facet of reality only at the price of to that extent disregarding what is. "I say, ye are gods." Of course. How could it be otherwise? Ye are also rocks, and sky, as actors in a movie might be said to be individual actors but might be also said to be "part of" that movie. Is either view of things untrue? Is either view the only valid way to see it?

We say to you, see things as they are. The only way to do that—since neither the one viewpoint nor the other is the only correct way to describe reality—is to alternate from one to the other, or to overlap them (dealing with the slight resultant confusion and fuzziness), or to *see* one way, while *remembering* the other way. Then you will be whole.

Appendix I

Monroe's Toolbox

Hemi-Sync tapes and CDs

Gateway albums. The six albums of Gateway tapes (36 tapes) are designed to provide experience with Focus 3, 10 and 12. In general, long-standing TMI policy precludes sale or circulation of tapes containing Focus 15 or higher, with the exception of the "Going Home" series. However, there is no need to succumb to focus envy! The tapes employing Focus 10 and 12 are designed to significantly enhance your ability to access unusual states of consciousness and do useful work there. And the newly released Wave VII Gateway series includes exercises in Focus 21.

Going Home. Bob Monroe's last project, the "Going Home" series of tapes is designed to assist the dying and their family to make a smooth and peaceful transition.

H-Plus. The various H-Plus (Human Plus) tapes are each geared toward a specific ability or task. Hence, for instance, Concentration, one of my all-time favorites.

Metamusic. Hemi-Sync beneath music of various kinds: classical, jazz, New Age. I use these a lot, often when I'm writing or reading, sometimes late at night.

TMI residential programs

The Gateway Voyage is the introductory program that teaches access to Focus 10, 12, 15, and 21. Probably most people hope that Gateway will lead them to have an out-of-body experience. Sometimes it does. But TMI has a saying that "people get what they need from Gateway," and in my experience this is true. They seem to get whatever their internal guidance (Upstairs) knows they need at that time—which is often significantly different from what Downstairs thinks they need!

Guidelines concentrates heavily on helping participants develop their access to internal guidance, which may come in the form of heightened intuition, telepathy, "channeling," or other forms, seemingly more mundane but equally useful.

Lifeline explores the worlds on the other side of the veil, what TMI calls Focus levels 23–27; what others call the "afterlife." To the extent that participants internalize what they experience in this program, I would expect that they find their fear of death greatly lessened or eliminated. But in my experience, exploring these other focus levels can bring unexpected benefits. In my case, the insights and positive benefits of being enabled to help others who became confused in passing over brought very tangible benefits to my emotional life, as I have described.

It should be obvious from the story I have told that I highly recommend Gateway, Guidelines, and Lifeline. I have not taken Exploration 27 or Heartline, so I can't write from experience; the following is my understanding of the structure and goals of those programs:

Exploration 27. The park at Focus 27, Monroe was told, was created infinitely long ago by humans for the sake of humans. This course promotes exploration not only of the park but of other parts of Focus 27, and moves on to the place of The Gathering, at Focus level 34–35. The Exploration 27 affirmation states, in part, "it is my intent through these explorations to contribute to the expansion of human consciousness by experiencing and acquiring knowledge of the realms beyond ordinary consciousness. It is my intent to observe and bring into conscious awareness the process of bridging these realities."

Heartline is billed as "an invitation to [the left brain, or rational self] to open, allow and welcome the heart, the feeling connection, to come into balance." Aimed at those "who are serious about looking within," Heartline explores the areas that block self-trust and self-acceptance, with the goal of helping participants to move into greater wholeness and expanded self-awareness.

The Dolphin Energy Club

The Dolphin Energy Club of The Monroe Institute is a volunteer on-call service network coordinated by TMI. Those requesting to be added to the healing list receive two weeks' efforts at distant healing from ten club members, who are given only the person's first name, physical location, and medical condition to be addressed. After the period is up, the recipient is asked to provide feedback on anything positive or negative noticed during the period.

What I think is very unusual is that not only is the service free to the recipient; group members pay an annual fee in order to belong. About the only material benefit they receive for their membership is a TMI tape reverse-engineered from the brain patterns of healers, to help them work. The other benefits come in the form of satisfaction. Think of a club of healers who provide a free service to those who need it, and who are not only unpaid, but pay an annual fee to be able to do so!

Distant healing sounds as unlikely as anything else I have been talking about in this book. All I can tell you is that I and my friends have been on both ends of it, and it works.

To contact The Monroe Institute,
call 1-800-541-2488,
e-mail monroeinst@aol.com
or write to:
The Monroe Institute
62 Roberts Mountain Road
Faber, Virginia 22938

Appendix II

Mapmakers

People you ought to know, and why. I count them as friends I never met—except that in a few cases, I *have* met them. These personal favorites of mine will lead you on to others, by their own reference and with a little help from your friends Upstairs.

Dion Fortune: six novels, very British, very much of the interwar period, very absorbing. Perhaps try *The Sea Priestess* first, though it was not her first. She also wrote much nonfiction, including *Psychic Self-Defense*. You'll have to overlook her disturbing British racism. Much of her nonfiction presently is coming back into print in this country.

Joan Grant: novels and nonfiction. Her autobiography, *Far Memory*, is perceptive, funny, and fascinating. Her first novel, *Winged Pharaoh*, is an all-time classic.

Carl Jung: psychology. Start with *Modern Man in Search of a Soul*, perhaps, or his autobiography, *Memories, Dreams, Reflections*.

Bruce Moen: A series of three books on his personal exploration of the reality of the afterlife. *Voyages Into the Unknown* begins with a strange recurring dream he had as a very young child, and continues on through The Monroe Institute residential programs that taught him how to explore. *Voyage Beyond*

Doubt carries on the story of his explorations. *Voyages Into the Afterlife* brings it farther yet.

Robert Monroe: *Journeys Out of the Body*, the story of his first explorations. *Far Journeys*, how his out-of-body travels began to provide him with a larger view of the world. *Ultimate Journey*, in which he wraps up his cosmology in one stream-lined package. I highly recommend them all.

Peter Novak: *The Division of Consciousness: The Secret Afterlife of the Human Psyche*. Novak's startling thesis is that, at death, the conscious mind goes one way, the unconscious mind goes another, and the result clears up a good deal of mud-dled concepts and contradictory reports over the years.

George Ritchie: *Return from Tomorrow* and *Ordered to Return*. Two books by the same man about the same experience. One was embraced by Christian publishers, the other shunned. Yet the message is the same. *Ordered to Return* changed my life.

Jane Roberts (Seth): *Seth Speaks; The Nature of Personal Reality; The Education of Oversoul 7* (a novel), and other books. Perhaps the best channeled material ever brought across.

Evelyn Underhill: *Practical Mysticism*. Short, simple to understand, straight from the shoulder. No attempt to mystify, no conjuring tricks, but a straight description of the process and the rewards of going inside and discovering the true well-springs of life.

Laurens van der Post: novels and nonfiction. This man's depth of soul and feeling, of thought and experience, suffuses all he writes. A wonderful man altogether. I came to him via *Jung and the Spirit of Our Time*, and that's a wonderful place to start. His autobiography, *Yet Being Someone Other*, is another natu-ral introduction. His novels include the twin books, *A Story Like the Wind* and *A Far-off Place; The Hunter and the Whale; Flamingo Feather; The Face Beside the Fire* (perhaps my all-time favorite); and others. Some of his novels are inexplicably out of print.

Colin Wilson: novels and nonfiction. Colin Wilson can't seem to write an unreadable sentence or a dull page. His lively mind moves from here to there and carries you with him. He lives in a *wider* world than most, which is a continual breath of fresh air. He has written eighty or so books, and I doubt there's a used bookstore or a public library in an English-speaking country that doesn't have at least one, and usually more. His newer books can be found in any bookstore of reasonable size. *The Outsider* is a classic, and a renewed delight whenever I reread it. Among my favorites of his novels are *The Philosopher's Stone*, *The Mind Parasites*, and *Necessary Doubt*. But you can hardly go wrong anywhere.

Appendix III

Author's Note

I am interested in hearing about your experiences. Obviously I cannot engage to discuss these things over the telephone, but I will attempt to respond to mail or e-mail—e-mail especially, as it is easiest. If you don't hear from me right away, please be patient. My life, like yours, is filled with many things, not all of which may be put off from moment to moment. But I *am* interested.

Write to:
Frank DeMarco
c/o Hampton Roads Publishing Co., Inc.
1125 Stoney Ridge Road
Charlottesville, Virginia 22902

Or e-mail: *demarco@hrpub.com*

Index

A
Andersonville, 286-288
astral sex, 185-186
Atlantean life, 55-56
auras, 28
automatic writing, 22-23

B
belief, 39-40
Bond, Frederick Bligh, *xiii-xiv*
The Boss, talks with, 75-99

C
C1, 119-120
Carter, J. Edwin
  contact with Bob Monroe, 259-
  260
  death of, 305-306, 312-314
  Hampton Roads involvement, 247
  last consultation with TGU, 306-
  312
  relationship with, 89-90
chance, 5, 352
Clio, 48-49
coincidence, *xv*, 5
Colburn, Ginna, 312-313
Cotten, Clara
  as John's (Frank's) wife, 146
  death of, 324-325
  finding, 283
  Frank's first vision of, 138-139
  name of, 147
Cotten, John, 172-173, 282-284

D
Danger Is My Business, 44-46
DeMarco, Frank

as sister (Katrina) to Mary
  (Marcus), 208-210
automatic writing, 74
Colin Wilson's influence on, 17
Downstairs existence, 15-16
dreams of, 62-72
Focus 27 reports, 286-291, 292-
  297
Gateway experience, 132-168
  anticipations of, 126-127
  reflections on, 168-173
Gateway tapes work, 91
Guidelines experience, 217-234
Hampton Roads startup efforts,
  87-88
healing by, *xxvi*, 195, 214, 226
hypnosis by, 46-47
hypnosis of, 47-48
incarnations summarized, 346-
  347
journalism work, 32, 72-73
Jungian analysis, 61-62
Lifeline program 1, 252-297
  expectations going in, 252-253
  Focus 22 and 23, 255-259
Lifeline program 2, 320-339
Mary
  healing, 195
  meeting, 102
  paired intuitive questioning
  with, 237-243
  relationship with, 190-192,
  236, 243-244
  'seeing' house of, 142, 143
  telepathy test with, 244-245
  work with, 105-109, 112, 190-
  193
Downstairs/Upstairs, 8-11

Index

dreams, 61-62
Dunbar, Suni, 59-60, 299

E
Elena, 195-196, 202-205, 213, 236-237
Emerson, Lidian, 154-156
Emerson, Ralph Waldo, 110-111, 154-155, 353
Emily
    concern for, 147, 156, 157
    first talk with, 143-144
    Frank in relation to, 159, 162-163
    massage from Frank, 166-167

F
Far Journeys, xi
Fortune, Dion, 88, 361
Fran, 61

G
Gateway Voyage, 128-173
Grant, Joan, 361
Guidelines experience, 217-235
    advice from Bob Monroe, 218-219
    lab sessions, 219, 228, 233
    paired intuitive questioning, 221-224

H
Hampton Roads Publishing Company
    Carter's involvement in, 247
    move to Charlottesville, 288, 290-291
    startup efforts, 87-88
Holmes, Penny, 132
human beings
    as psychic, 43
    connectedness of, 339, 342
    nature of, 21, 341, 342
    purpose of, 23
    well-balanced, 64

I
INSPEC, 347, 353
    See also larger being

J
Jacobs, David, *xviii*
Johnson, Mary. *See* Mary
Journeys Out of the Body, 116
Joyce
    discussing Katrina with, 265-266
    finding her Upstairs, 317
    grip on Frank, 316
    illness and death, 299-305, 324
    Rich and Frank with, 266
Jung, Carl G., 2, 347, 361

K
karma, 318
Katrina, 274-276, 282-293, 292
Kennedy, John F., 66-67
King, C. Daly, xiv

L
lab sessions, 219, 228, 233
larger being, *xxii*, 342-345, 347, 353
Lifeline program, 252-297
Living Body Maps, 253
Living Is Forever, 89
Lliteras, Danny, 94
Long, Max Freedom, *xii-xiii*
Louis, 314-318
love, 182-183, 212, 213
Lucy, 322, 327, 328-329

M
Mary
    as brother (Marcus) to Frank (Katrina), 208-210
    book rejection by Hampton Roads, 100
    books published by Hampton Roads, 193
    Charlottesville visit, 101-102, 105
    expulsion by Elena, 237
    Frank
        beginning work with, 105-109, 112
        healing by, 195
        meeting, 102
        paired intuitive questioning

with, 237-243
relationship clarified, 196
telepathy test with, 244-245
work with, 190-193
move to Virginia, 236
move to Williamsburg, 237
sitar concert recipient, 201
testing, 200-201
materialism and materialists, 39,
340, 349
McMoneagle, Joe, 148-149
'Megahertz scale,' 293
Merton, Thomas, 88-89
Messenger, ix
The Mind Parasites, 4, 17
Moen, Bruce, 301, 361-362
Monroe Institute
accommodations at, 129-130
contact information, 360
residential programs, 358-359
techniques used by, 114-115
Monroe, Robert
appearance at Gateway, 140
books by, 362
death of, 248
Frank's memories of, 234-235
implied cosmology of, 115-125
memorial service for, 248-250
on learning, 335
terminology chosen by, 118
work of, *x-xi*, 113-114, 115
My Life After Dying, 96

N
Nancy Penn Center, 129-130
Novak, Peter, 362

O
old house
finding, 168-169
returning to, 217-218, 337
visions of, 138-139, 142, 146
Ordered to Return, 95, 96
Owen, David. *See* Poynter, David
Owen

P
paired intuitive questioning, 221-
224, 238-243
past life stories, 56-58
Patrick tape, 158
Peterson, David. *See* Smallwood,
Josiah
Poynter, David Owen
influence on Frank, 187
initial vision of, 50-54
life details of, 205-208
Mary and Frank session on, 238-
243
partial story of, 104
vision about his death, 151-153
psychic powers, 3-4, 182
psychics, 41-42, 192
Psychics Disease, 41

R
religion(s), *xxiv-xxv*, 348-349
religious wars, 348
remote viewing, 148-149
Return From Tomorrow, 95
Ritchie, George, 95, 96, 362
Roberts, Jane (Seth), 187, 362
Russian prison camp, 280-281

S
saints, 223-224
Schlachter, Dave, 11-14
science, *xxiv-xxv*
Senji-san, 54-55
Seth (Jane Roberts), 187, 362
"Shaping" excerpt, 79-80
Shaw, George Bernard, 2
Shirley MacLaine's Higher Self
Seminar, 32, 34-38
Smallwood, Josiah
at Gettysburg, 246
Frank writing as, 110-112
influence on Frank, 187
journeys of, 109-110
name of, 184
partial story of, 103-104
visiting Emerson, 154-155
Swedenborg, Emanuel, x-xi, 349

T
teachers, 3
telepathy test at Monroe Institute,
244-245
TGU (The Gentlemen Upstairs), 17-
18
TMI (The Monroe Institute). *See*
Monroe Institute
Tucker, Barbara, *xv*

U
Ultimate Journey, xi
Underhill, Evelyn, 362
Upstairs
contacting, 18-20
protections in, 21-22
Upstairs/Downstairs, 8-11
Urbito, Alex, 301

V
van der Post, Laurens, 362

W
Wallis, Dave, 13-14
wave-vibration concept, 117
Wilson, Colin, 8, 363

Y
Yeats, W.B., 294-295

Hampton Roads Publishing Company

. . . for the evolving human spirit

Hampton Roads Publishing Company
publishes books on a variety of subjects,
including metaphysics, health, integrative medicine,
visionary fiction, and other related topics.

For a copy of our latest catalog, call toll-free
(800) 766-8009, or send your name and address to:

Hampton Roads Publishing Company, Inc.
1125 Stoney Ridge Road
Charlottesville, VA 22902

e-mail: hrpc@hrpub.com
Website: www.hrpub.com